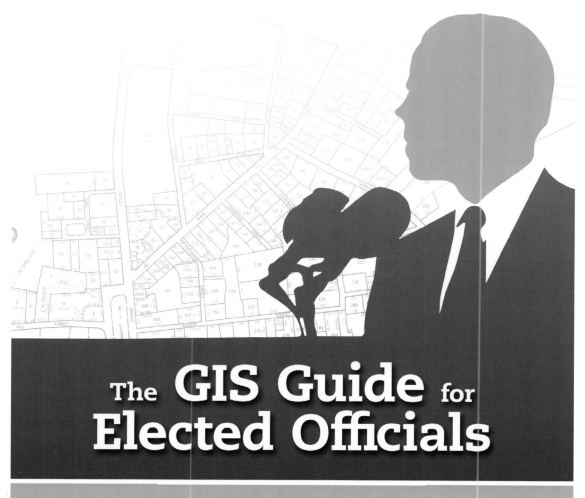

The **GIS Guide** for **Elected Officials**

edited by **Cory Fleming**
International City/County
Management Association (ICMA)

Esri Press
REDLANDS|CALIFORNIA

Esri Press, 380 New York Street, Redlands, California 92373-8100
Copyright © 2014 Esri
All rights reserved. First edition 2014
Printed in the United States of America
18 17 16 15 14   1 2 3 4 5 6 7 8 9 10

Library of Congress Cataloging-in-Publication Data
The gis guide for elected officials / edited by Cory Fleming, International City/County Management Association, ICMA.—First edition.
     p. cm.
  Includes bibliographical references.
  ISBN 978-1-58948-272-2 (pbk.)—
  ISBN 978-1-58948-353-8 (electronic)
  1. Local government—Information technology—United States. 2. Local government—Technological innovations—United States. 3. Geographic
     information systems—Political aspects—United States. I. Fleming, Cory, 1963–
  JS344.E4.G57 2014
  910.285—dc23   2013024370

Contents

vii   Foreword by Jack Dangermond

ix   A note from Robert J. O'Neill Jr.

xi   Acknowledgments

xiii   Contributors

1   **Part 1. Understanding GIS**

Geographic information systems (GIS) technology offers vast analytic capabilities. Part 1 highlights the evolution of GIS technology and includes interviews with leaders in government who discuss advances in the use of GIS technology for a wide variety of purposes.

17   **Part 2. Using GIS to support policy decisions**

From making decisions about land-use planning or managing natural resources to identifying where food deserts exist in an urban area, GIS gives decision makers an important tool for better understanding the effects of their decisions and explaining those decisions to their constituents. Part 2 features case studies that highlight the many different GIS applications that governments at all levels have developed to make better policy.

79   **Part 3. Streamlining government operations with GIS**

Part 3 focuses on how GIS technology can help streamline government operations. From a groundbreaking study that explores return on investment (ROI) resulting from the development of the GIS program in King County, Washington, to numerous examples of how new efficiencies were achieved using GIS, the case studies in this section offer important lessons in what can be accomplished with a little creativity and innovation.

163   **Part 4. Building a strong GIS program**

The final section of this volume outlines what elected officials need to know in order to provide much needed support to their own GIS programs. Decision makers need not become technical wizards themselves in order to make decisions that result in a robust GIS program.

Foreword

Our quality of life as individuals depends greatly on the health and sustainability of our communities. From streets and roads to playgrounds and parks to transit systems to sanitation services, government provides us with the services we use nearly every day. We depend on our government leaders to set wise policies and plan for the smooth delivery of these services.

Geographic information systems (GIS) technology, the subject of this book, enables spatial analysis of place-based data through the creation of easy-to-understand maps. A robust GIS program can significantly enhance the ability of government leaders to make better decisions and improve the delivery of services in our communities. GIS applications have introduced a wide range of innovations, both small and large, into government business processes. These innovations have resulted in new and improved services, time and cost savings, and greater accuracy and transparency in the way government works.

This book, *The GIS Guide for Elected Officials*, will assist government leaders in understanding how GIS technology can aid their work. We believe it may even help bridge the gap when elected officials and GIS staff come together to discuss what GIS data is available to the community—be that a town or city, county, state, or regional coalition of governments—and what applications are needed or would be desirable to improve the quality of life in our communities.

If you are an elected leader reading this book, we hope you will let us know how we can continue to aid you in your work.

Jack Dangermond
President
Esri
Redlands, California

A note from Robert J. O'Neill Jr.

In 2014, the International City/County Management Association (ICMA) will celebrate its one-hundredth anniversary as a professional association for local government managers. From its very beginning, ICMA has believed in and promoted the concept of peer-to-peer information sharing. Learning from the experiences of our peers not only saves time and effort, but can also identify potential challenges early on before they can overwhelm a project.

The case studies that form the foundation of this book offer an important opportunity for us to learn from our peers in government. GIS technology touches nearly every aspect of government work in some way or another now. The work featured here represents critical advancements in the field and promotes a greater understanding of the effect government decisions have on our constituents.

ICMA is proud to have Esri as a Strategic Partner and is pleased to have collaborated with Esri in the development of this book.

Robert J. O'Neill Jr.
Executive Director
ICMA
Washington, DC

Acknowledgments

This volume has been designed to provide peer-to-peer information sharing on the benefits of geographic information systems (GIS) technology. Literally hundreds of people have contributed to its development in one fashion or another, sharing their knowledge, their experience, and, most important, their excitement about GIS technology and the benefits it can offer governments. It has been my honor and privilege to work with many creative and innovative individuals on this project, and I have learned much from them. I cannot adequately describe my appreciation for the time and effort they put into helping develop the many case studies that are featured in this volume.

I would especially like to thank Christopher Thomas, Esri government industry manager, and Britney Hinthorne, who served as Esri government marketing coordinator, for their support throughout this project. Their suggestions, feedback, and terrific sense of humor made this project fun! I also want to thank the Urban and Regional Information Systems Association (URISA) for the many case study suggestions it provided.

Finally, I would like to dedicate this volume to the memory of my father, Donald A. Fleming, who passed before this project was complete.

Cory Fleming
Editor
ICMA
Washington, DC

Contributors

Part 1. Understanding GIS

Decisions in the public realm

Generating excitement about GIS in the State of Oregon
> Interview with Cy Smith, Geographic Information Officer, Oregon Geospatial Enterprise Office (GEO), Salem, Oregon

How GIS works

Promoting GIS technology use in local government
> Interview with Randy Johnson, Commissioner, Hennepin County, Minnesota

Growing a GIS program in Honolulu, Hawaii
> Ken Schmidt, GIS Administrator, City and County of Honolulu, Hawaii

Types of GIS

The World Wide Web and Web 2.0

Mobile

Logistics

Thinking about data

Data standards

Data sharing

Data interoperability

The future of GIS technology

Crowdsourcing

Cloud computing and software as a service (SaaS)

Web services, or "maps and apps"

Part 2. Using GIS to support policy decisions

Traditional uses of GIS

Land parcels and the value of verifying what's there: GIS works for Bethel, Maine
> Donald Bennett, Town Selectman; James Doar, Town Manager; and Sarah Tucker, GIS Analyst, Town of Bethel, Maine

Using GIS to prepare for a possible disaster: San Antonio's CBIRF exercise
> Chris Stokes, GISP, Special Projects Manager; and James Mendoza, CEM, Assistant Emergency Manager, City of San Antonio Office of Emergency Management

GIS for decision support and policy making

GIS-ing flood data: Polk County, Florida, makes valuable information in paper studies available
> Mehdi Mashud Khan, GIS Supervisor, Polk County BoCC IT/GIS, Florida

Examining the fiscal impact of new development for the Ohio-Kentucky-Indiana Regional Council of Governments
> Della G. Rucker, Principal, Wise Economy Workshop

Quantifying visual quality in the Province of Newfoundland, Canada
> Doug Piercey, GeoInformatics Analyst, Natural Resources Canada–Canadian Forest Service, Newfoundland

Using GIS to understand and engage constituents

Preserving open space and parks through urban Greenprinting in Deschutes County, Oregon
> Breece Robertson, National Conservation Vision and GIS Director; Kelley Hart, Associate Director of Conservation Vision; and Kristin Kovalik, Oregon Project Manager, The Trust for Public Land

Making it easier for citizens to have input in development plans in Ireland's Dún Laoghaire-Rathdown and Fingal County Councils
> Based on an interview with Dermot O'Kane from Esri Ireland, and a case study by Esri Ireland

Collecting and using municipal census data for planning services in St. Albert, Alberta, Canada
> Tammy Kobliuk, GIS Coordinator, Corporate Geographic Information Services, City of St. Albert, Alberta, Canada

Assisting the special-needs community during emergencies in Fort Worth, Texas
> Robin Britton, GIS Lead; Shaun Campbell, Lead IT Programmer/Analyst; and Randy Westerman, Public Education Specialist, Office of Emergency Management, Fort Worth Fire Department, City of Fort Worth, Texas

Matching GIS to community trends

Growing a healthy economy: How GIS supports Littleton's economic gardening program
> Chris Gibbons, Director; and Eric Ervin, Marketing/GIS Analyst, City of Littleton Business/Industry Affairs Department, Littleton, Colorado

Looking at food deserts in Chattanooga, Tennessee
> Lori Quillen, Policy Analyst, the Ochs Center for Metropolitan Studies, Chattanooga, Tennessee

Going mobile in Redlands, California
> N. Enrique Martinez, City Manager; and David L. Hexem, Chief Information Officer, Department of Innovation and Technology (DoIT), City of Redlands, California

Matching GIS to policy interests

Promoting active living with the Trail and Recreational Information Portal (TRIP) in Carver County, Minnesota
> Peter Henschel, GIS Department; Randy Maluchnik, Commissioner; and Tracy Bade, Public Health and Environment Division, Carver County, Minnesota

Building a virtual emergency management network in Multnomah County and the State of Oregon
> Amy Esnard, GISP, GIS Manager, Multnomah County IT Department, Multnomah County, Oregon

The benefits of GIS from the perspective of a newcomer to the field
> Interview with Judy Shiprack, Commissioner, District 3, Multnomah County, Oregon

Land conservation and preservation in Scottsdale, Arizona
> Kroy Ekblaw, Preserve Director; Robert Chasan, Geographer/GIS Analyst; and Scott Hamilton, Preserve Planner, City of Scottsdale, Arizona

Part 3. Streamlining government operations with GIS

Return on investment and the benefits of GIS

Show me the money: What was King County's ROI from twenty years of using GIS?
> Greg Babinski, GISP, Finance and Marketing Manager, King County GIS Center Seattle, Washington, and URISA President, 2011–12

Considering the benefits of GIS and ROI: Moreno Valley's participation in the 2010 Local Update of Census Addresses (LUCA) Program
> Michael K. Heslin, GIS Administrator; and Bonnie Flickinger, Mayor, City of Moreno Valley

City of Airdrie implements a secure, real-time, and virtually paperless online census
> Esri Canada

Getting the job done

Improving efficiency and flexibility in the development process in Mono County, California
> Nate Greenberg, GIS Coordinator, Mono County and Town of Mammoth Lakes, California; and Susan Kirk, BasicGov

Emergency management service (EMS) investment returns big for Lexington County, South Carolina
> Brian Hood, Lexington County EMS Coordinator; Jack Maguire, Lexington County Planning and GIS Manager; and Tony Bradshaw, Bradshaw Consulting Services

Visualizing a ten-year capital plan in Niagara: Time savings, improved communications, and increased collaboration
> Esri Canada

Applying GIS to business problems

The need for SPEED: New York City's real estate and environmental GIS search engine promotes brownfield redevelopment
> Daniel Walsh, PhD; Lee Ilan; and Shaminder Chawla, Mayor's Office of Environmental Remediation, City of New York, New York

Locating vulnerable populations in Broward County, Florida
> Ginny Hazen, Broward County Emergency Management Division; Carolyn Rodriguez, Broward County Human Services Department; Hillary Hinds, Broward County Enterprise Technology Services; Roberto Castillo, Broward County Enterprise Technology Services; Bob Humple, Broward County Emergency Management Division; and Tami Price, Broward County Emergency Management Division, Broward County, Florida

GIS tied to workflow and business processes

Tracking Comprehensive Plan amendments in Fairfax County, Virginia
> Indrani Sistla, Department of Planning and Zoning; and Thomas Conry, GIS Manager, Fairfax County, Virginia

Streamlining the permitting process in Delaware, Ohio
> David M. Efland, AICP, Director of Planning and Community Development, City of Delaware, Ohio; and Matt Harman, Project Manager, Azteca Systems

Using GIS data for identifying and cataloging brownfield sites in Wauwatosa, Wisconsin
> Nancy Welch, Director of Community Development, City of Wauwatosa, Wisconsin, and Principal Urban Planner, NLW Consulting

Integrated GIS

Adding value to 311/CRM data in Hartford, Connecticut
    Brett Flodine, GISP, GIS Project Leader, Metro Hartford Information Services; and Andrew Jaffee, Director, Emergency Services and Telecommunications, City of Hartford, Connecticut

Putting Quebec City on the map
    Esri Canada

Work management and GIS: Identifying where the work is in Corpus Christi, Texas
    Michael Armstrong, Chief Information Officer, City of Corpus Christi, Texas

Performance measurement and accountability

Opening up the redistricting process in the State of Utah
    Based on an interview with John Cannon and Chris McClelland, Office of Legislative Research and General Counsel, State of Utah

Using GIS to promote city services in Rancho Cucamonga
    Ingrid Bruce, GIS/Special Districts Manager; and Solomon Nimako, GIS Fire Analyst, City of Rancho Cucamonga

Opening up the liquor license process in the State of New York
    Based on an interview with Joshua Carr, Deputy Commissioner, New York State Liquor Authority

The right tools for the job

Responding to the needs for a regional GIS in central Florida
    Claudia Paskauskas, MCSD, GISP, 6 Sigma Green Belt, PMP, GIS Manager, East Central Florida Regional Planning Council, Altamonte Springs, Florida

Traffic safety: How GIS is improving the safety of streets in the city of Carson, California
    Barry Waite, Director, Economic Development, City of Carson, California

The Mobile Office Initiative: Trailblazing changes in Alberta's resource management
    Esri Canada

GIS is changing

Working toward greater GIS access in Cape Girardeau, Missouri
    Anamika Anand, GIS Coordinator, City of Cape Girardeau

Information is key in Newton County, Georgia
    Kathy Morgan, Chair, County Commission; Lynn Parham, GIS Manager; and Ernie Smith, GIS Coordinator, Newton County, Georgia

The evolution of a regional GIS program: eCityGov Alliance, Washington
    John Backman, Executive Director, eCityGov Alliance; and Emily Arteche, Senior Planner, City of Sammamish, Washington, and Chair, NWMaps.net Business Committee

Three-dimensional GIS

Designing the future with Virtual Fairfax
    Thomas Conry, GIS Manager, Fairfax County, Virginia

Part 4. Building a strong GIS program

Developing a vision

GIS visioning workshop and strategic plan in Boone County, Missouri

> Karen Miller, County Commissioner; and Jason Warzinik, GISP, GIS Manager, Boone County, Missouri

Building a solid foundation: Data

Building a solid data foundation through the GIS Infrastructure Group (GIG), Washington County, Oregon

> Preston Beck, GIS Coordinator and IT Project Manager, Financial and Information Services, City of Tigard; Jay Leroux, IS Manager, City of Hillsboro; and Nels Mickaelson, GIS Coordinator, Washington County, Oregon

Devising an implementation plan

Consolidating and integrating GIS into the business of Boise, Idaho: Ushering in a culture change

> Jim Hetherington and Garry Beatty, Information and Technology Department, City of Boise, Idaho

Moving Novi's online mapping service to the cloud

> Christopher Blough, MPA, PMP, City GIS Manager, City of Novi, Michigan

Sustainable applications

Moving to self-help GIS services in Salina, Kansas

> Keith Ganzenmuller, GIS Supervisor; and Mike Fraser, Director, Department of Public Works, City of Salina, Kansas

Using GIS to deploy smart meter technology in San Marcos, Texas

> William Flynn, Public Services GIS/Technology Manager, City of San Marcos, Texas

Case studies by population size

Part	Jurisdiction	State/Province	Country	Population*
2	Bethel	Maine	US	2,614
3	Mono County	California	US	14,202
3	Airdrie	Alberta	Canada	28,927
3	Delaware	Ohio	US	34,753
3	Cape Girardeau	Missouri	US	37,941
2	Littleton	Colorado	US	41,737
4	San Marcos	Texas	US	44,894
3	Wauwatosa	Wisconsin	US	46,396
4	Salina	Kansas	US	47,707
4	Novi	Michigan	US	55,224
2	St. Albert	Alberta	Canada	60,138
2	Redlands	California	US	68,747

(continued)

Part	Jurisdiction	State/Province	Country	Population*
2	Carver County	Minnesota	US	91,042
3	Carson	California	US	91,714
3	Newton County	Georgia	US	99,958
3	Hartford	Connecticut	US	124,775
2	Deschutes County	Oregon	US	157,733
4	Boone County	Missouri	US	162,642
3	Rancho Cucamonga	California	US	165,269
2	Chattanooga	Tennessee	US	167,674
3	Moreno Valley	California	US	193,365
4	Boise	Idaho	US	205,671
2	Scottsdale	Arizona	US	217,385
3	Lexington County	South Carolina	US	262,391
3	Corpus Christi	Texas	US	305,215
3	Niagara	Ontario	Canada	427,421
2	Province of Newfoundland and Labrador	Newfoundland and Labrador	Canada	505,469
3	Quebec City	Quebec	Canada	525,376
4	Washington County	Oregon	US	529,710
2	Polk County	Florida	US	602,095
2	Multnomah County	Oregon	US	735,334
2	Multnomah County (J. Shiprack Interview)	Oregon	US	735,334
2	Fort Worth	Texas	US	741,206
1	Honolulu	Hawaii	US	953,207
3	Fairfax County (CPATS)	Virginia	US	1,037,605
3	Fairfax County (Virtual Fairfax)	Virginia	US	1,037,605
1	Hennepin County (R. Johnson Interview)	Minnesota	US	1,152,424
2	San Antonio	Texas	US	1,327,407
3	eCityGov Alliance	Washington	US	1,524,111
3	Broward County	Florida	US	1,748,066
3	King County	Washington	US	1,931,249

(continued)

Part	Jurisdiction	State/Province	Country	Population*
2	OKI Regional Council of Governments	Ohio	US	1,999,474
3	State of Utah	Utah	US	2,763,885
3	East Central Florida Regional Planning Council	Florida	US	3,172,380
3	Province of Alberta	Alberta	Canada	3,290,350
1	State of Oregon (C. Smith Interview)	Oregon	US	3,831,074
3	New York City	New York	US	8,175,133
3	State of New York	New York	US	19,378,104
2	Dún Laoghaire-Rathdown County Council and Fingal County Council		Ireland	DLR County Council 206,261 Fingal County Council 273,991

* **Note:** US population totals from 2010 Census (US Census Bureau), and Canada population totals from 2006 Census (Statistics Canada).

Part 1. Understanding GIS

Takeaways:

- GIS data and spatial analysis provide elected officials with critical input for policy and decision-making processes.
- GIS technology has gone mainstream, with many applications available that require no special training to use.
- A robust GIS program requires strategic planning to determine what key datasets are needed and can be used for the greatest number of applications.
- Cloud computing and web services represent the next generation in GIS technology.

Decisions in the public realm

Vision. The voting public expects elected officials to have a vision of the future, no matter what level of government they serve. What will this person do while in office? How will he or she make this a better world for all citizens? What programs and services will this official support? What are his or her spending priorities? How will the decisions an elected official makes affect the average person's daily life?

Responding to such questions—helping people understand what decisions are being made and why—is a challenging task. Elected officials work every day to represent the best interests of their constituents and make decisions that create positive change for their communities. To do so, they must consider a huge volume of data and information in their decision-making process. Sorting through all the information, understanding

the various implications, and, in turn, explaining those implications to the public is a laborious and complicated process. They face a diverse and complex range of issues that require thoughtful decision making.

Geographic information systems (GIS) provide a comprehensive framework for discussing public issues and challenges. All forms of government are place and location based, whether town and city, county, state, or federal. With that geographic element comes the ability to map a wide variety of data related to specific locations. The belief that planning and land-use issues are the primary beneficiaries of GIS technology doesn't hold true anymore. As Commissioner Randy Johnson from Hennepin County, Minnesota, observes, "I have yet to find a county function that couldn't be improved by use of GIS analysis." GIS technology can make the task of decision making less complicated.

> **"When you can tell a story with a map versus telling a story with words, your citizens understand it better." Karen Miller, Commissioner, Boone County, Missouri**

Consider the various types of everyday questions constituents ask elected officials, advises Christopher Blough, the GIS manager with the City of Novi, Michigan. He suggests that many, if not most, questions require location-based information to answer them. For example:

- Where do citizen calls for service originate? Does the jurisdiction have responsibility for responding, and how long do the calls require for resolution?
- Are calls for service originating from the same neighborhood about the same problem? If so, why?
- Can work crews respond more efficiently to service calls if they receive the locations of work orders while in the field?
- Where do police and fire department calls for service originate, and where are response times exceeding acceptable levels?
- Does citizen satisfaction with city services vary across the community?
- Where have capital improvement projects been scheduled in the community over the next five years?

The range of uses for GIS technology extends nearly as far as the imagination goes. This book offers evidence of the vast uses of GIS in part 2, which describes how government leaders use GIS for determining potential markets for start-up businesses in Littleton, Colorado; for responding to the needs of special population groups within the community during a disaster in Fort Worth, Texas; and for identifying urban food deserts in Chattanooga, Tennessee. In the early days of GIS, much of the analytic work focused on spatial

relationships, or what was located where in a community or in a state. Increasingly, though, policy makers use GIS technology to model future scenarios, run simulations, and forecast what the effect of a given decision might be. GIS helps answer the age-old question, "What happens if we do this?"

> **"GIS has been a fundamental tool in our Economic Gardening program in Littleton for over a decade. It is a sophisticated way of identifying markets by demographics, lifestyles, and consumer expenditures. By providing direct and tangible support to our local emerging growth companies, we have been able to double our job base and triple our sale tax revenues without spending a single cent on recruiting or incentives." Chris Gibbons, Director of Business/Industry Affairs, City of Littleton, Colorado**

This volume is designed as a peer-to-peer information-sharing effort to enable governments to learn from the experiences of others. Dozens of governments contributed to the development of this volume, which is by no means a technical or how-to manual, but rather a reference guide to illustrate the power of GIS technology. As an introduction, part 1 looks at the evolution and growth of GIS technology. Parts 2 and 3 feature a wealth of case studies on how governments across North America use GIS to study options, develop policy, and better manage the business of government. Finally, part 4 reviews what it takes to build and maintain a strong GIS program, especially in light of rapidly changing technology and shrinking government budgets.

The Great Recession of 2008–2009 has changed—and continues to change—the way governments do business. The great challenge right now for elected officials is to develop a new vision based on the economic realities created by the recession. Governments at all levels need to rethink and reengineer the processes that deliver services to citizens. In order to lower costs over the long term and maintain service quality, governments will need to make a fundamental shift away from manual systems that use up critical staff time and move toward the greater and smarter use of technology. GIS technology, with its spatial approach to analysis, provides a common foundation for working with widely divergent types of data. Having common GIS datasets and layers that can be used by any department or any agency allows governments to take advantage of opportunities when they arise and serve citizens in new ways, as Cy Smith, geographic information officer with the Oregon Geospatial Enterprise Office, explains next.

Generating excitement about GIS in the State of Oregon

Interview with Cy Smith, Geographic Information Officer, Oregon Geospatial Enterprise Office (GEO), Salem, Oregon

Level of government: State
State/province: Oregon
Country: USA
Population: 3,831,074

High-profile projects generate excitement, and the State of Oregon's Geospatial Enterprise Office (GEO) has undertaken several such projects since 2009. Working closely with the governor's office, staff at GEO have developed an array of new GIS applications that allow citizens to track how and where stimulus funds received from the American Recovery and Reinvestment Act (ARRA) of 2008 are being used. Citizens can go online to see how the Recovery Act is impacting their community and how state agencies are meeting the needs of Oregonians.

Figure 1.1 Cyril Smith, geographic information officer of the Oregon GEO. Courtesy of Cyril Smith.

The new applications have generated numerous hits on their respective websites, as well as provided background information for news articles that discuss how stimulus dollars are influencing job creation and workforce training, education, community services, and a number of other vital services.

Although the applications are being well used, Cy Smith, who leads the Oregon GEO, cautions that the success they have experienced developing and pushing out these applications has not come about overnight. "In order to make that happen, you have to have a solid foundation. My group has spent the last ten years building that foundation. As it's become more and more developed, we've been able to use it to take advantage of opportunities," explains Smith.

A decade ago, GEO developed a strategic plan and an implementation plan that laid out a GIS enterprise approach for the state. GEO staff looked across the board at all the business processes being performed by state agencies and other key stakeholders, including local governments (both cities and counties), regional associations of governments, academic institutions, private-sector businesses, and federal agencies. After examining the state's geospatial data needs and seeking feedback and collaboration from stakeholders, GEO began to lead the development of the necessary foundation of data and information layers that enabled stakeholders, in turn, to develop applications they need.

Smith elaborates, "If you have the technical and data infrastructure in place to support an enterprise approach, you can take advantage of new opportunities fairly quickly and inexpensively. But if you don't, you're looking at spending considerable time and money on development costs, sometimes redundantly, prior to attempting to meet those new needs. If you're already set up with the necessary data layers, then time and money can be spent on the businesses processes themselves."

In other words, the current success of and excitement about the new GIS applications did not come about overnight, but rather are the result of a long-term strategic and systematic effort on the part of GEO to collect the basic reference data needed by a large number of state agencies and other stakeholders. In order to achieve this critical foundation of data and information layers, GEO collaborated with the state stakeholders to let them know what the state's plans were, and then listened to what the stakeholder groups, particularly local governments, were doing.

Smith explains, "We look for opportunities where we can have the biggest impact. In the case of ARRA, we were able to talk to all the state agencies and the governor's advisers, who were looking at all the different policy areas, and show them what was possible with GIS in terms of showing the impact of federal expenditures. When we did that, immediately the light bulbs started going on. People began to see how the data could be used and adapted for their particular projects, many of which were not ARRA funded."

They also began to ask questions about what else could be done using other data from GEO. For example, one agency contracted to have a website developed that demonstrated the impact of lottery dollars spent on the statewide salmon recovery program. When a vote came up on whether lottery dollars should continue to fund that program for another five years, the agency administering that program could demonstrate the impact of the program over the last ten or fifteen years. The public voted in favor of extending the program.

GIS started as a program in the Department of Energy nearly twenty years ago, but as other state agencies saw what the technology could do, they, too, wanted to take advantage of the technology's analytic capabilities. The state established a GIS service center to meet some of the demand for the technology, but over time, with lower computer costs and easier-to-use GIS programs, many of the other agencies started developing their own GIS applications, and the service center could not support itself. Approximately ten years ago, the state opted to close down the service center and established GEO to coordinate enterprise GIS activities.

Located within the office of the state's chief information officer (CIO), GEO's role has been one of promoting and encouraging the use of GIS technology among the state agencies and other stakeholders. As more government agencies use GIS technology, more data is developed, and more information becomes available for all the agencies. GEO supports the governance structure for the state's GIS infrastructure. Much of the work initially was organized around data, including the development of fourteen reference (or base layer) datasets. GEO has established protocols to ensure that the data is shared in a standardized manner and has developed an operational basis that cuts across the work of all the state agencies.

The office has also begun to create teams to work on areas of mutual interest and applications other than data, such as public safety. (See the related case study on Multnomah County, Oregon, in part 2.) Representatives from multiple agencies and other stakeholder groups have formed committees to manage applications related to topics of mutual interest using a common operating picture. The governance structure institutionalizes the working relationships that are needed across agencies and their respective programs in order to fully address issues of mutual interest.

Smith has found that being able to illustrate how a policy-level decision can be aided by a GIS analysis has been the most effective tool in generating excitement about the technology. Offering examples of GIS applications that provide what a policy maker needs to make key decisions helps generate new ideas and brings out people's creativity. "GIS technology has the unique ability to bring together governments at all levels to work collaboratively on issues of common concern and connect their respective business processes. It sets us up to deliver services in a new way to citizens," says Smith.

How GIS works

Consider a basic road map and all the information it contains on paper—cities and counties, highways and roads, lakes and rivers, parks and forests, camping sites, boat launches, and historic sites. In a GIS, all these different types of data can be organized and stored in a computer as data layers that can be added to or taken away from a basemap depending on the requirement of the analysis being conducted. If a city council wants to know, for example, where the Federal Emergency Management Agency (FEMA) floodplains are located in relationship to a proposed new development, that data layer can be added to the basemap instantly. If the city council then wants to see how the development is situated in relationship to existing residential neighborhoods, it can add a data layer that visualizes the existing land uses in the analysis. This ability to look at different and multifaceted combinations of data layers nearly instantaneously makes GIS technology a very powerful tool for elected officials grappling with the possible ramifications of complex policy decisions (see, for example, figure 1.2).

Figure 1.2 The City of Westbrook, Maine (the editor's home), provides its GIS online so citizens can easily look up their properties to determine where lot lines lie or which type of zone they live in. Courtesy of City of Westbrook, Maine.

Agencies handling issues related to land use and planning have long used GIS technology, but increasingly other fields are taking advantage of the software's analytic capabilities. If a state legislative committee wants to study the effectiveness of crime prevention programs for juveniles, support staff can create a series of maps that show juvenile crime rates in relation to the state's population demographics and available program resources. Likewise, a governor proposing to expand broadband access in her state might ask to review an inventory of current coverage, and then look at barriers to broadband adoption on a county-by-county basis.

Although once the exclusive stronghold of the technologically gifted, GIS has gone mainstream in the last decade. In much the same way that it is no longer necessary for a person to learn programming languages such as BASIC or Fortran to use a computer, using GIS technology no longer requires an individual to be fully proficient in the sometimes confusing language of parcels, vectors, and points. New means for accessing GIS technology, such as cloud computing, software as a service (SaaS), and web services, make it possible for anyone to take advantage of the analytic capability of GIS. As Commissioner Randy Johnson of Hennepin County, Minnesota, points out next, a person doesn't have to be a computer programmer to use GIS technology anymore.

Promoting GIS technology use in local government

Interview with Randy Johnson, Commissioner, Hennepin County, Minnesota

Level of Government: County
State/province: Minnesota
Country: USA
Population: 1,152,424

Commissioner Randy Johnson, who represents District 5 in Hennepin County, Minnesota, has been an advocate of GIS technology nearly since its inception. In the early 1970s, Hennepin County developed one of the first GIS software programs. The application, developed by the county's Public Works team, plotted where the county's roads and highways then existed and where future roads could be built. It also showed boundaries for parcels in the county's tax base.

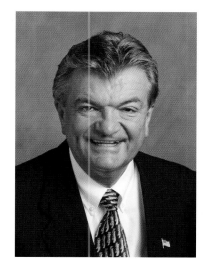

Figure 1.3 Randy Johnson, commissioner.

Since that time, according to Johnson, GIS technology has become a critical decision support tool for policy makers. When the software was first introduced in the market, it was used primarily by computer programmers and engineers, he recalls. No real applications supported the work of elected officials at that time. "Now, [we seldom have a] board meeting that doesn't involve some type of GIS presentation. My eyes get bright when I hear one of my fellow commissioners comment, 'I'd like to see how that looks on a map.' For example, just recently we [Hennepin County board] were considering where to locate health clinics around the county in relationship to population needs. The GIS presentation provided us with concrete data to determine the best locations for serving our constituents," says Johnson.

Johnson has a deep love of maps that goes back to his childhood. "From the time I was about eight years old, I was always the navigator on family trips," says Johnson. This longtime fascination with maps may be part of the reason that he uses GIS to create his own maps. "I once created a map using ZIP Codes in the county that plotted the addresses of individuals and families receiving food stamps. I used this as a rough indicator of financial need in the county," says Johnson. "What I was able to determine is that financial need is not just an inner-city problem, but it [is] a problem throughout the county." Although most of Johnson's fellow commissioners aren't quite as motivated to create their own maps as he is, he does note that they frequently use the property and parcel maps, election results maps, and the park locator maps, both for themselves and their constituents.

Johnson maintains most county government programs would benefit from GIS analysis. "I have a favorite story I like to tell that illustrates the real potential of GIS. About ten years ago, I offered a free lunch to anyone in Hennepin County government who could find a county function that couldn't use or be improved by GIS. To this day, I have yet to pay for a lunch," says Johnson. "Once a hospital employee said she understood how GIS and GPS could help us manage our ambulance fleet, but she questioned how it could help patients once they were admitted to the hospital. I pointed out that our hospital, like most large hospitals, occasionally 'loses' patients. Combining GIS with RFID [radio-frequency identification] patient bracelets could solve that problem, and it could also help us keep track of the location of expensive equipment and even gurneys!"

Johnson is particularly excited about recent developments in GIS technology and equates the evolution of GIS to that of the automobile. "When the automobile first came on the market, it was a pretty simple thing operationally, but you had to be your own mechanic to keep it running. These days we have ABS brakes, satellite radio, GPS, rear-end cameras, and more that makes the driving experience safer and more enjoyable, but I don't need to look under the hood in order to use all those features," says Johnson. "The same thing is happening with GIS. It is becoming easier to use and very intuitive to learn. For example, it takes about ten minutes to learn how to use the GPS unit in my car. There is very complex programming behind the technology, but I don't need to understand the programming language to use it. When you look at the new iPhone and iPad and other applications coming out now, you don't need to be very computer savvy at all to use those."

Johnson points out that almost everything local governments do is location based. "We, as elected officials, need to encourage our staff people to make presentations more graphically. Maps aid our own understanding of an issue as well as help communicate information about the issue to our constituents," says Johnson.

The City and County of Honolulu, Hawaii, was an early pioneer in developing a GIS program, and it has continued to take advantage of new innovations in the technology. The history of its GIS program showcases how the technology has propelled local governments to improved service delivery and smarter ways of doing business.

Growing a GIS program in Honolulu, Hawaii

Ken Schmidt, GIS Administrator, City and County of Honolulu, Hawaii

Level of government: City and county
State/province: Hawaii
Country: USA
Population: 953,207

The City and County of Honolulu first adopted a GIS application in 1988—five years after discussions about the benefits of adopting a system started—in an effort to provide better data for land-use planning and information efforts. By 1990, it had hired a full-time GIS coordinator, which facilitated the growth of the GIS from basic data delivery to more advanced applications that allowed for the retrieval of tax assessment and property ownership information.

Since its implementation, the system has continued to expand, both in terms of the number of departments using it and its functionality. Today, Honolulu Land Information Systems (HOLIS), which manages Honolulu's GIS efforts, has thirteen staff members and a budget of $1.2 million (for fiscal year 2011). The GIS unit is a hybrid, with a centralized database and coordinating function through several major city agencies, including the Department of Planning and Permitting, Environmental Services, and Tax Assessment, as well as the Police and Fire Departments. These agencies also each have at least one GIS specialist on staff.

New and evolving uses

Since its inception, the GIS has "become more embedded in the mission-critical operations of the city," says Ken Schmidt, the GIS administrator for the City and County of Honolulu. "Individual

The GIS data has allowed for an automated permitting system, HonLINE, through which residents can apply for, pay for, and print building permits online. In 2010, nearly 25 percent of all building permits—or 3,209 permits—were issued using HonLINE, and it generated close to $375,000 in revenue. In addition, the city estimates that it saved 300 personnel-days.

CASE STUDY > > >

agencies have really developed their capabilities where they have become more independent to utilize and employ GIS." The GIS is now embedded in the city's police dispatching, public safety, utility management, and permitting operations. Honolulu has also increased the web presence of its GIS, making the technology easily accessible for both city agencies and the public.

An important evolution in the GIS has occurred with the development of HonLINE, an online permitting process (figure 1.4). David Tanoue, director of the Department of Planning and Permitting, explains that "HonLINE is key to our technology initiatives for improving our customer services and for establishing more efficient and cost-effective permitting operations. By allowing for certain standard permits to be issued online, our personnel can focus on the more complex applications. This eliminated bottlenecks in the permit application workflows by reducing the volume at the front counter, while enabling revenue-generating services." The GIS data has allowed for an automated permitting system in which residents can apply for, pay for, and print building permits online. The GIS and the integrated permitting system allow the applications to be checked to ensure that they are in compliance with zoning codes and other regulatory requirements. In 2010, nearly 25 percent of all building permits—or 3,209 permits—in the city were issued using HonLINE, and it generated close to $375,000 in revenue. In addition, the city estimates that it saved 300 personnel-days.

Figure 1.4 Honolulu's public GIS interface links directly with building permit data and a wide range of land record data to assist in parcel and property research. Courtesy of City and County of Honolulu, Hawaii.

The biggest challenge Honolulu faces with its GIS, according to Schmidt, is the maintenance of all the information. But, he adds, "maintenance of GIS is a continuous cycle, built into the business process. It is required for city services to make decisions."

CASE STUDY > >

Collaboration and community use

Honolulu's GIS system is a collaborative effort between the city and various state and federal agencies. The City and County of Honolulu comprises the entire island of Oahu and, as a result, all of the government agencies and departments work closely together. "There has been a great deal of collaboration between our agencies," Schmidt says. "We are 'local' as we like to say. We have much less complexity in that area." However, although they often talk about what other local governments in the state are doing, HOLIS does not necessarily work with them because it does not often have a need for their data because the jurisdictions are island environments. Honolulu does participate in a statewide program called the Hawaii Geographic Coordinating Council (HIGICC), and there is a significant amount of coordination and collaboration through the state agencies.

Honolulu has been working to expand the public GIS website and improve its functionality for users, and it has received strong and positive feedback from the community about the system. The website is heavily used, receiving 238,500 visits in fiscal year 2010, or approximately 660,000 page views. The local realtors associations are major users of the online data, because it helps provide a sense of a property's location as well as regulatory influences and requirements of a given location (e.g., if it is in a flood zone). Additionally, the online system links directly into the permitting program for researching history of a particular property.

Moving forward

Honolulu is continuing to expand and improve its GIS. HOLIS's next major effort is to enable the electronic submission of building plans associated with a permit. The e-plan initiative will allow the actual building plans to be submitted online, where they will be stored in a web-based interface that will allow direct communication with the developers. This will allow the city and county to move toward electronic permit-plan review and will greatly expand the current capabilities of HonLINE. The system is also being updated to associate permitting data, which is currently referenced to a parcel or lot, to the structure or to a site identifier to make the information more specific.

Honolulu is also working on developing specific address-based information that would provide specific references for the entire island of Oahu. This information has previously only been available for the urbanized area of the island. In addition, HOLIS is focusing on updating its cadastral basemaps. The current basemaps were developed before the advent of high-resolution geographic imagery, and, as a result, lot and parcel boundaries are not always identically referenced. This basemap update will help improve the accuracy of parcel boundaries and lot lines, which will enhance city services.

GIS and Honolulu's local government agenda

Honolulu's GIS has influenced the local government's agenda by providing more information to decision makers. It has helped local decision makers evaluate the return on investment of the decisions they want to make and has helped identify what the ongoing costs and benefits of those policies will be. "The information value it provides really can improve the services of local governments to help reduce the cost of local government and maintain the efficiency that is needed," says Schmidt.

CASE STUDY >

Local elected officials are generally interested in information generated by the GIS due in large part to its visual content. "It's really being able to tell a story with a graphic or presentation in a very quick way. You need to have simple information displays," Schmidt notes. "It is also important to have advocates in the agencies to help them present to the mayor the importance of the information."

For example, the GIS is currently being used to develop tsunami evacuation zones. Through the GIS, local officials and first responders have been better able to define those areas of the island that would need to be evacuated in the case of a tsunami event. The GIS not only helps generate this information, but also helps graphically convey the information to both local officials and residents. It provides a significant benefit—through public safety agencies—in terms of making decisions related to what areas need to be evacuated and protecting citizens. These maps are being presented through the news media, included in neighborhood meetings, and distributed throughout the community via libraries and other organizations to visually educate residents on the potential hazards of a tsunami.

Lessons for other local governments

Honolulu has a very complex and advanced GIS. As a result, HOLIS's experiences can provide lessons and insight for local governments looking to implement or expand their own GIS. Schmidt uses the development of HonLINE, the online permitting process, to draw out these lessons. To begin with, he emphasizes a focus on the business processes of the permitting process—which can be very complex—and the importance of designing systems that can be flexible.

In addition, it can be helpful to have a business process review performed by consultants. HOLIS had consultants look at "key choke points" in the permitting process to determine where inefficiencies were occurring. When HonLINE was started, front-end data entry was a system choke point, and they worked to improve the system capabilities. Now, the plan review process is the choke point and, as discussed above, HOLIS is working to refine this process to allow for online plan submittal.

Workflow diagramming can be essential for looking at where complexities exist and where there is a lot of transfer of information back and forth, as well as how improvements can be made. Although workflow diagramming can be immensely useful, it is not necessarily needed for all the information systems, but rather for the general businesses processes. "When you find these areas of where you want to improve your business process or practice," Schmidt says, "your system needs to be flexible to be modified without requiring major reconfiguration of the system."

Finally, during reviews of the GIS and its capabilities with city departments, it is important to have members of the GIS unit present to serve as technical experts to policy makers and operations managers. Being part of strategic planning teams helps in answering questions as to whether certain proposed updates or additions to the GIS can be implemented. Weekly meetings with executives to discuss operational processes and issues have been extremely useful in communicating the technology capabilities and in coordinating system development with the business process improvement initiatives.

CASE STUDY •

Types of GIS

Early in its history, GIS required the use of large main-frame computer systems usually available only through federal government agencies or universities. As computers have evolved and become more affordable and easier to use, so has GIS technology. Web-based online applications allow any individual to simply check the data layers he or she wants to look at on a map or type the address of a destination to get directions for the shortest route to a given location. Simply put, GIS technology is almost commonplace now. The technology has become part of the critical infrastructure needed for doing government business.

The World Wide Web and Web 2.0

The introduction of the World Wide Web revolutionized the way business works with an influence that is truly global in nature. Initially the web was used primarily for accessing information in an electronic, but still static, format. As the web has grown and evolved, it has become much more dynamic and interactive, and online GIS applications and Web 2.0 have become important business drivers for all levels of government. Developers and builders routinely use government GIS applications to scout for appropriate site locations. Real estate agents use GIS to look up property assessments, parcel boundaries, and other key information needed by clients. Citizens can check out trails and other facilities at nearby parks. One web application allows citizens to comment online on a community's development plan, specifically noting areas on a map where they may have concerns (see the case study on Dún Laoghaire-Rathdown County Council and Fingal County Council, Ireland, in part 2). Another allows developers to insert a model of a proposed building into the existing streetscape to see how the building will work with its surroundings (see the Fairfax County Virtual Fairfax case study in part 3).

For elected officials, online GIS applications can help explain complex policy decisions as well as provide greater transparency of how public funds are spent. They also respond directly to constituents' need for information.

Mobile

Wireless technology has made it possible to access the web via a computer virtually anywhere. Workers can access GIS technology on laptop computers or net-books in the field and provide real-time updates on what is happening at a location (see the case study on San Marcos, Texas, in part 4). The ability to pick up new jobs remotely without having to return to the office saves both staff time and money.

The popularity of smart devices has led to the development of a number of new applications that use GIS technology. As a result, GIS is being used for many new public purposes: citizen engagement, volunteerism, consolidation of services, and sustainability, to name a few. One application, for example, allows citizens to snap a photo of a pothole that needs repair or a traffic light that's out, and then send the picture, along with the GIS coordinates, to the city as a service request. (See the case study on Redlands, California, in part 2.)

Logistics

Increasingly GIS technology is used to better manage the day-to-day logistics involved in government work. Mobile devices with GIS technology are routinely installed in government vehicles. Although these devices can provide simple driving directions like the retail GPS units many car owners purchase, they can do much more. Complex routing, which takes into account the need for multiple stops and tracks the locations of multiple vehicles, is now possible. Even the required turn radius needed for larger vehicles can be calculated in selecting routes. Maximum allowable loads and the need to return to the home base to refill or refuel are also included in developing routes that ensure the shortest drive times and the most efficient use of resources.

GIS logistics technology allows emergency response vehicles to find the quickest routes based on current traffic conditions and avoid any possible impedance. Service vehicles that require having material supplies on board—such as street sweepers, street repair trucks, and snowplows—can determine how far they can go on routes before needing to return to home base to pick up additional materials. As a result, logistics are automatically integrated into departmental workflows and feed directly into work order management and scheduling.

This technology enables governments to be greener, reducing both carbon emissions and fuel costs. It also contributes to better resource management by increasing productivity and efficiency.

Thinking about data

Data is at the heart of GIS, and the volume of data involved in building a robust GIS program is substantial. The creation and maintenance of needed datasets can be labor intensive. Maintaining data quality and integrity is a deep concern for many in the GIS field. With good strategic planning, however, many of the datasets created for a GIS program can be used for multiple purposes, and data-sharing agreements can give jurisdictions access to much more data than they could afford to create on their own. Additionally, the open government movement and its push for more open data (`http://www.data.gov`) has begun to usher in a new era of publicly available GIS data that will be very inexpensive.

Data standards

With GIS becoming more mainstream and accessible, the need for data standards that are used by all employees is critical. Data standards provide guidelines to ensure that a data layer created by one department can work with a data layer created by another department. In much the same way that a recipe allows one cook to produce the same dish as another by detailing the exact amounts of the ingredients to be used, data standards allow analysts to use different datasets knowing that they will work in the same way to create an accurate GIS analysis. Consider the near impossibility of creating a national land-use management system if all states, counties, cities, and towns adopted their own unique symbology for roads, land-cover change, or other features.

Executive Order 12906, signed by President Clinton in 1994, established the National Spatial Data Infrastructure (NSDI) to provide a structure for the practices and relationships among data producers and users to ensure a consistent means of sharing geographic data. The vision behind NSDI is to have current and accurate geographic data readily available to respond to a variety of needs. The Federal Geographic Data Committee (FGDC) is responsible for guiding the development of the NSDI, but adherence to its guidelines is voluntary, not mandatory.

The open data movement represents the next frontier in GIS data. Government in any democracy can support transparency and accountability goals by making its data and information freely available for review by citizens. Currently, most governments post their budgets, program results, and other public information on websites where it can be viewed, but often the data and information appear in a static format, such as text or PDF files, which make the data difficult to manipulate for analytic purposes. It is the equivalent of being given all the ingredients for a cake without having a mixing bowl, measuring cups, and spoons to actually make the cake. The open data movement promotes making government data available in an open format that is easily usable by citizens, the business community, and governments themselves. Many US cities and states have launched open data portals, where GIS and other data files can be easily accessed.

Looking to the future, elected officials should adopt policies to guide the development of local data standards that are coordinated with the FGDC efforts and contribute to the development of NSDI in order to realize savings for data collection, enhance the use of data, and support better decision making. Officials will also need to consider adopting open data policies that make data produced by the government more accessible to the general public.

Data sharing

Political boundaries clearly exist on maps; however, in the real world, they are not so readily apparent. Roads don't just stop at a state line, and economic development requires the resources of a region, not just a single city. In the early days of GIS, many governmental organizations initially hesitated to provide their data to others, preferring instead to maintain tight controls over its release and use in order to better maintain data quality. Additionally, many datasets exist that include information that legitimately should be kept confidential and secure.

Data-sharing agreements, however, provide governments with access to far more data than they could realistically hope to create and maintain on their own. State government could not begin to provide the same level of resolution of data for a city as the city itself, whereas a state can provide aerial imagery or historical survey maps that many local governments might not be able to afford to purchase or create on their own. Furthermore, it makes little sense for a city and a county to both maintain sets of the same types of data—for example, property tax assessment parcels or street addresses—if they can achieve the desired results by sharing their data with each other. Intergovernmental agreements among participating governments, which detail the terms and conditions of data-sharing arrangements among partners, ensures that the data is used appropriately and fosters both greater collaboration and stronger working relationships among member governments.

Data interoperability

Data interoperability refers to the ability to exchange and transfer data freely between systems. Consider a car that requires a repair. It shouldn't matter whether the parts required for the repair are made by one manufacturer or another; they should be interchangeable and work in the car no matter which manufacturer produced the part. The concept of data interoperability builds on the need for data standards and data sharing to promote the development of data that can be used no matter what type of system is being used. In other words, the data should work equally well whether being used in a traditional desktop program, an online web service, or a mobile application. The data user should need little to no knowledge of the unique characteristics of the data in order to use it. Again, just as elected officials should adopt policies to ensure that

common data standards are followed and data-sharing agreements are encouraged, they should also support the use of GIS practices that promote greater data interoperability.

The future of GIS technology

The evolution of the web has facilitated the exchange of data and information at an unprecedented pace over the last twenty years, and GIS technology has made the creation of and access to data related to specific geographic locations immense. In a sense, the tools have been created and refined up to this point in time. The future of GIS technology lies in understanding how to make the best use of these tools and to use them in new ways. The need to do so is confirmed by the fact that the US Department of Labor has identified geotechnology, including remote sensing, GIS, and GPS, as one of the leading fields of growth in the coming years.[1]

Crowdsourcing

Crowdsourcing, which involves individuals feeding data into a central system, allows GIS analysts to quickly compile and analyze a situation on the ground in nearly real time. The Gulf oil spill in the Gulf of Mexico in May 2010 resulted in the largest deployment of field GIS technology in any emergency response effort in history. Teams of GIS professionals collected critical response information for shoreline assessment and response planning. The quicker an emergency response can be developed, the less widespread and severe the damage. Agencies such as Florida Fish and Wildlife, the US Coast Guard, and various response teams within BP used ArcGIS for Mobile to feed incident command with critical information needed to plan response efforts.[2]

Cloud computing and software as a service (SaaS)

Cloud computing refers to a host of new web-based services that are delivered to the customer through a web browser. Software as a service (SaaS) is one of the most common components of cloud computing, where the vendor provides a single application for use by customers. Web e-mail service, where the user goes online to access his or her e-mail rather than using a program installed on a local computer, is a familiar example of a SaaS application. Using a SaaS application allows governments to move away from the need to continually update equipment and software in-house. Rather than selling new equipment and software that will eventually become obsolete, companies provide the application as a service online as well as needed technical support, program updates, and security upgrades. Cloud computing allows governments to store their GIS datasets and layers offsite and work with them on the web. Doing so requires less upfront investment in servers and other equipment; it offers greater storage capacity and access to additional services and data. It also enables users to work with the application from any computer with Internet access.

Web services, or "maps and apps"

Closely related to SaaS, web services allow a company to offer business services online, selling the service as a monthly pay-as-you go arrangement as opposed to the one-time purchase of a disk that requires installation on a local computer. Web services go beyond traditional web hosting, where space is rented on a server for the purpose of maintaining a website. Web services enable businesses to communicate with each other and with clients to share business logic, data, and processes. Essentially web services allow the hand-off of data and information from one application to another without the need for lots of additional computer programming. Consider that the location of a building can be expressed in half a dozen different ways—from a US National Grid reference number to a city parcel number to a street address, to name just a few ways to identify a location. Web services make it possible to use any of these different types of spatial data; data created in one application can be reused in another. The emergency management field, in particular, has benefited from the development of these "maps and apps" that provide dynamic, real-time data feeds for monitoring emergency situations. For example, weather data or flood stage data can be viewed in combination with traffic data to determine evacuation routes. Or the location of at-risk populations in a community can be viewed with data on bed space available at area hospitals in the event that individuals with special needs have to be relocated.

GIS technology continues to evolve with new innovations springing up on a daily basis to address needs and challenges that would not have been recognized even a few short years ago. Dr. Roger Tomlinson, often referred to as the "father of GIS," points out that "all of the major problems that we face throughout the world today—overpopulation, food shortages, reduced agricultural production, adverse climate change, poverty—these are all quintessentially geographic problems. These problems are all concerned with the human relationship to the land, and this is where GIS can make its biggest contribution."[3]

Endnotes

1   Virginia Gewin, "Careers and Recruitment: Mapping Opportunities," *Nature* 427: 376–377, doi: 10.1038/nj6972-376a.

2   Jeff Shaner, "Gulf Oil Response Update," blog entry, August 1, 2010, http://blogs.esri.com/Dev/blogs/mobilecentral/archive/2010/07/31/Gulf-Oil-Spill-Response-Update.aspx.

3   Jim Baumann, "Roger Tomlinson on GIS History and Future," *GEOconnexion International Magazine*, February 2009, 46–48.

Part 2. Using GIS to support policy decisions

Takeaways:

- GIS technology has expanded beyond its traditional uses (planning, zoning, and property assessment) to address a growing number of human services and social science policy issues.
- Using GIS to promote greater citizen engagement is an emerging trend in the field.
- Defining the right questions for GIS analysis is a critical element in using the technology to support public policy decisions.

In the public realm, elected officials have the responsibility for diagnosing problems and challenges that need to be addressed, determining what alternatives exist to respond to these challenges, and making decisions from among these alternatives. These decisions become public policy. Constantly changing economic, social, and political conditions makes the task of setting policy an unending job, as does the wide range of issues requiring attention. In order to accomplish these tasks, elected officials must have access to good data and solid analyses on which to base their policy decisions.

Spatial thinking itself—the desire to understand what's happening on the ground in a specific location—isn't new. Dr. John Snow is often cited as an early pioneer in spatial analysis for his groundbreaking work to identify the cause of London's cholera epidemic in 1854. Dr. Snow mapped cholera deaths on a London street map along with the locations of the public water-pump wells. One well proved to be located at the epicenter of a large number of the deaths. Once the suspect well was closed, the number of cholera deaths in London decreased dramatically.[1]

GIS technology offers the ability to delve deeper and to consider more variables and alternatives as part of a spatial analysis. Spatial data provides a common starting point and framework for conducting GIS analyses on a wide variety of societal issues. Certain basic datasets and layers provide a common foundation for many types of GIS analysis, whether an analysis involves determining potential markets for start-up businesses (see the case study on Littleton, Colorado, later in part 2) or making the location of area recreational facilities and trails more easily accessible to residents in order to encourage more active lifestyles (see the case study on

Carver County, Minnesota, later in part 2). Census data, labor force and employment data, street and road locations, district or ward boundary lines, and many other types of data can all be used for multiple purposes.

The challenge in using GIS technology is to consider what questions need to be asked in order to better understand a particular policy issue in a spatial context. Before beginning the development of a new GIS application, elected officials need to first define their policy goals, and then define the questions they need answered in order to achieve those goals. For example, if a state or province wants to determine the best location for building a new road, policy makers must first determine what the overriding priorities for building the road are:

- Lowest cost?
- Shortest distance?
- Easiest construction?
- Safest design?
- Least disruption to landowners?
- Least disruption to landscape and wildlife habitat?
- Or some combination of all of the above priorities?

Based on these questions, GIS analysts can develop an application to demonstrate how possible site alternatives for the new road might best meet the policy priorities. It is critical, though, to first know the desired end goal(s).

The case studies in part 2 illustrate how GIS technology can be used to support the development of government policy. More important, though, the case studies illustrate the very wide range of policy issues GIS technology is being used to address.

Traditional uses of GIS

Many GIS programs first began in the planning and zoning, engineering, or property assessment departments. These departments remain heavy users of GIS technology because they have a direct need to document and verify what exists on the ground. Even the smallest of governments, such as Bethel, Maine, find value in digitizing existing town maps for these uses. The emergency management field also recognized the value of GIS technology early on; San Antonio, Texas, for example, took advantage of the analytic power of GIS when running a Chemical Biological Incident Response Force (CBIRF) exercise with the US Marine Corps.

Land parcels and the value of verifying what's there: GIS works for Bethel, Maine

Donald Bennett, Town Selectman; James Doar, Town Manager; and Sarah Tucker, GIS Analyst, Town of Bethel, Maine

Level of government: **Town**
State/province: **Maine**
Country: **USA**
Population: **2,614**

Bethel, Maine, began its GIS program in 2006 using funds received through a grant from the Maine GeoLibrary. The first task the town took up was digitizing its parcel maps. Bethel received the grant in January 2006, and the work on digitizing parcel maps was completed in December 2007.

CASE STUDY > > >

Prior to the implementation of Bethel's GIS program, the town relied on static Mylar maps to define land parcels in the community. Information included in the maps quickly became dated, which often required that land parcels be surveyed to ensure that the information was correct before decisions such as property tax assessments or valuations could be made. "You'd have information that was historical," Don Bennett, town selectman, says. "You usually had to go out and have a landowner survey their own property. And surveying costs money. But a lot of times, you needed more facts before you could make a decision."

Bennett elaborates further: "From a selectman's perspective, some of the things that you want to see are the clarity in your whole mapping system and the ability of citizens to understand tax maps. This whole idea of being able to see things in a true accurate form is the basis of it all. We have a great map of all the smaller towns that we deal with around here. It's tough to go to some of those town offices and try to find information—for example, the land lots and where they [lie]—and find things that are accurate. My focus for Bethel is to have something that is accurate and provides a true picture of what's out there on the land."

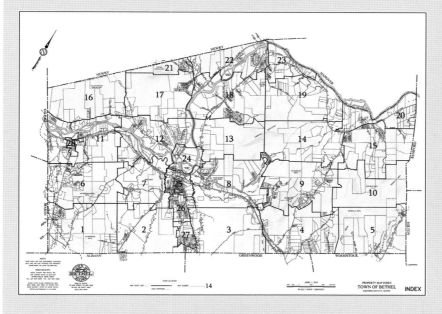

Figure 2.1 The need for greater accuracy led Bethel, Maine, to digitize all of its parcel maps. Courtesy of Town of Bethel, Maine.

The community had tried to venture into GIS technology prior to 2006, but only in a small way, and without much success. The town credits much of the success of the GIS program to its GIS analyst, Sarah Tucker. A former planning assistant for the town, Tucker first learned about the Maine GeoLibrary's grant initiative through the area's regional planning agency, the Androscoggin Valley Council of Governments. Tucker had heard of GIS as part of her planning job, but had never worked with the software in any capacity. The grant application required a local match, so Bethel paid for

Bethel operates its GIS program with Tucker working part time as a GIS analyst and an annual operating budget of approximately $2,500 that pays for a software license and mapping work.

Tucker to take a GIS course at the local community college. Tucker has continued her education since that time and will soon have an associate's degree in GIS. Having someone on staff trained to use GIS and someone who is enthusiastic about the technology have been two keys to making the new program successful.

Bethel operates its GIS program with Tucker working part time as a GIS analyst and an annual operating budget of approximately $2,500 that pays for a software license and mapping work. Many of the data layers used by the town come through data-sharing agreements with the Androscoggin Valley Council of Governments and the Maine GeoLibrary.

In spring 2007, the town went through a revaluation process for property taxes, the first since the establishment of the GIS program. The revaluation process cemented the town's commitment to GIS because it was incredibly helpful during the hearings. When citizens came in to talk about their properties, the assessors were able to use GIS to pull up aerial photos, wetlands designations, and other data layers related to the properties. The program proved so useful that the town's Select Board decided to

Figure 2.2 Having the maps with complete information and in digital form greatly aided discussions with citizens about property assessment. Courtesy of Town of Bethel, Maine.

CASE STUDY >

allocate $20,000 over the course of four years to pay for a map upgrade from level 2 to level 3 data standards. (Level 3 data standards for parcel data require a greater degree of accuracy, including linking the parcels to orthophotography images and actual physical features that can be identified from aerial photographs.) This action enabled the town to retire all of its old Mylar maps, and in 2010 PDF files of all the town's tax maps were placed online.

With the availability of level 3 data, which the town is using for ongoing assessment work, Bethel is considering its other mapping needs, including snowplow routing and capital improvements planning, particularly that related to road maintenance, sewer planning, and other infrastructure-related needs. The code enforcement officer has been using the digitized parcel data to produce floodplain, shoreland, and wetland maps. "The really cool thing about this is that GIS gets people asking questions: Can we do this? How about this? People get more and more excited about what [it] is possible to do. It gets you thinking about how we can do this. I think that's the attraction to GIS," says James Doar, town manager.

CASE STUDY •

Using GIS to prepare for a possible disaster: San Antonio's CBIRF exercise

Chris Stokes, GISP, Special Projects Manager; and James Mendoza, CEM, Assistant Emergency Manager, City of San Antonio Office of Emergency Management

Level of government: City
State/province: Texas
Country: USA
Population: 1,327,407

The City of San Antonio, Texas, has experienced its share of disasters, providing local first responders and emergency managers with substantial real-world experience in managing and organizing complex emergency events. This real-world experience has taught the city's emergency management team that planning and preparing for such events is critical in reducing injuries and saving lives. In 2012, the city, together with the US Marine Corps CBIRF unit,[2] conducted a tabletop exercise to underline the roles and responsibilities of local first responders, state agencies, and US Department of Defense (DoD) search and extraction units. The scenario selected for the exercise was a tornado causing widespread destruction as well as radiological and chemical contamination throughout a large portion of the city.

CASE STUDY > >

> **"The fusion of GIS technology and emergency management has revolutionized the way we provide emergency response in San Antonio by marrying cutting-edge technology with prudent emergency planning and response. This exercise demonstrated how our Emergency Management program, together with the Department of Defense and federal responders, creates a powerful union of skills, resources, and programs to save lives and protect property during a catastrophic disaster. Our citizens are the direct beneficiaries from the lessons learned from exercises like this one."**
>
> Julián Castro, Mayor, City of San Antonio, Texas

The exercise focused on defining the tactical levels of local, state, and federal emergency responder actions, critical decisions, and appropriate integration of state and federal assets necessary to save lives and protect public health and safety. The CBIRF exercise showcased the San Antonio Office of Emergency Management's (SAOEM) robust GIS program and its capable delivery of actionable, reliable, and timely information to leadership. The ability to integrate GIS analyses in support of all four phases of comprehensive disaster/emergency management—preparedness, response, recovery, and mitigation—proved to be crucial in the success of the exercise.

For example, SAOEM's Planning and Analysis Section helped exercise planners by preparing spatial analyses of the tornado's path and provided demographic information and critical infrastructure and key resource (CI/KR) reports for the affected area. Questions always arise during such events: "Where are the nursing homes?" "Do we have locations of pharmacies?" "Is there a helipad in that area?" Leveraging the city's vast CI/KR data catalog provides public safety leadership with the capability to answer these questions that are geographic in nature. Local capacity to produce such mission-critical data and information allows state and federal resources to be allocated appropriately. The geospatial intelligence chief for CBIRF, Sgt. Brock Everts, notes that not all cities are as capable of supplying GIS data to support identified mission objectives. Simply knowing the locations of fire hydrants for decontamination stations, for example, becomes critical during emergencies.

Use of the US National Grid (USNG) data had been invaluable in past search and rescue efforts, and it is the standard grid mapping system for all DoD planning and response activities. The exercise planning team felt it imperative to incorporate this tool into the exercise to increase awareness about the significance of using this standardized system. DoD staff shared an Internet-based map application that provided different levels of data resolution; SAOEM had also adopted this standard grid system, which greatly aided the ability to communicate between systems. SAOEM uses WebEOC Mapper as its geographically based common operating picture as recommended by the National Search and Rescue Committee. WebEOC uses the USNG map service, published by Esri. In addition

CASE STUDY >

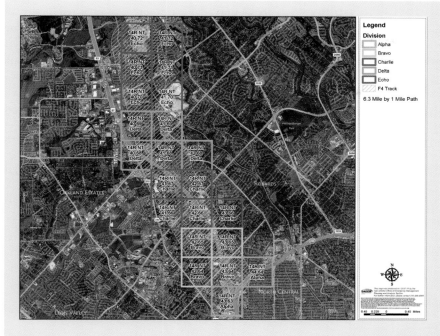

Figure 2.3 The city was able to leverage the USNG data to create CBIRF division assignments. Courtesy of City of San Antonio Office of Emergency Management.

to providing greater awareness, the USNG data proved instrumental in allowing the team to quickly implement its operational plan by creating division assignments for the affected area, which enables field crews to undertake a thorough search and rescue effort for surviving victims and recovery of the deceased.

The exercise planning team also requested information on the impacted area that would assist with response and recovery. A primary tool used by SAOEM was Esri Business Analyst Online (BAO). BAO was a vital application not only in planning for the exercise, but for actual responses as well. The ability to have rich demographic data in the hands of local incident commanders and emergency managers in near real time has been essential to successfully managing various types of incidents. The reports and maps provided assistance in allocating search and recovery resources for the exercise, shelter, and mass care coordination, as well as determining transportation issues in regard to evacuations. Although BAO is frequently used as a tool for making educated real estate and business decisions, it has also proved to be an indispensable application for public safety as well. This functionality, like the USNG data, has also been incorporated into WebEOC Mapper, providing a central location of web-based analytical tools.

The exercise's after action report will give San Antonio's team an opportunity to identify lessons learned and determine where improvements in planning and preparation may be needed. The city intends to share these lessons to enhance preparedness nationwide. The use of GIS has become a staple within the city, and there is constant advancement and development of new tools in the field. Leveraging social media and GIS technology as well as smartphone/mobile device applications for preparing for and managing emergencies are all new areas being explored.

CASE STUDY •

GIS for decision support and policy making

Policy makers often have decisions brought before them where data needs to be created in order to run a GIS analysis that will help them understand the implications of their decisions. In some cases, this means going through historical records and maps to capture data not currently available in a digital format, as in the case of Polk County, Florida. In other cases, it requires creating an evaluation system that can be used to develop quantitative means for considering possible answers to policy questions, as was done in Newfoundland. Finally, the Ohio-Kentucky-Indiana Regional Council of Government needed GIS to create a fiscal impact model to evaluate the potential costs new development might have on regional road networks.

GIS-ing flood data: Polk County, Florida, makes valuable information in paper studies available[3]

Mehdi Mashud Khan, GIS Supervisor, Polk County BoCC IT/GIS, Florida

Level of government: County
State/province: Florida
Country: USA
Population: 602,095

Government—and more specifically Polk County, Florida—provides various services to its citizens and also establishes standards and regulations for various businesses, activities, and developments to serve and better protect its residents. Government adopts policies to ensure that this goal of serving and protecting its citizens occurs not only in the present, but also in the future. Analyzing present data to understand existing knowledge and facts and to visualize or predict the future is very important in formulating policies. Because GIS can provide insights by answering the what, how, where, and when, it can help enormously in creating, framing, improving, or shifting policies for the better. Polk County's work on moving flood studies from paper to GIS data layers demonstrates the potential of GIS in better implementing and shaping the future scope of current policies.

> **Because GIS can provide insights by answering the what, how, where, and when, it can help enormously in creating, framing, improving, or shifting policies for the better. Polk County's work on moving flood studies from paper to GIS data layers demonstrates the potential of GIS in better implementing and shaping the future scope of current policies.**

CASE STUDY > > > > >

Flooding is one of the most common natural hazards in Polk County, as it is in many other parts of the United States. Approximately 46 percent of the county is located in one of the FEMA Special Flood Hazard Area (SFHA) designations. A significant percentage of the county's population lives or works in areas that are at risk of flooding. Because Polk County is in Florida, it is also susceptible to seasonal hurricanes, which also can cause severe flooding. In 2004, three hurricanes passed through the county, resulting in standing water across the region and causing rivers to overflow into adjacent communities. Any prolonged rainfall has the potential to result in flooding. The county's flat topography, combined with expanding development, causes storm water to reach buildings quickly because water moves across the surface more rapidly than it can be absorbed into the ground. These same factors also delay the departure of floodwaters.

Mitigation activities

To minimize flood damage, Polk County has undertaken flood protection activities (e.g., periodic ditch and channel cleaning and maintaining flood-prone areas as open space) and introduced new flood protection regulations. As part of this effort, the county requires that new residential buildings or buildings that are substantially improved be elevated one foot above the base flood elevation (BFE). This ordinance requires that information on the flood zone and the base flood elevation for a site must be known for these properties. To help determine the flood zones and BFEs, FEMA provides paper and online maps. In some cases, these maps may supply sufficient information. However, in many instances, FEMA maps lack sufficient detail because they were prepared ten or more years ago using five- to ten-foot contour data. At that scale, a parcel or a small piece of land can easily be lost. Although FEMA maps were updated in 2000, many of the updated maps are based on maps originally prepared in 1983. FEMA maps might recognize a potential flood hazard area but lack detailed information such as BFEs or the extent of flooding. In a worst-case scenario, FEMA maps may have completely inaccurate information or lack any information at all.

The county has acquired a significant number of detailed local flood studies over the last twenty years. These studies—the result of a county requirement—are being converted from paper documents to GIS layers to provide valuable flood protection information to county residents.

County response

The county has addressed this issue by requiring detailed flood studies for any proposed development larger than five acres or fifty lots. Over the years, the county has acquired a significant number of studies for many developments within its jurisdiction. These studies, submitted and stored by the county in paper format, are a great resource not only for the developments for which they were created, but also for future developments in the same area. Because flood studies are based on topographic features, these studies can provide flood-specific information for adjacent areas and supply required information for future developments. Even if a study is contained within that area, the study can be used as the basis for future studies of adjacent areas. In both scenarios, access to this information can substantially reduce costs. If existing studies are not available, residential and commercial developers

CASE STUDY > > > >

must perform expensive flood studies to determine the BFE for a site. To relieve individual parcel owners or developers with projects of fewer than five acres of this expense, the county also accepts an alternative method of compliance. It specifies that new structures be built three feet above the "highest adjacent grade" (i.e., the highest elevation on the lot) if a BFE is unavailable. Although this meets the county's requirement, a lack of information can result in requiring a parcel owner to pay a lot for flood insurance. Consequently, individual owners stand to benefit from going through old flood studies of adjacent properties. This information can not only save money on flood insurance, but also help property owners choose appropriate construction materials and techniques.

Figure 2.4 Some areas of concern are not shown on FEMA maps. The area marked by red dots shows that the localized flood study (rendered in green hatch) identifies potential flood zones that were not included in FEMA maps (rendered in solid gray). Courtesy of Polk County, Florida.

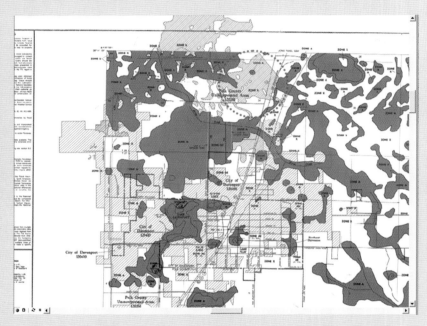

Making studies accessible

Currently, many of the flood studies are available only as paper documents. To respond to a request to determine if a property is located in an area prone to flooding (and therefore must meet FEMA floodplain management requirements), legal descriptions are used to locate a parcel on an appropriate study and get pertinent information. This process, which is tedious, lengthy, and wastes staff time, has all the limitations of paper-based media in terms of archiving, organizing, and searching flood studies. Sometimes flood studies are divided into parts and represented in several drawings. It is inconvenient to combine these paper drawings so the whole picture can be seen. It is also challenging to view these studies in conjunction with other data. This is a long, painstaking, manual process.

To use these studies more effectively, the county's Land Development Division decided to convert them from paper to a digital format so the department could find the information quickly and make

CASE STUDY > > >

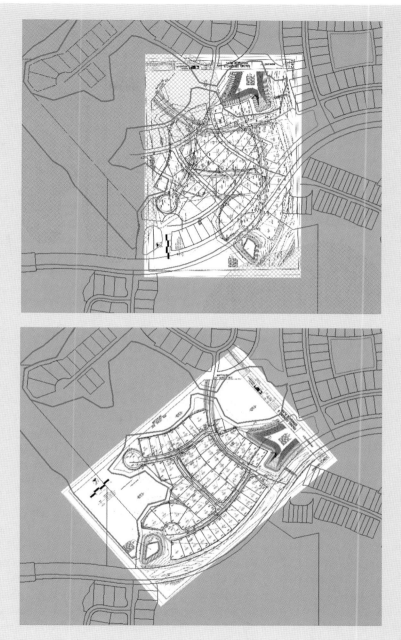

Figure 2.5 The top image is a scanned, unaligned study area that needs to be georeferenced. The bottom image shows the same area georeferenced. It has been rotated, stretched, and aligned. Courtesy of Polk County, Florida.

flood studies more accessible to a wider audience. The hope was that the new digital maps could be seamlessly analyzed and explored in the context of other relevant data. GIS was the obvious answer. Converting these flood studies to GIS layers would allow users to take advantage of sophisticated analysis tools so that they could be explored in conjunction with other relevant GIS data. Departments could store these studies in a relational database management system, thus making it accessible through the county network. The county could also provide this information to the public through web GIS and eliminate the labor associated with the older manual process.

Better data, dependable information, better policy

As discussed earlier, just converting the paper-based studies into GIS has some obvious benefits. It saves significant employee hours in analyzing and retrieving flood data. And if published through the web, citizens and professionals have access to this very useful data, easily saving them time and money.

But the significance of this conversion goes beyond the obvious. For example, the county participates in the National Flood Information Insurance Program (NFIP), a program initiated by FEMA that offers reasonably priced flood insurance for communities that comply with its minimum standards for floodplain management. The Community Rating System (CRS) for this program provides incentives for communities that exceed minimum standards by reviewing four key factors: public information, mapping and regulation, flood damage reduction, and flood preparedness. The conversion of paper studies to a GIS format has the potential to improve all four factors, resulting in a better CRS rating for the county and lower flood insurance rates for the county's homeowners and residents.

Currently the county's policy requires a higher standard than that required by NFIP for managing the floodplain. Having flood data easily available for the whole county—the ultimate intent of this project—would systematically raise the bar for floodplain management. It would definitely push policy makers to set the standards even higher; for example, the county currently requires that a new building be built three feet above the highest elevation level of the lot if there is no BFE available. Because the BFE is unknown in many instances, there is still a chance for new buildings to be built in flood-risk areas that might cause property damage and require higher flood insurance. If countywide data were available, the standard could specify the exact height based on the locations instead of an arbitrary requirement of "three feet" above the highest elevation. This new standard would save money for builders and homeowners either by providing real protection in a flood-prone area or by not requiring the construction of additional heights if unneeded.

The county's policy also requires the creation of new floodplains if a new development affects existing floodplains. Once countywide floodplain data is available to developers, county planners, and other real estate professionals, it will be easier for all groups to determine where, how, and how many floodplains need to be created for a given development. It may well push policy makers to come up with new policies for new developments because they would have the better and bigger picture of the county's floodplains.

It would also help the county's emergency management team to better predict the flood-risk areas and how a flood would impact those areas. Because emergency responders would be able to better visualize and estimate the effects of a disaster, it would definitely contribute in their planning to address an emergency situation.

CASE STUDY >

Location, economy, development

This project, once completed, will also help with the county's economic development efforts. Developers and homeowners will have data readily available that would otherwise cost them significantly, making the county more competitive for development. Under the current scenario, it may be difficult to locate data if the name of the development has changed since the flood study was performed. If the same data is available spatially, this issue does not matter anymore, because the geographic location never changes. Detailed flood data will help a developer better predict costs and select appropriate construction materials for a given location. Insurance companies will be better able to determine their rates, and homeowners will be better informed about the risks of a particular location.

Conclusion

Sound and successful policies demand information—the ability to analyze information to foresee the future. Polk County is taking advantage of GIS technology to better represent the present, to realize the reality of potential risks, and to foresee the unforeseen. GIS has an enormous potential to reshape present policy and provide a solid framework for decision making on how to conduct business in the future.

CASE STUDY •

Examining the fiscal impact of new development for the Ohio-Kentucky-Indiana Regional Council of Governments

Della G. Rucker, Principal, Wise Economy Workshop

Level of government: Region
State/province: Ohio, Kentucky, and Indiana
Country: USA
Population: 1,999,474

The Ohio-Kentucky-Indiana (OKI) Regional Council of Governments is made up of more than 110 local governments and organizations from across an eight-county region in three states. In 2009, OKI completed development of a regional fiscal impact model that uses a GIS platform to integrate parcel data, auditors' land-use data, and property assessments for an initial set of four counties, five cities, and one township within the OKI region. The model generates detailed estimates of costs and revenues resulting from proposed land-use changes, which elected officials use when considering the approval or denial of a proposed new development. A robust GIS platform was central to making the model possible.

Most jurisdictions in this tristate region maintain control of their own land use, and exurban development has resulted in a far-flung metropolitan region that is almost entirely auto dependent.

CASE STUDY > > > > >

OKI, however, plays a central role in managing the region's road and highway infrastructure; as the Metropolitan Planning Organization (MPO), OKI receives and administers most transportation funding from the state and federal governments.

In 2005, OKI convened a broad cross section of citizens and leaders to develop a regional strategic land-use plan. During the planning process, leaders determined that the current land-use patterns in the region could not be sustained because the amount of road and highway demand would quickly outstrip even the most optimistic projections of future funding. The 2005 strategic plan, titled Where Do We Grow From Here?, outlined these projections and a variety of related concerns and identified a number of strategies for helping the independent local governments understand and account for the ramifications of their land-use decisions.

One of the primary tools that gained considerable attention was the concept of a fiscal impact model. Although fiscal impact studies had been developed for a small number of jurisdictions in the OKI region, these studies were static examinations of "typical" revenues and costs to local governments resulting from various types of land use. Such studies can be valuable, but they cannot be applied readily to a specific development, and present particular challenges in evaluating the mixed-use developments that were becoming more common in the region. OKI leadership determined that, to truly help local governments understand the fiscal impacts of land-use decisions, OKI should provide a tool that created estimates of the costs and revenues that could result from specific development proposals.

The OKI design team initially looked at the handful of fiscal impact models that existed across the country at that time. After reviewing those models, the team spoke with elected officials as well as personnel of the member jurisdictions. Based on their research, OKI staff developed a vision of what was needed from the new model. Among the priorities identified for the new tool were:

- A web-based interface, which would both make the model easy for community members to use and allow OKI to maintain management of the data
- A robust analytical system, allowing for more nuanced results than a straight mathematical model could generate
- A method that used data specific to the community being analyzed, rather than relying exclusively on broad averages and rules of thumb

At this point, OKI leadership determined that outside assistance in designing and creating the model was needed and released a request for proposals. A team consisting of the Jacobs Engineering Group and the University of Cincinnati's Center for Economics Research and Education, which included two professors from the university's School of Planning, was selected. The team worked in close partnership with OKI staff and web design professionals for more than a year to design and create the model, which was launched in June 2009.

How the model works

The team developed an application that drew from a wide variety of datasets and used a series of nested calculations to determine costs and revenues associated with proposed development projects. Many of the jurisdictions did not have adequate data to determine their costs, but the goal

CASE STUDY > > > > >

was to develop a reasonably reliable estimate of what revenues would occur from a proposed development and what kinds of costs would be incurred. The model was designed to work for greenfield or infill locations, and it had to accommodate large and small jurisdictions of a variety of types across three states with significantly different legal structures.

Typically, the process starts with an application for rezoning, variances, or financial incentives associated with a specific development. A planning or development staff member logs into the website and defines the basic parameters of what is on the property using one or more of sixteen land-use categories that were developed to address the differences in typical fiscal impact found among different types of development. Data entered into the model to represent the property's present use includes the acreage, assessed value, and building square footage associated with each of the land uses. Developing information about current property uses allows the model to generate a net statement of fiscal impact, rather than giving the mistaken impression that the existing land uses do not generate costs and revenues themselves.

As a simple example, let's say that the proposed development site currently consists of a farmhouse sitting on ten acres of property. The one acre with the farmhouse is entered as a single-family residential land use, and the other nine acres are entered as agricultural land use. If the user chose to stop here, the application would provide an estimate of what the local government is receiving in revenue from that property today, as well as an estimate of what costs it is incurring to provide public services to that property.

After the user has entered the information about the existing land uses associated with a property, the user will move to the next entry page and enter the similar information for the proposed development. Again, the information needed to complete the data entry consists of the amount of acreage, building square footage, and market value that will be distributed across one or more of the sixteen land-use categories. The user guide for the model provides detailed guidance regarding how to allocate the properties.

Although early development of the model envisioned very detailed data requirements, including such factors as tax incentives and average employee salaries, the design team decided to limit the data requirements to the bare minimum necessary to perform the calculations. Given the wide variety of jurisdictions that the model needed to address, it became clear that a number of the more rural communities were not comfortable with asking for that level of detail.

After the information on the proposed development is entered into the online form, the model generates several estimates. The first table provides a summary of the net estimated costs and revenues associated with the proposed development, while subsequent tables provide more detailed breakdown by specific revenue and cost type. Because of the wide range of communities, many of which have different permissible revenue streams and cost obligations, the cost and revenue categories are defined in terms of five different types of revenues and seven different categories of expenses.

A nominal membership fee helps to offset data maintenance costs, such as updating census data, budgetary data, and other, similar data.

CASE STUDY > > > >

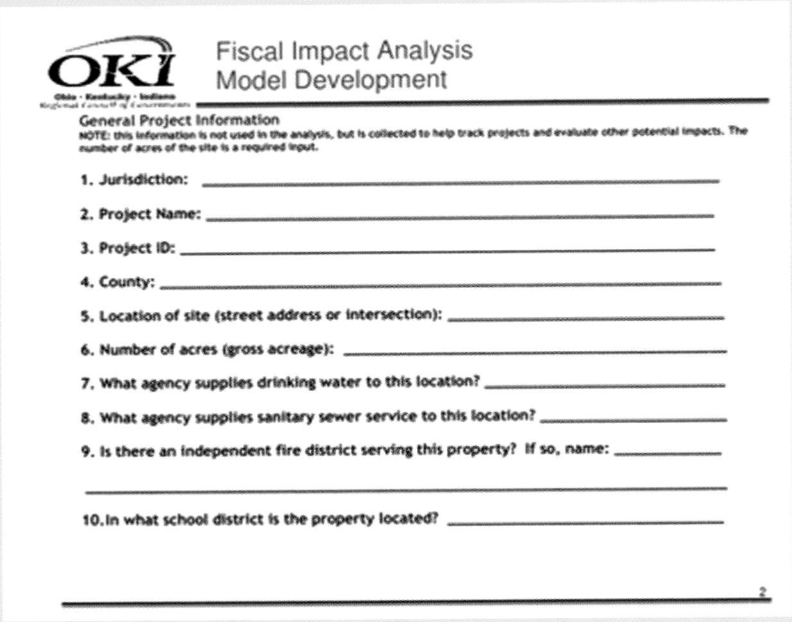

Fiscal Impact Analysis
Model Development

Ohio · Kentucky · Indiana
Regional Council of Governments

General Project Information

NOTE: this information is not used in the analysis, but is collected to help track projects and evaluate other potential impacts. The number of acres of the site is a required input.

1. Jurisdiction: __________
2. Project Name: __________
3. Project ID: __________
4. County: __________
5. Location of site (street address or intersection): __________
6. Number of acres (gross acreage): __________
7. What agency supplies drinking water to this location? __________
8. What agency supplies sanitary sewer service to this location? __________
9. Is there an independent fire district serving this property? If so, name: __________
10. In what school district is the property located? __________

2

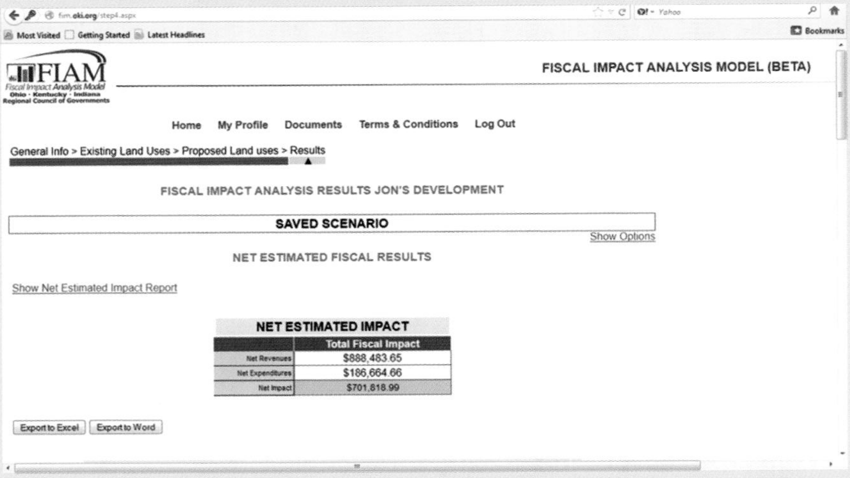

Figure 2.6 The Fiscal Impact Analysis Model, illustrated in these three screen captures, allows community leaders to input data about a proposed project to calculate what the potential fiscal impact might be on the local government. The model uses GIS technology to integrate data for selected properties. Courtesy of Ohio-Kentucky-Indiana Regional Council of Governments.

CASE STUDY > > >

Figure 2.6 continued.

Land Use	Existing Revenues	Existing Expenditures	Existing Fiscal Benefit / Loss
Agricultural	$2,544.40	($188.18)	$2,732.59
Estate Residential	$3,926.83	$578.27	$3,348.57
Single-Family Residential	$0.00	$0.00	$0.00
Multi-Family Residential	$0.00	$0.00	$0.00
Neighborhood Shopping Center	$0.00	$0.00	$0.00
Community Shopping Center	$0.00	$0.00	$0.00
Sit-down Restaurants	$0.00	$0.00	$0.00
Hotels & Motels	$0.00	$0.00	$0.00
High Traffic Retail	$0.00	$0.00	$0.00
Office	$0.00	$0.00	$0.00
Consumer Oriented Office	$0.00	$0.00	$0.00
Light Industry	$2,307.04	$326.73	$1,980.32
Manufacturing	$0.00	$0.00	$0.00
Education and Government	$0.00	$0.00	$0.00
Religious	$0.00	$0.00	$0.00
Parks, Cemeteries, Utilities, Parking Structures and Vacant Land	$333.36	$736.94	($403.58)
Not Attributed to LU Categories	$42.15	$0.00	$42.15
Total	$9,153.79	$1,453.75	$7,700.04

The model's structure and the role of GIS

Although the model appears very simple on the surface, it integrates four different datasets, three of which contain thousands of individual items of information. These datasets are:

- Parcel data, including the parcel size, building footprint, and existing land use for each property
- Tax assessment data for each parcel, including the assessed value and the assessment category assigned to it
- Census data, including disaggregated, nonsuppressed data relating to businesses, which was available to OKI as a result of its responsibility for administering federal funds
- Budget data for each jurisdiction.

Using a series of correlations derived from an extensive database of budget and census information from a dataset of reference communities, the model differentiates between land-use types based on a series of correlated impacts and applies the estimated proportions resulting from those calculations to the specific revenue and cost distributions demonstrated in the community's budget.

The use of GIS systems to manage and refine the enormous volume of parcel-related data became one of the key elements that differentiated the OKI Fiscal Impact Analysis Model from other approaches. Typically, fiscal impact models have largely relied on generic data, such as averages from other studies or broad totals drawn from tax assessment records. Because virtually the entire OKI region is covered by one of several GIS mapping systems, the OKI Fiscal Impact Analysis Model could be based on detailed, parcel-by-parcel data, instead of averages. This increases the accuracy and relevance of the model's estimates.

One of the key challenges associated with the model's development was finding a way to directly compare parcel, tax assessment, and census data for each community. Each community used a different existing land-use classification system, and although Ohio and Indiana use a system of land-use categories for tax assessment purposes that includes several hundred categories, these did not match up readily with any of the existing land-use categories. To further complicate matters, Kentucky uses an entirely

CASE STUDY > >

different system of tax assessment classification, one that varies by county and that in many cases uses as few as five categories. If the model were to be able to reliably estimate the costs and revenues associated with a given property or land use, it would be necessary to fit parcel and assessment data together.

The region's GIS systems proved instrumental to solving this challenge in two ways:

1. First, the team's staff was able to export the data for each parcel in the ten jurisdictions, creating a master attribute table, or table of the information associated with GIS layers, for each jurisdiction. Because these attribute tables included parcel identification numbers for each parcel, it became possible to attribute each property's assessment data, including the amount, the assessment category, and the ownership information, directly to the parcel. This meant that an exhaustive dataset of the three pieces of information needed to generate a fiscal impact estimate—acreage, building size, and value—which covered every parcel, was available to every jurisdiction using the model.

2. As with most large datasets, the information developed from the combination of parcel and assessment data included errors, such as incomplete parcels or parcel files that did not reflect recent lot splits or subdivisions. By integrating the GIS files with aerial photography, team members could physically adjust parcels to make certain that the data reflected current conditions as accurately as possible.

As noted previously, the model defines land use in terms of sixteen land-use types, which correlate to the types of impacts that different types of businesses and developments typically have on local government costs and revenues. For Ohio and Indiana, each of the hundreds of tax assessment categories (and, as a result, each of the thousands of parcels) needed to be assigned to one of the fiscal impact land-use categories. Because of the GIS attribute tables, the team was able to analyze the common characteristics of a community's properties in each assessment category (such as typical size and value of the property) and assign each of the assessment categories to an appropriate fiscal impact land-use category. For Kentucky, a different challenge presented itself: the Kentucky counties typically use only one assessment category for all types of commercial development, but the fiscal impact land-use system differentiates between seven different types of commercial development, each of which has different revenue and cost impacts. The OKI team was able to use aerial photography overlaid with the parcels to visually examine and manually assign the Kentucky counties' commercial parcels to one of the sixteen fiscal impact categories. "If we hadn't had access to those very robust GIS systems, we never would have been able to do that," notes one team member.

Impact of GIS systems

In the future, designers hope to expand the model to allow direct GIS mapping of the estimated fiscal impacts. The current diversity in data standards being used by the different GIS programs did not allow for designers to develop such an application. At present, the model is being used to help local government decision makers evaluate whether a proposed development would be in the community's best interest, and at least one community is using the model to estimate the fiscal impacts of long-range, community-wide development scenarios as part of its comprehensive planning process. Other stakeholders are evaluating strategies for using the model to evaluate the overall factors that may affect whether a given type of development supports a community's fiscal sustainability.

CASE STUDY >

The OKI Fiscal Impact Analysis Model provides a decision-making support tool for local government officials and a means of developing a reliable, numerical assessment of the impact that a future development or land-use pattern could have on a community's ability to provide the services that its residents and businesses expect. The Fiscal Impact Analysis Model gives community leaders a way to replace guesses and assumptions about the fiscal impacts of their decisions, but OKI frequently cautions its users to remember two points. First, the model creates an estimate, which can vary from what actually happens if the development project has unusual characteristics. Second, fiscal issues are only one of the factors that should be evaluated in terms of a development or land-use change. In many cases, other factors (such as impact on the local economy, social justice, or other factors) may mean that a project for which the fiscal impact model does not show a positive return on investment could be a good idea after all.

The need to understand the fiscal ramifications of decisions is on the public agenda at all levels of government, particularly since the global recession of 2008. Tools such as the OKI Fiscal Impact Analysis Model give decision makers the ability to better negotiate with developers on the public investments that are made when any new development is built, whether that be for street lighting, traffic signage, landscaping amenities, or other measures that can help offset costs.

CASE STUDY •

Quantifying visual quality in the Province of Newfoundland, Canada

Doug Piercey, GeoInformatics Analyst, Natural Resources Canada–Canadian Forest Service, Newfoundland

Level of government: Province
State/province: Newfoundland
Country: Canada
Population: 505,469

Management of the forested landscape in western Newfoundland has become more complicated over the years. Although the traditional pulp and paper industry is still a very important component of the region's economy, more nontraditional values have been identified, and the number of demands being placed on the forest has increased. New uses attributed to the landscape include protected species habitat, outdoor recreation and tourism, hunting, fishing, and resort development. Determining how to measure the value of these new uses is subjective by nature and can be difficult to quantify.

The challenge is to provide elected officials with the tools and resources they need to make objective policy decisions given the new uses. Ensuring the long-term sustainability of the forested landscape is

CASE STUDY > > > >

a central concern. Maintaining sustainability, both ecologically and economically, within such a multivalue landscape involves taking an ecosystem-based management (EBM) approach. Policy makers need to be able to take into account multiple perspectives—economic, ecologic, and social—across multiple spatial and temporal scales with the goal of identifying the impact of changing conditions on the values present. The Natural Resources Canada–Canadian Forest Service (NRCan-CFS) lab in Corner Brook, Newfoundland, is working in partnership with provincial government, industry, and academia to produce the knowledge and tools necessary for effective EBM using GIS technology.

Identifying the impact of a changing landscape on resources or values that are quantitative in nature is relatively straightforward. For example, the volume of timber available to be harvested or the area required for animal habitat can be directly attributed to changes in particular forest characteristics and can be mapped relatively easily within a GIS. However, it is more difficult to identify impacts for some of the qualitative values on the landscape. Visual quality is one such value. Visual quality acts as an indicator for many of the nontraditional uses mentioned previously. The problem is how to make visual quality, which is a very subjective value, more objective so that the impacts on it by a changing landscape can be measured quantitatively.

The solution is to define a conversion between landscape components and the public perception of visual quality. This conversion can be termed a visual quality index (VQI). It essentially identifies what people like and do not like about landscapes as they contribute to visual quality and attaches a quantitative value to them.

Although some VQIs have been developed, there are issues when considering them. First, most of these indexes involve manual examination of multiple paper maps and still require some subjective interpretation. The second problem with existing VQIs is that they are not area specific. For example, a VQI developed for national purposes may not reflect local perceptions of visual quality. In a large country such as Canada, there are many different landscape types. The perception of a flat prairie landscape by someone who lives in such an environment is likely different from someone who grew up in a rugged, coastline setting.

NRCan-CFS sought to develop a new VQI that considered visual quality in an EBM framework while accounting for the issues and limitations associated with existing indices. The steps taken during development are illustrated in figure 2.7.

A literature review identified indices that already existed. Because it was important to quantify visual quality spatially, the new index started with landscape components that were already available as spatial layers. The landscape elements selected for the new index include:

- Relative relief
- Topographic variety
- Dominant water type
- Percentage water
- Vegetative variety
- Degree of alteration
- Type of alteration

Each of these components contributes to a total visual quality. The ratings for each component as they contribute to the total value for two different landscapes are illustrated in figure 2.8.

CASE STUDY > > >

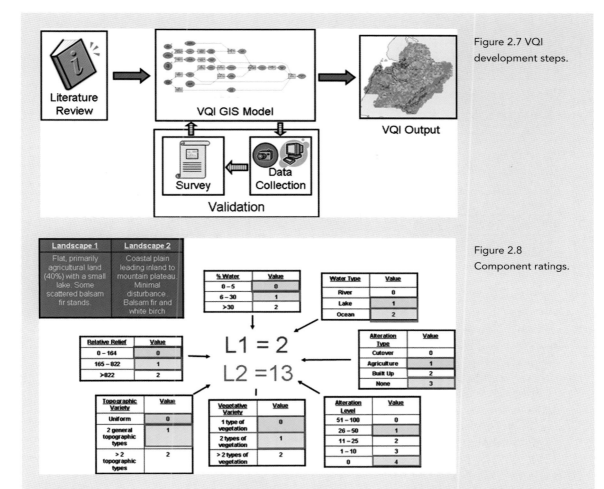

Figure 2.7 VQI development steps.

Figure 2.8 Component ratings.

The next step was to develop a GIS-based model based on these components that would calculate a total visual quality for each defined mapping unit over the area of study. In this case, the area was divided into equal-sized hexagons. By using GIS layers and a GIS-based model, subjectivity is removed and automated processing is possible.

For the VQI to be considered appropriate for use within an EBM framework, it had to satisfactorily represent public perception of visual quality. To validate the index and account for local preferences in visual quality, a public survey was conducted. The basis of the survey was a collection of photographs that were rated using the same landscape components included in the new VQI. Respondents were asked what they liked and did not like about each of the scenes, and then were asked to assign a rating based on a scale of one to ten (with one representing poor visual quality and ten representing high visual quality). Survey participants were also asked some demographic questions. By comparing survey ratings with modeled ratings, NRCan-CFS analysts were able to determine whether the VQI

CASE STUDY > >

represented public perception. A comparison of the VQI rating, survey mean, and survey mode for thirty-two photographs is illustrated in figure 2.9.

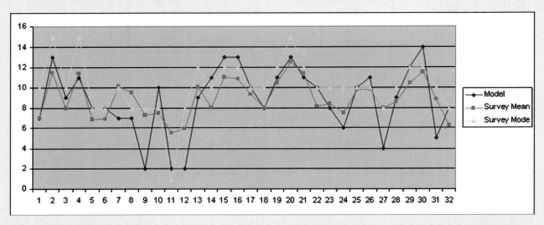

Figure 2.9 Comparison of VQI rating, survey mean, and survey mode for thirty-two photographs.

From this analysis, it was noted that the VQI performed well in comparison with the public ratings. In cases where it did not perform well, the NRCan-CFS team was able to look at what respondents liked and did not like about the scene, and then make adjustments to the model, if possible. Some adaptations were made to account for previously harvested forest areas and agricultural areas that were not deemed to be a negative influence on visual quality. This helped in modifying the VQI to better suit local perceptions and producing a final GIS-based VQI.

NRCan-CFS has used the new VQI to predict changes in visual quality under a variety of different management scenarios. Figure 2.10 shows a simple example. On the left is the study area at

Figure 2.10 Using VQI to analyze the change in visual quality in the future under different management scenarios.

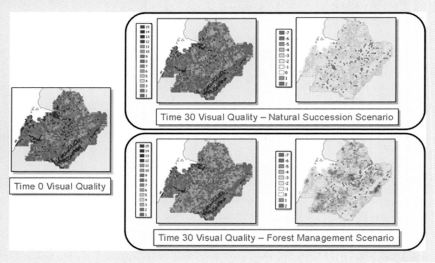

Time 30 Visual Quality – Natural Succession Scenario

Time 0 Visual Quality

Time 30 Visual Quality – Forest Management Scenario

CASE STUDY >

time zero. On the right side at the top are the visual quality value (left) and the change in visual quality value (right) thirty years into the future based on natural succession. On the bottom right are similar maps showing visual quality and change using a forest management scenario in which regular forest-harvesting schedules are applied. By comparing two possible future landscapes in terms of visual quality, policy makers can see the impacts and make decisions as to whether such impacts are acceptable.

It is important to note that this is only one value of many that were identified for the Newfoundland region, and more will be identified in the future. A model such as the VQI cannot be used in isolation, but instead must be considered along with other values in an EBM framework. It is, however, a valuable tool to assist decision makers by making a subjective landscape value objective and usable when considering land-use trade-offs.

CASE STUDY •

Using GIS to understand and engage constituents

Elected officials represent the interests of their constituents. Understanding the needs and desires of citizens and engaging them in critical public policy discussions helps ensure support for the decisions that are made. GIS analyses can help citizens better understand the context of decisions being made, as happened in Deschutes County, Oregon, or provide their own input into policy discussions, as was done in Dún Laoghaire-Rathdown and Fingal County Councils in Ireland. Other GIS analyses can document the characteristics of specific populations and their needs in a community, as was the case with St. Albert in Alberta, Canada, and Fort Worth, Texas.

Preserving open space and parks through urban Greenprinting in Deschutes County, Oregon

Breece Robertson, National Conservation Vision and GIS Director; Kelley Hart, Associate Director of Conservation Vision; and Kristin Kovalik, Oregon Project Manager, The Trust for Public Land

Level of government: County
State/province: Oregon
Country: USA
Population: 157,733

Deschutes County is located in central Oregon between the Cascade Mountain Range to the west and the high desert to the east. The county faces tremendous development pressures. Although there

CASE STUDY > > > >

Greenprints help communities make informed decisions about land conservation and encourage community stakeholders to work toward common goals. The Greenprint process combines traditional methods of citizen engagement with GIS mapping and modeling.

are several national forests located in and near the county, as well as many state parks, the county and its municipalities could preserve complementary outdoor space, wildlife habitat, and outdoor recreation amenities through a variety of means, including land conservation measures. In 2009, The Trust for Public Land approached the county commissioners about the possibility of introducing a public financing measure for land conservation, but no comprehensive work had been done at that point to identify possible lands for acquisition. The commissioners encouraged The Trust for Public Land to undertake a plan to establish priorities. The challenge kicked off the start of the Deschutes County Greenprint process and a unique joint effort with the county, as a county commissioner, the county planning director, and staff members all actively participated in the Greenprint.

Developed by The Trust for Public Land, the Greenprint uses community-driven prioritization processes and state-of-the-art computer models created with GIS software to analyze community-based data. Greenprints help communities make informed decisions about land conservation and encourage community stakeholders to work toward common goals. The Greenprint process combines traditional methods of citizen engagement with GIS mapping and modeling. The process has five steps:

1. Identify local goals and assemble data. What are the issues? What are the threats? What do community members love? What do they want to conserve in their community? Usually five to ten major goals emerge from the process.
2. Translate data into a "priorities map" for each conservation goal. Priority maps are expressed in terms of conservation values ranging from low to high across the region.
3. Assign relative weightings that reflect community or regional priorities.
4. Create alternative scenarios by adding additional criteria or modifying the relative importance of existing criteria.
5. Combine the building blocks into a composite conservation priority map.

Before beginning the Greenprint process in Deschutes County, a steering committee comprising representatives from the county; The Trust for Public Land; the cities of Bend, Redmond, Sisters, and LaPine; the Deschutes Land Trust; and the Bend and Redmond Park and Recreation Districts agreed to lead the process. A core team developed a list of the different interest groups in the area that might care about open spaces, parks, trails, or wildlife conservation. From this list, it created a larger stakeholder group that represented a multitude of local groups with an interest in the project. The stakeholder group, based on input from the larger community, helped determine what the conservation goals of Deschutes County should be.

CASE STUDY > > >

Participants in the Greenprint process contributed many hours to the effort. The group met three to five times over the course of the project. The citizen engagement efforts associated with the project were extensive. Over the course of the project, the group sought public input through two telephone polls, two online surveys, in-person interviews with community members, and an information table at various community events.

Through these traditional means of citizen engagement, Deschutes County identified eight goals as part of its Greenprint. Once the goals were agreed upon by the stakeholders, a GIS map and model associated with each of the goals was developed. The goals were translated into more specific criteria as part of developing a GIS map and model (figure 2.11). Because scientific knowledge is involved in determining many of the criteria needed to support the goals, a technical advisory team, composed of seven to ten local people, was formed to help determine how to develop a GIS map and model to illustrate each of the selected goals. Team members who were subject-matter experts related to the selected goals helped determine what goal-related data was available.

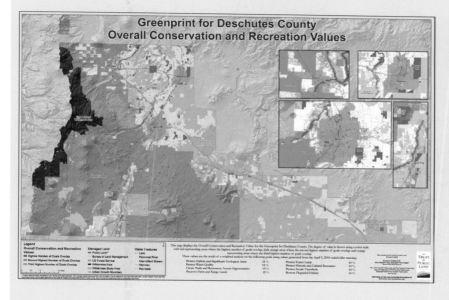

Figure 2.11 The "Overall Conservation and Recreation Values" map displays in red and orange the areas that are most critical for protection in Deschutes County. The community identified and weighted the goals that were combined to create this map. Courtesy of The Trust for Public Land.

Criteria for the goals were weighted based on the level of importance and the quality of the data available. The maps were taken to the stakeholder group for review. With the GIS maps projected from the computer on to a screen in the meeting room, participants used keypads to vote electronically on the goals and criteria, pulling data onto the maps in real time to see the impact of different decisions. The process depended heavily on local knowledge of opportunities and constraints. People could see how their votes made a change on the map, and the group was able to move through a discussion of priorities more quickly than if more traditional voting methods had been used. A discussion ensued as people contributed their local knowledge of the landscape to the information on the maps. Having the maps available in the room and being able to visualize alternatives aided the group decision making.

CASE STUDY > >

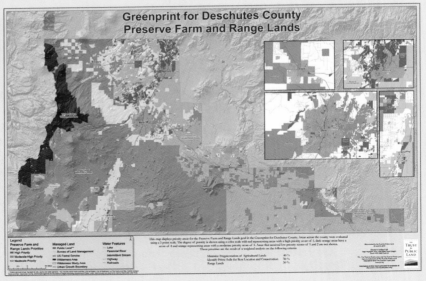

Revisions and updates to the data in the GIS models were performed after the meeting, and the final maps went back to the stakeholder group. The maps were shared with the larger community during listening sessions and other meetings that allowed the public to see the results of the Greenprint process. A master map that combines all the goals became the primary map for the project.

An online mapping site was also created as part of the Greenprint process. Stakeholders who were involved in the project can access the data used to create the maps. Query functionality is built into the application as well as more general map features such as zoom in/zoom out, drawing, and measuring, and data layers can be turned on and off. The Oregon State University (OSU) created the site and demonstrated it at a stakeholder meeting, and it continues to host the site.

When the county began to update its comprehensive plan in 2010, it included the Greenprint data and process in the natural resources section of the plan due to the extensive citizen engagement effort and significant amount of information collected through the Greenprint process.

CASE STUDY •

Making it easier for citizens to have input in development plans in Ireland's Dún Laoghaire-Rathdown and Fingal County Councils

Based on an interview with Dermot O'Kane from Esri Ireland, and a case study by Esri Ireland[4]

CASE STUDY > > >

Level of government: County Council
Country: Ireland
Population: DLR County Council 206,261; Fingal County Council 273,991

With a population of nearly 4.5 million people, Ireland is a small country where the commitment to active citizen engagement is deeply engrained. National law requires local councils to submit development plans every six years to guide development strategy in their respective regions. As part of the process, local councils must provide community residents with up to four opportunities for public input and comment on the development plans before they are finalized. Collecting and compiling citizen feedback on the plans is a complicated and immense task, especially for councils located in urban areas. For two councils in County Dublin—Dún Laoghaire-Rathdown (DLR), with a population of 206,261 (2011 Census) and Fingal, with a population of 273,991 (2011 Census)—the desire to be more accessible to constituents combined with the need to systematically collect and compile citizen feedback in a useful format led to a unique innovation.

In 2010, the DLR County Council migrated its development plan to a GIS platform to make it easier to manipulate and update. The DLR council was particularly keen to make the development plan maps available to the public via the Internet. The system had primarily been paper based, with large books of paper maps available at the council offices for citizens wanting to review development plans for their neighborhood. The idea was to give people the ability to review the maps online in their own homes rather than having to schedule a trip to the office.

At the same time, the Fingal County Council had begun to discuss a similar concept. Fingal had moved to a single continuous, seamless geodatabase in its Planning Department and had started using GIS as part of its development plan process as far back as 1996. It had fully migrated to a GIS platform prior to its 2005 development plan. The new technology gave the council a wealth of options in how the plan could be used, one of the most significant being the ability to put the plan online and create an online submissions application for the public (figure 2.13). Such an application would

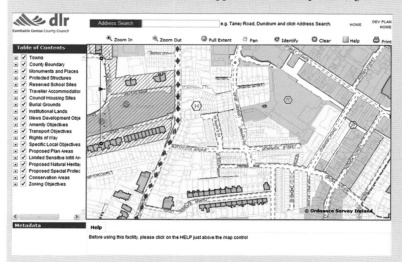

Figure 2.13 The online submissions application was designed to allow people to review the maps online. Courtesy of Esri Ireland.

CASE STUDY > >

make it easier for members of the public and other interested parties to participate in the required consultation process by enabling them to view and submit comments on development proposals as time permitted.

As the idea was discussed further, staff determined another benefit of such an application would be improving the council's internal efficiency. At the time, technicians had to digitize any submissions received by traditional mail or e-mail and cross-reference them with the development plan, which was a time-consuming process. The concept of an online application began to gain support. The Fingal County Council knew the direction it wanted to go, but had not determined how to deliver the new capability.

Both councils sought to maximize their investments in GIS technology. Because the councils were customers of Esri Ireland, in close proximity to each other, and on roughly the same time schedule for producing their development plans, a joint collaboration seemed inevitable. With the two councils working together on the project, they could split costs, share development ideas, and run tests that had to be carried out on a number of platforms under a range of different conditions.

Using the new online submissions facility, individuals or their agents can enter a summary of their concerns or proposals, make a full-text submission, mark the boundary of the area relating to their submission directly onto the plan, and attach up to five supporting documents. When the submission is completed, the solution automatically provides a confirmation message and a unique submission reference number. The new online submissions facility went live in May 2009, in time for public consultation by both councils' development plans.

The application is very intuitive and does not require any special training to use. However, staff from Fingal held a number of predevelopment plan workshops throughout the community and gave demonstrations on the new tool to citizens. The council also invited local media representatives to attend and use the new application.

Figure 2.14 Citizens can view different scenarios for development plans during stakeholder meetings. Courtesy of Esri Ireland.

Fingal County Council calculated that a quarter of the submissions it received were made via the Internet. The council estimates that it saves ten to fifteen minutes for every submission received online, where the citizen has captured the boundary through the submissions process. In the next round of public consultations, the council expected to receive in the region of 1,200 submissions. If all these comments were submitted online, the council could save sixty to eighty hours (based on the assumption that approximately one quarter of those submissions would have a boundary captured by the citizen).

CASE STUDY •

Collecting and using municipal census data for planning services in St. Albert, Alberta, Canada

Tammy Kobliuk, GIS Coordinator, Corporate Geographic Information Services, City of St. Albert, Alberta, Canada

Level of government: City
State/province: Alberta
Country: Canada
Population: 60,138

Many municipalities conduct their own censuses in Canada. In the Province of Alberta, municipal censuses are conducted under the Determination of Population Regulation of the Municipal Government Act. Counting assumptions and methodologies must be approved by the province in order for the final population number to be accepted as official and superseding that of the last federal census. For growing municipalities, waiting five years for the next federal census can mean lost revenue to support delivered services. Grants from the provincial and federal governments are often based on the total population count. All other information is generally collected for the purposes of municipal service planning and delivery.

Unlike a federal census, resident participation in a municipal census is not mandatory. However, municipalities often consider their census information to be more accurate than the federal census. This is due to the control they have over the data collection and their in-depth knowledge of the community, which enables them to correct assumptions and spot errant records. It is also the only census information to which the municipality has access to the address-level information. When St. Albert opted to conduct a municipal census in 2010, it achieved an overall census response rate of 98.6 percent. Only eighty-five residences refused to provide any information to the city. One of the key findings of the municipal census was that the city of St. Albert had passed the 60,000 population mark, an internal milestone for local civic officials.

CASE STUDY > > > > > >

Prior to 2008, St. Albert's municipal censuses were conducted mostly to find the total population and general age profile of the community and used paper forms that were then electronically scanned and counted. Previous census information had never been mapped or analyzed at a level smaller than neighborhood. Census analysis took place immediately following the census time period, with no further analyses being done.

The service departments within the city had a demonstrated need for more detailed information on population densities within the city. For example, the Transit Department wanted to know where the optimum locations were for new roads in the city, and the Social Services Department needed to know which neighborhoods needed which types of services. It was a matter of allocating resources appropriately as well as providing equitable service delivery to the residents of St. Albert. Additionally, there was a strong desire on the part of city leaders to obtain more value from the money spent on conducting the census. Although documenting the city's overall population is important, city leaders wanted to use census information in new and innovative ways.

The census map (figure 2.15) revealed the following trends and patterns:
- Population is not evenly distributed across the city.
- Population is not evenly distributed within neighborhoods.

Figure 2.15 This population density map shows that population is not evenly distributed across the city, nor within neighborhoods, and that the use of neighborhood averages should be used only where internal varied concentrations will not present an issue. Courtesy of Corporate GIS City of St. Albert, Alberta, Canada.

Population Density

High
Medium
Low

CASE STUDY > > > > >

- Pockets of multifamily complexes (smaller hotspots) can easily be identified.
- Single-family homes in newer neighborhoods (such as the ones at the top of the map) contain larger families than older neighborhoods in the heart of the city. The primary reason for this is that younger families with children at home tend to buy houses in the newer neighborhoods; families in older neighborhoods are often composed of empty nesters.

In 2009, the city's corporate GIS business area conducted a proof-of-concept project to demonstrate that the 2008 census data could be mapped out to the address level. The responses to individual questions were mapped out along with a demonstration of how information from the various questions could be combined and displayed on a map. This initiative was intended to determine the amount of work involved in creating a GIS-enabled census land base and to demonstrate the power of displaying the information at a very detailed level. This exercise also illustrated that the answers to simple census questions could supply much more information about residents than the previous general reports indicated.

In December 2009, the mapping of the 2008 census land base was completed and was used to create an up-to-date 2010 census land base. Although the conducting of a 2010 census was not officially approved by the council until January 2010, planning for the census began in the summer of 2009. The city was eager to move forward with newer technology but was reluctant to make too many changes at one time. The decision was made to move forward with the online citizen response option but to hold off on deploying handheld data collection units with field staff. Field staff followed up at residences that did not supply an online response.

The capture of a GIS census land base layer proved to be a key change from previous censuses because GIS data and technology were, for the first time, used to generate the master census address list. This provided a significant time savings in generating the master address list and was considered to be much more accurate than compiling addresses from tax and utility databases. The GIS land base also enabled much more accurate planning of enumeration areas because it was much more accurate in determining the number of residences in each enumerator district.

The benefits from geocoding the 2010 census data were numerous. By mapping out the results, the city was able to achieve greater accuracy and a greater level of detail on its population. The city also has a more reliable residential address list for future censuses. Most important, St. Albert has new address-level information—detailed demographics, employment, and student information not previously available—that can be combined with other spatial data to provide useful information for specific programs and allow for ad hoc analyses that can be done on an as-needed basis.

Figure 2.16 illustrates the challenge faced by the community in that the concentration of school-aged children shifts across the community over time, leaving schools that were once in the midst of young families now in a sea of empty nesters. This increases the need for busing children to schools, because many children no longer live within walking distance. The shifting demographics are very difficult for municipalities and school boards when it comes to planning schools, playgrounds, and park amenities.

The majority of municipal services are tailored to meet the current and planned populations of a municipality. Roads, wastewater systems, public transportation, and community services are all

CASE STUDY > > > >

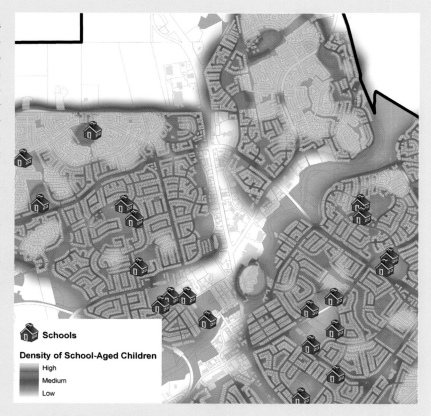

Figure 2.16 This map shows the distribution of school-aged children in relation to current school locations. In St. Albert, children tend to be concentrated in newer neighborhoods that may not yet have schools. The current schools often exist in neighborhoods where children have aged out and are now adults. Census information shows this is a cyclical process and that older neighborhoods eventually show a trend of attracting young families again as seniors and empty-nesters move on. Courtesy of Corporate GIS City of St. Albert, Alberta, Canada.

Schools

Density of School-Aged Children

High
Medium
Low

designed based on the size and demographics of the population they are to serve. The more accurate the picture is of that population, the more precise the planning can be for the delivery of those services. The new data will support the GIS analyses required for the planning of a number of municipal services. Table 2.1 details the many ways the city plans to use the data.

Table 2.1 Planning services using municipal census data

Planning service	GIS analysis
Fire services long-term planning	The analysis will look at where populations are concentrated and predict where future needs will be. The analysis will help ensure that service growth is properly planned instead of responding to unanticipated workloads. Future station locations will be identified so that land can be acquired in the short-term at a lower cost.

CASE STUDY > > >

Planning service	GIS analysis
Affordable housing planning	The analysis will determine how many of each high-risk family type the city has and the neighborhoods where the families currently live. Being a higher-income community, St. Albert has a strong interest in ensuring that the community continues to be affordable for all, particularly young families and seniors. The municipal census provides a raw database from which to test and validate assumptions and hypotheses about the number and distribution of assumed family types.

Family and community support services planning	The analysis will identify where at-risk families live to help determine where the city's support services are required. Sample questions the city can now answer include the following:
	• How many single-parent families are there?
	  • Where do they live?
	  • What type of housing do they live in?
	  • Are they renters or owners?
	  • How many children are in those families?
	  • Are they headed by a male or female?
	  • Are they headed by a senior?
	  • Is the head of household working?
	
	• Where do the seniors over the age of 75 live?
	  • Are they evenly distributed across the city or do they live in certain areas and facilities?
	  • Are they singles or couples?
	  • Are they renters or owners?
	  • How long have they lived at their current address?
	  • Are they working?
	  • Are they still living in their own homes?

Playground and park planning	The analysis will ensure that park amenities match the needs of the surrounding populations. For example, if an area of the city has few children, perhaps the neighborhood park infrastructure will concentrate on developing amenities desired by adults and seniors rather than building playgrounds for young children.
Land-use density analyses	Planning for future growth requires the city to review its land-use classes and validate the population densities associated with each. Based on the density analyses, the city can better determine where infrastructure investments may be desirable.

(continued)

CASE STUDY > >

Planning service	GIS analysis
Wastewater model validation	The city has an extremely good detailed record of flow volumes. Existing flow models can be calibrated against address-level populations to allow for more accurate flow predictions in growth areas.
Transit planning	The city's transit department can obtain a detailed demographics analysis of the capture area for each bus stop and bus route. This allows for better estimations of the demand for public transportation services and allows for better modeling of required services in new neighborhoods.

St. Albert's elected officials (the mayor and six council members) depend on GIS analysis for making numerous policy decisions and are big users of city maps, such as basemaps, land-use maps, and development/rezoning maps. They make use of the city's GIS program mostly through requests for reports, maps, presentations, and analyses generated or supported by GIS. Beyond the GIS analyses using the municipal census data that are already planned (see table 2.1), the city leaders have indicated a desire to use the data in other ways:

- Marketing the community: St. Albert is the third most populous municipality in the Alberta Capital Region and lies on the northwest boundary of the much larger city of Edmonton. Geographically small, the city of St. Albert relies heavily on residential taxes to supply city services. Regional competition is strong for attracting both residents and businesses, and the city must compete with other nearby municipalities for these potential tax dollars. It is important to know what types of residents the city has been successful in attracting and where the gaps are, the makeup of the retail customer base, and what type of resident-employee supply there is for businesses that would like to locate there.
- Neighborhood development: Like most cities, St. Albert is generally safe, but there are neighborhoods that bear extra attention. Census information is used to assist in understanding the demographic makeup of these areas and to ensure that services and solutions fit those neighborhoods' needs now and in the future.
- Understanding crime statistics: For areas undergoing an increase in crime, census information can help the police and municipal enforcement interpret the root causes of the crime and suggest solutions that the council may address.
- Performance monitoring: St. Albert has a rigorous performance measurement and management program designed to improve the efficiency and effectiveness of service delivery. For example, the new census data will assist with a review of fire and EMS response times to ensure that the city is meeting expected response time targets and providing a means to anticipate future response times as the city grows.

In short, the decision of St. Albert city leaders to use GIS technology to prepare for and conduct the municipal census will save time, energy, and money with future censuses, and the new geocoded

CASE STUDY >

data collected at such a detailed level will afford the city new opportunities to improve services planning for such critical issues as road capacity, public transportation, infrastructure planning for parks and recreation facilities, and potable water and wastewater capacity planning. The new data layers also offer faster public service due to easier access to information.

Figure 2.17 The planning of public transit routes needs to ensure that those demographic groups least likely to own a vehicle have adequate access to transportation to access important facilities and services. One of these groups is seniors (shown on this map). Courtesy of City of St. Albert, Alberta, Canada.

CASE STUDY •

Assisting the special-needs community during emergencies in Fort Worth, Texas

Robin Britton, GIS Lead; Shaun Campbell, Lead IT Programmer/Analyst; and Randy Westerman, Public Education Specialist, Office of Emergency Management, Fort Worth Fire Department, City of Fort Worth, Texas

Level of government: City
State/province: Texas
Country: USA
Population: 741,206

CASE STUDY > > >

Emergencies and disasters most often happen without warning, and mass confusion can ensue if communities are not prepared. Individuals with special needs require additional support during such a crisis, but first responders may not always be aware of where such residents can be found. In 2006, the City of Fort Worth's Office of Emergency Management (OEM) began development of the Special Needs Assessment Program, or SNAP, in response to the needs of the city's population. The goal of the program was to give the citizens of Fort Worth a venue to register the locations of citizens with special needs. Parents with special-needs children, in particular, have made use of the program. In the event of emergency, first responders can quickly identify individuals who require a priority evacuation or might need additional assistance, for example, if they were on oxygen. The SNAP system went online in 2008.

Figure 2.18 SNAP was developed to respond to the needs of the Fort Worth population.
Courtesy of Randy Westerman, public education specialist, Office of Emergency Management, Fort Worth, Texas.

Two years later, in 2010, the city began working with the North Central Texas Regional Council of Governments to expand the SNAP program to the sixteen-county area surrounding Fort Worth. When the system is fully implemented, more than 6.1 million people will have access to the program. Fort Worth had cooperative agreements in place with many of the surrounding communities for public safety, which paved the road for collaboration on SNAP.

Citizens who want to register for the program begin by logging on to the SNAP website `https://www.fortworthgov.org/applications/snap/` and completing an online form in four short steps:

1. Identify county of residence.
2. Establish an account and enter personal data.
3. Select disabilities or special needs from a drop-down menu.
4. Complete a free-form text space with notes on special needs not covered by the drop-down menu.

Registration is for one year and must be renewed on an annual basis to ensure that data in SNAP is current.

The SNAP website stores residents' geocoded addresses, information on the nature of their disabilities, and contact information in a SQL database that is linked to GIS. With this capability, the data can be used in a hazard analysis model that calculates potential hazards in the area along with the closest police and fire stations, hospitals, shelters, and community agencies and the quickest routes to each. The data also allows emergency management personnel to match residents to shelters or community facilities that can support their individual medical needs.

CASE STUDY > >

One of the enhancements to the program was to populate the SNAP data into the computer-aided dispatch (CAD) system. This allows 911 dispatchers access to the additional information should they receive a call that references a SNAP residence. In the event of a call to report a fire where the resident is confined to his or her bed or requires medical equipment, extra personnel and precautions can be taken when dispatching service vehicles to the site. This ensures the safety of the residents and the first responders who are there to assist them.

SNAP data is used for both planning and emergency response by the Fort Worth OEM. Data collected from SNAP registrations on the number of citizens who may need special assistance, as well as the types of disabilities, is used to ensure that special needs are addressed in community disaster planning. OEM also uses GIS extensively for planning and emergency response. SNAP data is captured as a GIS layer that has a variety of uses, such as helping to identify appropriate methods to notify special-needs residents of hazards such as flooding around area lakes.

Because of the confidential nature of the data, access to the database is limited. The corresponding linked GIS data also has security restrictions. Departments that have access to the data include OEM, Public Safety, Transportation and Public Works, and the Water Department. Departments outside the public safety arena use the data to notify residents when essential city functions may be impaired, such as when they have a major water main repair job or need to make emergency repairs.

Fort Worth places a high priority on disaster preparedness. Neighborhood associations are used for communicating information on the program to residents. Residents can sign up their neighbors for the program. Churches also offer support in getting the word out about the program. The city's Public Information Office attends local festivals and other public events as part of its ongoing public education efforts to make citizens aware of the support available. Randy Westerman from the OEM says, "It benefits the entire community on that part. It's a very simple way for people to help aid their family or friends or neighbors. This program has actually brought tears to people's eyes when I tell them about it." The program is a significant benefit to citizens, but it also benefits public safety officials and first responders. First responders have advance notice that there are people with special needs during an evacuation or any type of special emergency and can plan their actions accordingly.

The development team for SNAP offers a word of caution, suggesting that other jurisdictions consider the larger vision of such a program first as well as the goals that are accomplished.

> **Data collected from SNAP registrations on the number of citizens who may need special assistance, as well as the types of disabilities, is used to ensure that special needs are addressed in community disaster planning. OEM also uses GIS extensively for planning and emergency response. SNAP data is captured as a GIS layer that has a variety of uses, such as helping to identify appropriate methods to notify special-needs residents about hazards such as flooding around area lakes.**

CASE STUDY >

The City of Fort Worth developed SNAP in four phases, moving from the initial website development to CAD maps to GIS integration and finally going to a region-wide system. Instead of doing this in an incremental way, the team believes it would have been a better and more efficient deployment if it had been developed with the bigger picture in mind.

CASE STUDY •

Matching GIS to community trends

Grassroots movements often feed into the government policy process. What begins as an idea in one community spreads to others, and soon a new trend is born. Economic gardening is a concept that has gained tremendous interest among communities looking at effective strategies for strengthening their economic health. Littleton, Colorado, demonstrates how it has used GIS technology to strengthen its program. Chattanooga, Tennessee, has used GIS technology to help tackle the issue of urban food deserts. In Redlands, California, a new mobile application helps the city process service requests more efficiently.

Growing a healthy economy: How GIS supports Littleton's economic gardening program

Chris Gibbons, Director; and Eric Ervin, Marketing/GIS Analyst, City of Littleton Business/Industry Affairs Department, Littleton, Colorado

Level of government: City
State/province: Colorado
Country: USA
Population: 41,737

Small businesses have traditionally led the way in job creation and growth. Supporting local entrepreneurism and new or fledging start-up companies thus makes sense as a government economic development policy. In very simple terms, this is the concept behind a new trend called economic gardening that many communities are pursuing. The belief is that businesses and jobs grown locally have a greater tendency to stay local rather than move to a cheaper location, which often happens with industries recruited from elsewhere, because there will always be a less expensive location for their operations. One of the communities at the forefront of the trend is the city of Littleton, Colorado.

An economic gardening approach involves three primary elements: information, infrastructure, and connections. Littleton uses its GIS program to support the information element. "We use GIS for the standard uses like identifying markets, plotting customer locations, and seeing where the densities block up. We buy information to support those uses. We also use GIS for drive-time analysis as well as

CASE STUDY > > >

determining where a company should put its sales people," says Chris Gibbons, director of Littleton's Business/Industry Affairs Department. "All of those things go toward that information aspect of economic gardening."

"I think GIS is an essential and critical tool. Before I took this job, I used to do feasibility studies. I would go out and charge $30,000 and it'd take me six months, and I didn't have nearly as good data, [to do] something we can do today in hours."

Chris Gibbons, Director, Business/Industry Affairs Department,
City of Littleton, Colorado

Using GIS to assist local businesses

Littleton's Business/Industry Affairs Department provides a variety of services to stage 1 and stage 2 businesses. Stage 1 companies are generally defined as start-ups and have fewer than ten employees; stage 2 companies are in growth mode and have between ten and one hundred employees. When a company is at the stage 1 level, it primarily needs information on how to increase sales. Percentagewise, much of Littleton's GIS work focuses on defining markets for stage 1 companies. Start-up companies require basic data on demographics, household income, age, and gender.

Stage 2 companies need more sophisticated lifestyle data. With lifestyle data, a company can more fully refine its marketing program using data from census block groups, which are much smaller than census tracts or Zip Code areas. Anywhere from one to six census block groups might be located inside a census tract. If, for example, a company markets based on Zip Code data, it might do some direct marketing to households by offering coupons or perhaps put an ad in the local paper. Marketing in this manner costs a fair amount of money, especially if the firm really only wants to hit three of the neighborhoods in a particular Zip Code. Littleton also purchases consumer expenditure data, which allows it to determine "how much ketchup is sold in this neighborhood next to us," says Gibbons.

Littleton uses a standard four-step marketing approach in working with local businesses. Briefly, the first step involves building a customer profile during which the business determines who it wants to reach with its service or product. The second step determines where the market audience for that service or product is located. The third step defines the message that needs to go to that audience. During the fourth step, the media used to reach that audience is selected.

Customer profiles start with a fairly simple analysis and become refined over time as more data is added. GIS analysis helps with the refinement process to identify where companies should invest their marketing dollars to yield the best results. Potential customers often cluster in neighborhoods, because neighborhoods tend to be fairly uniform in terms of demographics and lifestyle profiles. But sometimes they're not. If the neighborhoods aren't uniform, the next step is to look for "watering holes." If members of a target audience are scattered throughout the neighborhoods, are there locations (aka,

CASE STUDY > > >

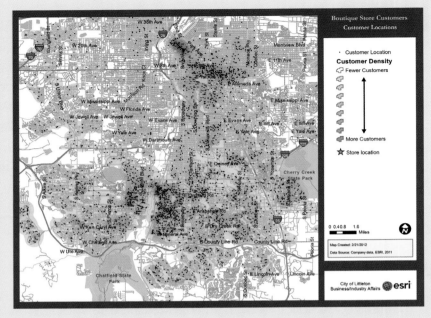

Figure 2.19 The first step in Littleton's four-step marketing approach involves building a customer profile product. Courtesy of Eric Ervin, City of Littleton, Colorado.

watering holes) where they come together? Do they all belong to an association? Do they all read the same things? Do they all go someplace at a particular time?

One method for refining a customer profile involves using an existing database of customers and plotting where those customers are located. Employing a density analysis technique, GIS technology can identify hot spots where customers are located. After identifying such hot spots, the key variables that make up the profile of the hot spot can be compiled. The resulting analysis includes the demographics, lifestyle, and other relevant information. That information, in turn, can be used to look for other neighborhoods with a similar profile. With that information in hand, the company can undertake a very targeted and well-directed marketing campaign to a new base of potential customers. It also has better information about what motivates the potential customer, and, in turn, can better craft its marketing to speak to those important motivations and create a more effective marketing message.

Beyond developing basic customer profiles for companies, Littleton has used its GIS to support and encourage local entrepreneurs with some sophisticated spatial analyses. One project involved work for a company that was making high-end gym bags that ranged in price from $250 to $400, a very targeted market. Using lifestyle information, Littleton staff identified a group of people who were both wealthy and active. This group has a very specific lifestyle name: Turbo Boomers.

A national spatial analysis showed that these individuals are located in only nine cities across the country, and then only in certain neighborhoods in those cities. Had the company decided to advertise in Minneapolis and Miami, for example, it would have missed these individuals because they don't live

CASE STUDY > >

in either city. The neighborhoods were in San Francisco, Denver, Dallas, Atlanta, and Washington, DC, among others. The GIS analysis enabled the company to do a highly targeted marketing campaign because it knew to look for a specific lifestyle group, and that lifestyle group only occurred in certain cities and only in certain neighborhoods in those cities.

The other example is a company that offers a software product for farm-implement dealers. The company knew that a lot of its potential customers were located in the Midwest, and it wanted to hire a salesperson who would be somewhat centrally located in relation to potential customers. The rough guess was that a location near Kansas City would be optimal because the city is in a prime agricultural area in the middle of the country. As Gibbons explains, "When we ran the data, we found all the farm-implement dealers in the Midwest, and it turned out that the best location was much closer to Indianapolis in terms of the center of density of the potential customer base. It's that kind of ability to provide them data-based decision support information that makes them a better company."

Economic instability, economic gardening, and the power of GIS

"GIS has been a fundamental tool in our economic gardening program in Littleton for over a decade. It is a sophisticated way of identifying B2C markets by demographics, lifestyles, and consumer expenditures. By providing direct and tangible support to our local emerging growth companies, we have been able to double our job base and triple our sales tax revenues without spending a single cent on recruiting or incentives."

Chris Gibbons, Director, Business/Industry Affairs Department,
City of Littleton, Colorado

During economically unstable times, an economic gardening approach fosters important opportunities for new companies. Consider that a significant number of great American companies first came into being during the Great Depression. Although initially that fact—great companies being founded during some of the worst, most turbulent times—may seem counterintuitive, when old structures break down, new prospects emerge. Great disruption allows new ideas and ways of doing business to emerge. New and different kinds of companies and products can gain a foothold in the market.

CASE STUDY >

> ## "Littleton's economic gardening program is the backbone of our economic development efforts. It is unmatched in its effectiveness and economic resiliency. The proof is in the results; in a downturn economy Littleton is growing jobs, decreasing unemployment, and running positive budget numbers."
>
> Debbie Brinkman, Mayor, City of Littleton, Colorado

These new companies need an increased flow of information to secure their foothold in the new market. GIS is one tool to get the information to the companies that need it. The technology makes it possible to take large amounts of data, manipulate it, and then display it in a very visual way. The speed and the quality of the information that can be generated today is a quantum leap from thirty years ago. "I think GIS is an essential and critical tool," Gibbons says. "Before I took this job, I used to do feasibility studies. I would go out and charge $30,000 and it'd take me six months, and I didn't have nearly as good data, [to do] something we can do today in hours."

CASE STUDY •

Looking at food deserts in Chattanooga, Tennessee

Lori Quillen, Policy Analyst, the Ochs Center for Metropolitan Studies,[5] Chattanooga, Tennessee

Level of government: City and county
State/province: Tennessee
Country: USA
Population: 167,674 (city) and 336,463 (county)

Obesity rates in the United States have skyrocketed over the past few decades. The issue has found a place on the policy agenda in many communities because obesity is a complicating factor in numerous diseases, such as diabetes, heart disease, stroke, cancer, and depression. Increased obesity rates and the resulting increase in these serious health issues has led to greater health-care costs, which, in turn, severely affect both private and public budgets. In 2009, the Ochs Center for Metropolitan Studies studied the issue of food deserts—areas that lack traditional grocery stores and supermarkets, and thus lack access to affordable healthy food—in the city of Chattanooga and Hamilton County,

CASE STUDY > > >

Tennessee, to give policy makers new data to consider in developing appropriate long-term strategies for addressing obesity rates in the region.

Findings from the Ochs Center study led one state senator, Andy Berke from Tennessee's District 10, to file a bill, the Food Desert Relief Act. Senator Berke described the issue of food deserts as one that people can get their hands around, and it has generated tremendous energy and support from the greater Chattanooga/Hamilton County region. He noted that since the report was released the Food Trust of Philadelphia has become engaged in bringing together different stakeholder groups to address what is a common concern for many in the community. The GIS analyses used in the report helped drive home the neighborhood implications of the problem.

"The real value of GIS is that you can see how neighborhoods in your district are impacted and understand what is at stake for your constituents. It strongly underscores the need to take action."

Senator Andy Berke, District 10,
State of Tennessee

Researchers began the study by looking at three questions related to food access in Chattanooga and Hamilton County: Where are supermarkets located in Hamilton County? Do low-income residents have to travel further to access supermarkets? Does the lack of supermarkets in some areas have an impact on food prices? In order to answer such questions, the researchers first mapped the location of larger supermarkets and grocery stores and calculated the percentage of neighborhood populations that lived within a mile of a supermarket. They also calculated the average distance to the nearest supermarket by neighborhood. Finally, they conducted a food pricing survey of eighty-five smaller corner and convenience stores and larger supermarkets throughout Hamilton County.

Previous research on grocery store access and development had established a density of one supermarket per 10,000 people as adequate for facilitating grocery store access. With more than fifty supermarkets in all of Hamilton County, the supermarket density per 10,000 for the entire county is about 1.7, well over the generally accepted standard. However, grocery stores are not distributed equally based on population in the county, and several subregions within the city and county have much fewer than one grocery store per 10,000 people, including Bakewell, Bushtown/Highland Park, East Chattanooga, and Harrison, all four of which had no grocery stores or supermarkets.

The percentage of each subregion's population that lives within one mile of a grocery store is another indicator of grocery store accessibility. A spatial analysis revealed that several neighborhoods—East Chattanooga, Birchwood, and Bushtown/Highland Park—had a lower than normal

Figure 2.20 This map
illustrates the location
of all corner stores and
supermarkets in Hamilton
County. Courtesy of the Ochs
Center for Metropolitan Studies.

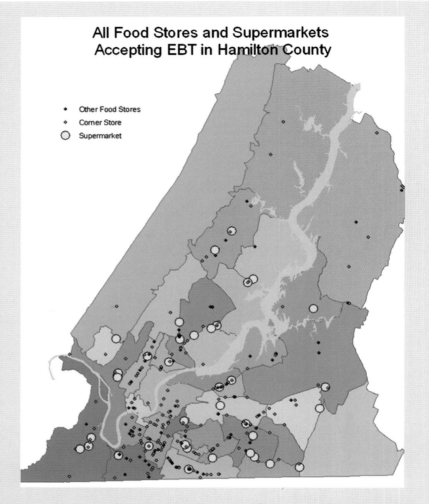

All Food Stores and Supermarkets Accepting EBT in Hamilton County

- Other Food Stores
- Corner Store
- Supermarket

percentage of their populations living within one mile of a grocery store. The analysis also looked at the average distance to the nearest grocery store or supermarket by subregion and found that subregions with the longest average distance to the nearest grocery store are those located in less developed parts of the county. Within the city of Chattanooga, East Chattanooga had the greatest average distance to the nearest grocery store, at 1.48 miles.

The final element of the analysis examined food prices. As a general rule of thumb, grocery stores and supermarkets have lower food prices than corner or convenience stores. The Ochs Center research proved no exception to the rule, finding that supermarket prices were up to 20 percent lower than those at corner stores. The analysis showed that residents in several subregions were at a distinct disadvantage in terms of the ease of access to and cost of healthy foods if they were solely dependent on

CASE STUDY >

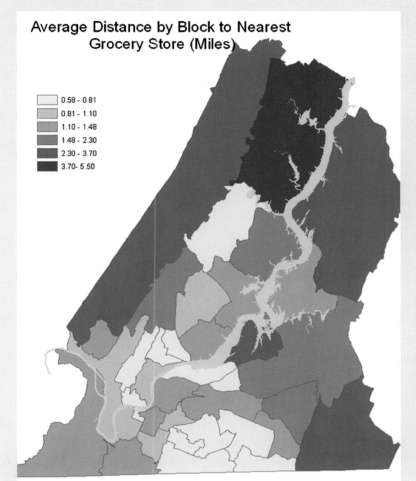

Average Distance by Block to Nearest Grocery Store (Miles)

	0.58 - 0.81
	0.81 - 1.10
	1.10 - 1.48
	1.48 - 2.30
	2.30 - 3.70
	3.70 - 5.50

Figure 2.21 This map shows the average distance to a larger grocery store or supermarket by region in Hamilton County. Courtesy of the Ochs Center for Metropolitan Studies.

neighborhood stores. The researchers determined that the neighborhoods of greatest concern were East Chattanooga, Bushtown/Highland Park, and South Chattanooga.

For a policy maker, the new information provides strong support for a variety of potential policy actions. For example, officials might determine that the lack of grocery stores in a given neighborhood justifies the city establishing a tax increment financing (TIF) district to help recruit such a business to the neighborhood. Alternatively, they could decide to establish community gardens on city-owned lands in the neighborhood or promote the idea of a farmers market for the community. Knowing where challenges exist is the first step to developing policies to address them.

CASE STUDY •

Going mobile in Redlands, California

N. Enrique Martinez, City Manager; and David L. Hexem, Chief Information Officer, Department of Innovation and Technology, City of Redlands, California

Level of government: City
State/province: California
Country: USA
Population: 68,747

In 2007, Redlands first began to feel the effects of the recession and subsequent stagnant economy. Employee furloughs, and ultimately layoffs, became necessary, and the city needed to be more efficient while continuing to provide the same level of services and lower its operating costs. Enrique Martinez, the city manager, determined that technology could help lead the city forward and opted to bring all departmental technology employees together under the management of one department, the new Department of Innovation and Technology (DoIT).

One of the immediate advantages apparent in the reorganization was that an enterprise GIS technology approach could provide solutions to the challenges the city faced. The City of Redlands began its GIS program in the mid-1990s, using the technology primarily for utilities management and crime analysis. Over the years, other departments took advantage of the technology and built needed assets for their work. The reorganization brought together all the GIS assets and inventory that had been developed by various city departments. Centralizing the city's technology assets and building an inventory of those assets allowed the city's chief information officer (CIO) to develop an overarching vision and strategic plan for how the city should move forward with GIS technology.

After reviewing what it already had in place, the city opted to expand its GIS program to leverage what it had and obtain greater value from what had been built. For example, it installed GPS monitors on its waste collection trucks. These monitors provided data not only on a truck's current location, but they also collected data on how long a truck's engine ran at a given location. The new data aided the city in determining how it could create new efficiencies.

From an organizational standpoint, Martinez views technology as the nervous system for the city, providing the connecting tissue among the service departments to make everything work together. He looks to the CIO to spot trends, recognize potential efficiencies, save costs, and identify shortcuts faster than any other local government official. "The CIO can tell me specifically and quantitatively what is going on, for example, with the garbage trucks," Martinez says.

In the long term, the city has a goal to implement a full customer service contact center, also known as a 311/CRM system (see the case study on Hartford, Connecticut in part 3). Although the city has not had room in its budget to implement a full system to date, city leaders do want to provide a means for citizens to contact the city with questions and concerns twenty-four hours a day, seven days a week. Redlands' Quality of Life Department handles most of the city's

CASE STUDY > >

field operations, with the exception of utilities, and receives the vast majority of service requests from citizens, including work orders for streetlights, potholes, tree trimming, and the like. The department's telephone system allows citizens to call and leave voice mail messages during off-work hours, but Redlands' leaders wanted a consistent way to take in information and use it internally to better understand the nature and location of how citizen requests come into the organization.

Given the city's past history of using technology to deliver services and lower costs, David Hexem, the CIO for DoIT, recommended looking at the opportunities offered by the multitude of new mobile reporting applications on the market. After researching available options, the city decided to work with CitySourced to build a Redlands 311 application (figure 2.22) that could be used by both citizens and Redlands employees to report service issues they find around the city. The application collects information from a smartphone (picture, video, audio along with location information). The resident then chooses from a preset list of issues (potholes, abandoned shopping carts, graffiti, streetlights out, and so on) and leaves any other comments on the issue before sending it to the city electronically.

The Redlands 311 application is being used in tandem with an outreach effort that involves dividing the city up into ten sections and assigning each department director to a section that he or she will be responsible for, for monitoring quality-of-life issues. Directors will look at sidewalks, curbs

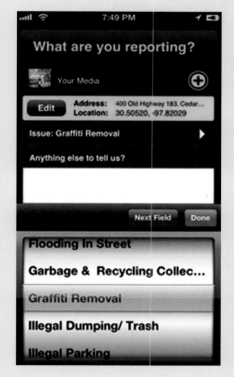

and gutters, graffiti, and potholes, among other issues, and will be able to create service tickets for any issues found in a quick and consistent manner using the Redlands 311 application.

The new application has received a positive response from Redlands citizens, especially younger residents who have embraced smartphone technology in a substantial way. The city has done some spot-checks and informal surveys of application users, and satisfaction rates with the application are high, generally ranging from 90 to 95 percent satisfied or very satisfied with the application.

The city introduced the Redlands 311 application in mid-February 2011 and received roughly 700 service tickets in its first seven months of operation. As smartphone use increases among the general population, the city expects those numbers to increase, but it is comfortable

Figure 2.22 Using the city's new mobile application, Redlands 311, the residents of Redlands, California, can report problems on a wide variety of issues, including illegal dumping, graffiti, and garbage collection. Courtesy of City of Redlands, California.

with a target of receiving 100 requests per month. City leaders believe that by combining this technology with an ongoing and highly visible presence of city personnel throughout the community, they can achieve the critical balance for securing the trust of Redlands citizens.

Initially, employees manually entered the service requests received from the Redlands 311 application into the Quality of Life Department's work order management system (Cityworks, developed by Azteca Systems Inc.). The city is working with CitySourced and Cityworks to integrate the new application so that requests are automatically fed into the work order management system. The Redlands 311 application is also being harmonized with the city's online service request forms, again with the intention of collecting data for service requests in a consistent and uniform manner.

The city intends to continue investing in technology in order to provide quality levels of service to its citizens. Both Martinez and Hexem see GIS as providing the foundation to build on. "Everything we do is spatial," says Martinez. "We need to get away from the programmatic silos we've developed over time and look at what's happening throughout the city. Solutions like the Redlands 311 application help prevent us from becoming separated from our customers."

Figure 2.23 The CitySourced application.
Courtesy of City of Redlands, California.

CASE STUDY •

Matching GIS to policy interests

Most elected officials have concerns that are of tremendous personal interest as well as important public policy issues. Such issues might have been among the reasons an elected official chose to run for office, or it may be an issue that arises after he or she has taken office. As such issues emerge and more is learned, policy makers should discuss the potential for creating GIS applications that can help foster more dialogue and shed new light on possible courses of action. In the case of Carver County, Minnesota, using GIS technology to create more connectivity among county and city recreational trails helped promote active-living health goals. The need for greater integration and sharing of emergency management data has become a focus in Multnomah County, Oregon, and the GIS application developed to support this policy interest (Bridge) has caught the attention of the entire Pacific Northwest region.

Promoting active living with the Trail and Recreational Information Portal (TRIP) in Carver County, Minnesota

Peter Henschel, GIS Department; Randy Maluchnik, Commissioner; and Tracy Bade, Public Health and Environment Division, Carver County, Minnesota

Level of government: County
State/province: Minnesota
Country: USA
Population: 91,042

In 2007, leaders in Carver County, Minnesota, began work on preparing the county's 2030 Comprehensive Plan. Carver County is one of the fastest-growing counties in the state, and the Planning Department wanted to address the potential impacts of that anticipated growth in the 2030 Comprehensive Plan. In order to do so, the Planning Department made a point of reaching out to other departments within the county to include them in discussions about how future development should occur. It also reached out to the eleven cities in the county. At the same time, the county's Public Health Department was considering what measures could be taken to support the county's chronic-disease prevention efforts. Obesity levels across the nation and in Carver County over the past decade had been rising, while physical activity levels had been decreasing. New local efforts were also underway in the county looking at the connection between health and the environment. For example, the Minnesota Health Department provided training on how to conduct Walkable Community Workshops. The vision of creating an environment to support active living in the county had found a spot on the policy agenda.

The Planning Department hosted a series of department meetings to talk about the 2030 Comprehensive Plan. During these meetings, some common goals emerged. In particular, four county departments—Planning, Public Health, Parks, and the Community Development Agency—came together to identify common goals around active living. Although the departments had worked together before, this was the first time they had come together on a project with such defined goals. After several conversations, and consulting with leaders and planning departments in the county's eleven incorporated cities, the multidisciplinary city and county team decided on three objectives:

- Incorporate active living principles into the county and all city comprehensive plans
- Provide connectivity within city trail plans, between city trail plans, and between city and county trail systems
- Increase community awareness of active living and promote walking and biking by encouraging the use of trails, sidewalks, parks, and facilities

CASE STUDY > > > >

> **"We can use [GIS] to promote the trails and parks and encourage people to get out, take a walk, and have a bit more healthy lifestyle. It makes it easy for people to go on their computers and find places they might like to take a walk, ride a bike, or play in our parks. . . . It's all a matter of communication and empowering citizens by giving them the tools to better utilize the amenities that are available. It provides easy access, and my constituents value and appreciate this service."**
>
> Randy Maluchnik, Commissioner, Carver County

The Public Health Department collects and maintains a considerable amount of data and had used GIS as one of its sources for analyzing and displaying data for a number of years. The department has sent staff members for training in GIS and actively uses the technology as a planning tool. The department led the multidisciplinary team that worked on the aforementioned objectives and identified the idea to develop a web-mapping application working with the GIS Department. The idea was to allow citizens to go online to see where all the parks, trails, and amenities were in Carver County as a means of promoting active living. When the opportunity to apply for a grant from Blue Cross/Blue Shield Prevention Minnesota arose, the Public Health Department decided to apply to support active living. The grant kicked off the start of Carver County's active living initiative.

Carver County created a GIS Department in 1996, but it initially focused on land records and other land-use data. The county had some regional parks and trails recorded in its GIS database when the active living mapping work first began, but it didn't have much data for the incorporated cities. The grant funds allowed the county to hire an intern to create a data model of all the cities' trail systems, including those that were recorded on paper maps or CAD drawings. The county started compiling information for the project in 2008, beginning with data to support the trails. Using the data model, the county was able to compile the information from the cities and eventually developed a network of 250 miles of trails and 130 miles of sidewalks that extended through all the cities.

> **"The best thing is to use [GIS] as a planning tool. It helps show the communities how we can connect to the regional Dakota Trail. Community planning takes a lot of time and effort, and GIS makes this a lot easier and more cost-effective. It also provides better quality work in planning. I'm very excited about it."**
>
> Randy Maluchnik, Commissioner, Carver County

CASE STUDY > > >

Cities in Carver County were particularly excited about the potential of a countywide web portal for active living. They reviewed the trails identified within their communities and corrected any information that was inaccurate. It gave the GIS team a good basemap for developing the application. The cities also contributed to the project with photos from the trails and parks.

The resulting web portal, Trail and Recreational Information Portal, or TRIP, provides several basic search scenarios. The application allows the user to search for a trail route, a park, or a lake using a drop-down menu. An address search feature is also available that allows the user to set a one-, two-, or five-mile buffer around his or her home to determine what facilities are available in the area. Basic map interaction allows the user to zoom in or out on the resulting map as well as scan the larger area. When the zoom function is used, photos pop up at different points and show actual pictures of the trails and parks to further intrigue the user.

Figure 2.24 This screen capture shows how a user would locate a park through the TRIP application. The user can search through the wizard on the left side of the application and locate parks by address, city, or the entire county. The pop-up window shows the park activities available through the icons and provides a slide show of pictures. The user can link the location of the park on Facebook or Twitter and get directions. Courtesy of Carver County, Minnesota.

A future release of the application is under development that will enable users to search for specific features or facilities within the parks. Users will be able to look for ice-skating rinks, playgrounds, skateboard parks, tennis courts, and beach areas, to name a few. The county is taking a long-range approach to the development of the applications and has discussed what new features should go in future versions.

The county and cities have been very active in updating the GIS data since the initial collection. Having quality data provides opportunities for community planners to improve trail connectivity throughout the county, designate safe routes to schools, and conduct walkability assessments to determine where problems (such as degraded sidewalks and lack of designated crosswalks) might exist. In the future, the county hopes to work with volunteers as a mobile force to improve data using GPS units

CASE STUDY > >

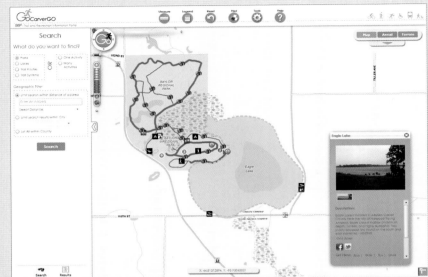

Figure 2.25 This screen capture shows the results of searching for a lake through the TRIP application. Pictures of the lake are available in the pop-up window, along with a brief description of the lake, directions to the lake, Facebook and Twitter links, and a link to the Minnesota DNR's Lake Finder website. Courtesy of Carver County, Minnesota.

or a smartphone application to collect more data from walkability assessments, which would save considerable staff time.

"Having only 3.5 employees in GIS and working on multiple projects, collaboration with the cities has been critical for the success of this project," says Peter Henschel, who is with the GIS Department. "We have eleven city editors checking the data on the website rather than one county person. We've been able to greatly expand the capabilities of the site as a result, and the cities are very excited about helping with the web editing and maintaining the data."

The trail and recreation application is part of a larger website, GoCarverGo.org, which has been steadily receiving hits since it was released. The site received more than 13,000 visits and 200,000 hits from April 2010 to March 2011. As might be expected, more hits come in the summer months when people want to be outside in Minnesota.

The shared expertise and resources between the multiple county divisions and the collaboration between the county and all the cities has led to the success of this project. In addition, having the support of the County Board of Commissioners has been instrumental in moving the active living program forward, both in terms of allocating resources and staff time and pursuing grant opportunities. The board's support and actual presence at events has made an impact on the larger community and emphasized the importance of the work. Many of the city mayors have served as champions for active living in their communities, which has resulted in plans being adopted and financial resources being allocated for active living objectives.

Commissioner Maluchnik notes, "Using GIS provided Carver County with a comprehensive map of existing and proposed trails. It also helped us identify possible connections between county trails and city trails. . . . We developed these things in GIS, which is great, but then we get the feedback from

CASE STUDY >

the people, and that makes it even better. As it's supposed to be in a democracy, the feedback from the people we serve drives our actions. It's enjoyable to obtain feedback from constituents on this project because the program has been so well received by the community. The taxpayers see this as an efficient and effective use of county resources."

Not only has this multidisciplinary team developed an innovative way of supporting health and quality of life for the residents of Carver County by utilizing the power of GIS, it also sees the opportunities for building on this success in the future to come. Take time to visit http://www.gocarvergo.org and check out how GIS can help make the connection between health and the environment.

CASE STUDY •

Building a virtual emergency management network in Multnomah County and the State of Oregon

Amy Esnard, GISP, GIS Manager, IT Department, Multnomah County, Oregon

Level of government: County
State/province: Oregon
Country: USA
Population: 735,334

Multnomah County's GIS program supports several departments, including Emergency Management. Up until 2010, the department had no means of accessing critical data that staff needed for situational awareness, response planning and mitigation, event tracking, and real-time monitoring during an emergency. Department staff considered purchasing a third-party application but ultimately decided to approach the county's GIS team to determine what could be built.

About the same time, the US Department of Homeland Security launched a new initiative, Virtual USA. Virtual USA had established a system for information sharing and collaboration

Multnomah County and its many regional, state, and federal partners brought together numerous critical and fundamental geospatial datasets, including transportation, critical infrastructure, and health data, as well as weather and traffic feed information. All were integrated into a web-based mapping situational awareness picture for emergency response.

CASE STUDY > > >

among the homeland security and emergency management community involving all levels of government. One of the applications rolled out by Virtual USA was VIPER, a situational awareness tool developed by the State of Virginia. VIPER merges real-time situational information with traditional GIS layers to create a comprehensive picture of current and developing situations. For example, the application can use precipitation data from the National Weather Service to predict what time a river might reach flood stage or display the location of special-needs populations in the event of a hazardous materials spill.

The Multnomah County team had an opportunity to see a demonstration of the application when the Oregon State Department of Emergency Management hosted a meeting for Virtual USA in 2009. Both Multnomah County Emergency Management (MCEM) and the State of Oregon had a need to see into every corner of their daily operations to prepare for a wide range of possible emergency scenarios. To do so required easy access to vast amounts of data ranging from operational data, such as vehicle tracking, road closures, and shelter status, to nonoperational data, such as the location of pipelines and hospitals. It also required demographic data to know where special-needs populations are located in the area. Additionally, stakeholders wanted to be able to share information about situational awareness, ongoing planning efforts, and emergency response with each other and their respective partners in nearly real time.

Another challenge was how to present the data in a consistent manner to all stakeholders. The state had half a dozen agencies ready to build their own operational viewers and dashboards to their specifications, whereas MCEM had a need for a common operating picture to integrate information and data from every business function. Interoperability among the many agencies involved requires everyone to have a consistent view of what is happening on the ground during an emergency while at the same time allowing for access to the specific information required by each agency.

The answer to these different missions was to develop a GIS-based information and analysis platform known as Bridge (formerly called VENOM). GIS technology provided a platform to affordably integrate the data provided by so many partners and independent systems. The visual aspect of mapping provided an intuitive view into complicated data and extremely robust analytical tools.

The Bridge platform integrates dozens of datasets from many organizations to create an information framework that can be leveraged by any public or private partner with a minimal investment. The common framework also prevented a dozen agencies from building a customized emergency management system that wouldn't work with other systems. The participating agencies can put their practice into action together in unison.

The Bridge platform uses four primary tools that can be used for multiple purposes. Tools available through the system include:

- Operational/situational awareness. The application shows in nearly real time what is occurring in the field—for example, a storm moving through a region or where heavy traffic might be located.
- Analysis. The application can help predict how an emergency situation might evolve, such as using a plume model to determine where a hazardous spill may move.

CASE STUDY > >

Figure 2.26 The Bridge platform enables the integration of different data types to aid emergency management personnel in planning for disasters of all types. Courtesy of Multnomah County, Oregon.

- Status updates. An executive dashboard allows personnel to quickly determine the current number of beds in county shelters or vacancy rates at regional hospitals.
- Planning. This tool allows the user to locate points on a map to show, for example, a bridge that's out or an evacuation route.

Multnomah County and its many partners brought together fifty critical datasets, including datasets for health, critical infrastructure (pipelines, roads, etc.), and organizational resources that can be used in a Bridge viewer. Many of the datasets are standardized, such as NOAA weather data, but some are not, which required a look at interoperability. To enable the integration of these many datasets, the development team designed a programming code that allows a user to easily switch back and forth between different types of data, regardless of the format. Data layers within the framework are both static and dynamic, providing the user with the option of viewing real-time data, such as weather feeds or operational status of shelters, or performing queries on static data, such as road centerline data.

One of the anticipated challenges of building out the system is balancing the needs of the local organization with those of the larger community. Prior to deployment of the application, the US Department of Homeland Security and the State of Oregon entered into a memorandum of understanding that enabled the state to maintain the basic framework used by the Bridge platform. Local government jurisdictions involved in the project entered into intergovernmental agreements with the state, supporting data contribution and data updates and enhancing data access. With this governance structure in place, data stewardship and accountability practices help to keep the system up to date and ensure the partnerships provide appropriate geospatial information support.

CASE STUDY >

Interest in the Bridge platform continues to grow. Having evolved from a county project to a multicounty project to a state pilot project, the application also now works in conjunction with a larger regional effort involving four states—Oregon, Washington, Idaho, and Montana—that participated in the Pacific Northwest pilot project for Virtual USA. In the winter of 2010, the application supported a demonstration exercise of data sharing across state boundaries. Each of the states had either adopted a Virtual USA template or worked with an existing application, but all were able to view weather feeds and infrastructure status changes, transferring data from one state to another during the demonstration.

The true beauty of the system, however, is that it can be used on a daily basis, not just in emergency situations. The Multnomah County commissioners have begun to use the Bridge platform for policy-making purposes (see interview with Commissioner Judy Shiprack). In short, the Bridge platform provides a model for the future for how local to federal public and private agencies can work together to build better services using fewer resources.

CASE STUDY •

The benefits of GIS from the perspective of a newcomer to the field

Interview with Judy Shiprack, Commissioner, District 3, Multnomah County, Oregon

Judy Shiprack first won her seat as the county commissioner for District 3 in Multnomah County, Oregon, in 2008. Although she wasn't new to politics, having served as a state representative for her southeast Portland neighborhood, it wasn't until she began her tenure as a county commissioner that she became a champion of GIS technology. Over the past ten years, her district in Multnomah County has increased in population, density, poverty, and racial diversity. "I am amazed by the ability to see data in a map context, layered with other data, and animated over time. GIS technology helps me demonstrate these changes visually on maps in ways that are easily understandable to general audiences. It helps me educate my constituents, my colleagues, and myself about how to improve the efficiency and effectiveness of programs we provide," says Shiprack.

Figure 2.27 Judy Shiprack, commissioner. Courtesy of CommissionerJudy Shiprack, Multnomah County, Oregon.

At the 2011 Esri International User Conference in San Diego, Shiprack had her first opportunity to focus solely on GIS and learn how it could help with her job. "I am learning about the ability to frame information a new way; it is going to help me both design policy *and* describe what the government I work for is doing in my community," she explains. "The power of visualizing data came home to me in a personal way as my plane flew in very clear conditions over Yosemite National Park on my way to the conference. I spent many childhood vacations there with my family, camping and backpacking on the John Muir Trail. Looking down and recognizing the familiar landscape, I imagined how fun, informative, and engaging a program based on geography would be. Geology, ecology, history, literature, recreation, art, wildlife, politics—all of these connections with the landscape I was seeing from the plane would be available on my computer."

"I see the problem-solving assistance of this GIS technology as being limited only by our imagination, our ability to ask the right questions, and our ability to analyze the information received."

Judy Shiprack, Commissioner, Multnomah County

Multnomah County faces many of the same policy issues that so many counties around the United States are facing. In the down economy, and with people trying to deal with joblessness and foreclosures, the county's service population has increased while its budget for providing services has diminished. GIS technology has been able to help address those challenges in a number of ways, Shiprack says.

"Our county owns a number of buildings, and we spend a lot of money on upkeep and improvements. GIS mapping can help us determine if these are the right locations for the services we provide, or if we should even have static locations for services when a mobile work force might be better for our clients as well as for our budget. We have used GIS to look at neighborhoods with a high number of prison returnees, to see if there is a way to target services to these neighborhoods. Do residents believe prison returnees impact crime rates in the community? We can map the relationship. Are there some Zip Codes where our services are not being adequately distributed? We will be able to map our service population and compare the location of the need with the distribution of the service," she says. "I see the problem-solving assistance of this GIS technology as being limited only by our imagination, our ability to ask the right questions, and our ability to analyze the information received."

Land conservation and preservation in Scottsdale, Arizona

Kroy Ekblaw, Preserve Director; Robert Chasan, Geographer/GIS Analyst; and Scott Hamilton, Preserve Planner, City of Scottsdale, Arizona

Level of government: City
State/province: Arizona
Country: USA
Population: 217,385

The McDowell Sonoran Preserve in Scottsdale, Arizona, offers 21,400 acres of unique geography and geology, including mountain ranges, cacti forests, and diverse desert wildlife. Located near a heavily populated urban area, the preserve protects critical open space and wildlife habitat from the pressures of development. The protection of the land through the creation of the preserve responded to a number of policy debates that emerged in the late 1980s and early 1990s, including preserving open space, maintaining scenic vistas, protecting wildlife habitat, promoting outdoor recreation, and supporting tourism in the community.

> **"Given the number of different ways we use GIS in developing and managing the McDowell Sonoran Preserve, the interoperability of programs like ArcPad and ArcInfo with Spatial Analyst and 3D Analyst has been a real benefit for us. We don't have to worry about converting data. The seamless transition from one program to the next makes life much easier, and it allows us to take raw data and put it into production almost instantaneously."**
>
> Robert Chasan, Geographer/GIS Analyst, City of Scottsdale, Arizona

The move to establish the preserve began as a citizen-led grassroots effort to protect the sensitive areas of the mountains from development. A public debate had emerged on the amount of growth appropriate for the area, the desired density levels, and overall quality of development. Consequently, to acquire land for the preserve, in 1995 the voters of Scottsdale approved a dedicated 0.2 percent sales tax. Then, in 2004, an additional 0.15 percent sales tax was approved by the voters to augment further acquisition of land.

CASE STUDY > > >

The original area for the preserve, or "recommended study boundary" determined by planners, consisted of more than 16,000 acres of mountain and desert land. In 1998, the Scottsdale City Council expanded the recommended study boundary to a total area proposed for natural desert open space of over 34,000 acres, or more than fifty-three square miles. In determining the location of the study boundary for the preserve, planners placed a high degree of value on connecting the preserve with other nearby publicly owned lands, including the Tonto National Forest (federal) and the McDowell Mountain Regional Park (Maricopa County).

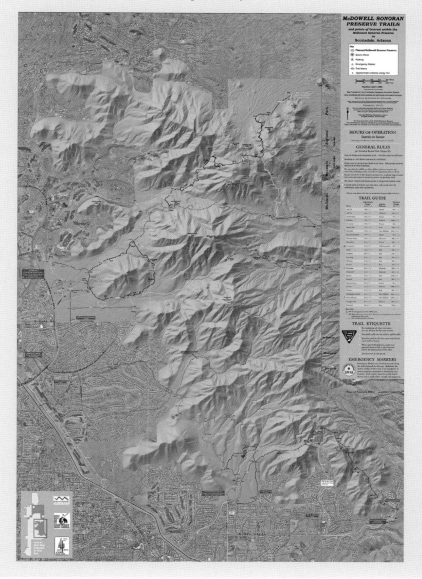

Figure 2.28 GIS technology has been used heavily in deciding where to develop new trails throughout the McDowell Sonoran Preserve. Courtesy of City of Scottsdale, Arizona.

Although GIS was not a component of the project when it began, it became readily apparent that the technology could play a very important role during the land acquisition phase in helping to determine priorities for parcel acquisition. Land desired for the preserve is evaluated based on access potential, unique geology, historical and archaeological features, wildlife habitat, scenic quality, potential for public recreation use (e.g., hiking, biking, rock climbing, horseback riding), and corridors for connecting open space areas.

Among the GIS data layers that city officials use most frequently to evaluate the desirability of possible purchases are slope analysis, topography, and natural drainage patterns. Using the software it is possible to integrate the analysis of these layers against the desirability parameters mentioned previously, such as connectivity and recreational use. The creation of maps and related products has assisted city officials in selecting parcels that offer the greatest value, perhaps not in the monetary sense, but in choosing lands valuable for conservation purposes.

The city also uses GIS software in the planning and development of multiple-use trails throughout the preserve. Maps produced with the software are used during the initial master planning process and are presented to the public for their input, as well as to various city boards and commissions, and the city council. Once a trail alignment is approved as part of the master plan, staff members begin the process of refining the alignment to a level where the trail can be constructed. This process involves extensive fieldwork, adjusting the master planned alignment to fit the terrain, ensuring that the route meets approved specifications, and taking advantage of opportunities along the trail to provide a high-quality experience for the user. Then, staff use GPS to determine the final flagged alignment and use GIS software to conduct an analysis of the route in preparation for construction bidding. Primarily, staff analyze the slope of the land that the route crosses to quantify the number of linear feet of the route located on various percentages of hill slope. This information is valuable in the bidding process because it informs contractors of the level of work that will be required for various portions of the trail. For example, it is more difficult to construct a four-foot-wide trail traversing a 20 percent hill slope than it is to construct one on a 5 percent slope. GIS software is also used to locate and quantify other cost items, such as switchbacks, drainage crossings and other areas where erosion control is needed, and construction access. Providing this information in a clear and concise manner allows potential bidders to better understand the project and establish more accurate cost estimates.

GIS technology is also used in the day-to-day management and maintenance of the preserve. The preserve, with its diverse recreational trails, is a popular destination site for area residents as well as tourists. As a result, maintaining trail signs is particularly important, so preserve staff have created a GIS database with an inventory of all the trail signs and their locations. Photographs of the signs are incorporated into the database as well, which allows staff to quickly produce replacements of signs upon reports of damage or defacement. Likewise, emergency markers have been placed throughout the preserve that are geocoded and assigned a unique alphanumeric value. The database with the emergency marker codes has been converted for use in the separate CAD systems operated by the police and fire departments. If a hiker encounters problems on the trails and calls 911, emergency personnel can quickly locate the individual by looking up the emergency marker code.

The city also uses GIS software to produce trail maps for users of the preserve. In 2011, the city produced and distributed more than 50,000 paper maps that highlighted the preserve's features

CASE STUDY >

and trails. Preserve users can also find trail maps online and download them from the preserve's website.

The preserve's work in habitat protection in partnership with the McDowell Sonoran Conservancy also makes use of GIS technology. Several research efforts are underway in the preserve, which include cataloging native plants and establishing transect corridors for conducting longitudinal research studies. Having this longitudinal data will enable researchers to monitor changes in the preserve's environment over time.

Finally, collecting data on long-term maintenance concerns—such as fence lines, signage, and control gates—within the GIS database has proven useful for budgeting purposes. Staff can maintain a database of the built assets, which can show on a preserve map where the assets are located and the history of repair and replacement costs associated with those assets in order to predict anticipated expenses for the year.

CASE STUDY •

Endnotes

1   Edward R. Tufte, *Visual Explanations: Images and Quantities, Evidence and Narrative* (Cheshire, CT: Graphics Press, 1997).

2   CBIRF is a highly specialized, self-sufficient unit that has the ability to respond to major chemical, biological, radiological, nuclear, or high-yield explosives situations worldwide, and is capable of deploying at a moment's notice, as demonstrated during Japan's Fukushima nuclear disaster in 2011.

3   Based on Mehdi Mashud Khan, Randall Vogel, and Ronald O. Edwards, "GIS-ing Flood Data: Making Valuable Information on Paper Studies Accessible." *ArcUser,* Fall 2010.

4   *Dún Laoghaire-Rathdown and Fingal County Councils: A Case Study* (Dublin and Belfast, Ireland: Esri Ireland, 2010).

5   *Food Access and Price: A Spatial Analysis of Grocery Stores and Food Prices in the City of Chattanooga and Hamilton County* (Chattanooga, TN: Ochs Center for Metropolitan Studies, December 2001).Promoting active living with the Trail and Recreational Information Portal (TRIP) in Carver County, Minnesota

Part 3. Streamlining government operations with GIS

Takeaways:

- Governments can realize significant new efficiencies and cost savings by developing GIS applications for their routine business processes.
- GIS analysis can benefit virtually every type of government program and service.
- Developing a solid data foundation for a GIS program will enable governments to take advantage of new opportunities as they emerge.
- Collaboration is critical to a successful GIS program.

Technology has long driven improvements in the productivity of workers, as well as the quality of their work, in both the private and public sectors. Consider how some of the tools in the workplace have changed over time:

Party lines → private lines → speaker phones and three-way calling → cell phones → smartphones

Manual typewriters → electric typewriters → mainframes → personal computers → laptops

Letters → faxes → e-mails → instant messaging and texting

Carbon paper → mimeographs → copy machines → scanners

Improved technology offers workers the opportunity to do their jobs better, faster, and smarter. GIS technology is no exception to this rule. The technology offers governments an important opportunity to rethink and reengineer the way they do business and deliver services to their constituents. As Bonnie Flickinger, mayor of Moreno Valley, California, points out, "GIS enables you to get access to data that you didn't know existed. It will provide eye-opening data and information that will make your decisions that much smarter."

Return on investment and the benefits of GIS

"GIS is not that costly and it can save you money by working with other entities."
Karen Miller, Commissioner, Boone County, Missouri

Introducing new technology into an organization requires an upfront investment of money and staff time. GIS technology is like any other IT program in this respect. Once in place, however, GIS technology provides significant return on investment (ROI) in the form of improved efficiency and cost savings. A few of the common areas for realizing cost savings and ROI include:

- Staff time. Labor costs are one of the most significant budget items in any organization's budget. GIS allows staff to better manage and maintain complex datasets and complete business analyses more quickly and efficiently, which gives employees more time to devote to other critical tasks.
- Asset management. Better scheduling of maintenance and repair of infrastructure and other community facilities yields cost savings and helps prevent expensive full-fledged failures.
- Routing. From street crews to police surveillance to emergency response, real-time GIS routing information helps lower fuel costs and saves staff time getting to and from sites.
- Economic development. Whether helping small businesses in the state better define their markets through demographic data or attracting new companies and industries with real estate data, GIS can help governments generate new jobs and spur economic growth.

This section highlights how governments have used GIS technology to save costs and demonstrate ROI. Leaders in King County, Washington, undertook a groundbreaking research study to demonstrate the ROI their GIS program has had for the county. Before the 2010 US Census, an address verification effort in Moreno Valley, California, revealed substantial differences between the population base identified by the US Census Bureau and the city. In Airdrie, Alberta, the city completed its annual municipal census online, increasing productivity and reducing costs.

Show me the money: What was King County's ROI from twenty years of using GIS?

Greg Babinski, GISP, Finance and Marketing Manager, King County GIS Center, Seattle, Washington, and URISA President, 2011–12

Level of government: County
State/province: Washington
Country: USA
Population: 1,931,249

King County is the fourteenth most populous county in the United States. Covering 2,000 square miles, the county is geographically diverse and includes highly dense urban areas such as Seattle and Bellevue (a growing rival suburban center across Lake Washington), forty other suburban communities, a large rural island in Puget Sound, a well-preserved agricultural green belt, and significant wilderness areas along the 7,000-foot snow-covered Cascade Mountains crest.

In the late 1980s, both King County and Seattle Metro (a regional transit and wastewater treatment agency separate from the city of Seattle) began tentatively exploring the use of GIS technology.

CASE STUDY > > > > >

In 1991, both entities began to develop GIS implementation plans. King County retained the services of PlanGraphics to develop its GIS business needs assessment, cost-benefit analysis, strategic plan, and GIS implementation plan. The firm prepared a report that included a present-value analysis that estimated that the implementation of a GIS system would break even after seven years and have a 1.49:1.00 benefit-cost ratio after ten years. The total cost of PlanGraphics' proposed GIS development was $22.5 million. The anticipated ROI was based on the development of approximately 126 specific business applications.

A return on investment study conducted by Dr. Richard O. Zerbe of the University of Washington's Evans School of Public Affairs found that compared with 2010 costs of $14.6 million to maintain, operate, and use GIS within King County, the annual benefits received from the program ranged from six to twelve times the program's annual costs.

The following year, however, the voters of King County and Seattle approved the merger of King County and Seattle Metro. In 1993, a joint county-metro committee developed a reduced GIS scope of work using a reduced funding limit of $6.8 million. The scope of work also included plans for integrating a separate $2.2 million metro GIS project. Work on the King County GIS (KCGIS) capital project began in 1993. By 1997, the project team completed the initial development work. Additional project funding brought the total capital cost for KCGIS to $10.6 million by 2001.

What KCGIS developed

A GIS has many components, including end-user hardware, data storage and application servers, high-speed networks, specialized GIS technology and database software, complex digital framework data, a highly trained core GIS staff to operate and maintain the system, a means of integrating agency spatial business data, and end-user applications. For any GIS benefit-cost analysis, major costs are associated with each of the preceding components. However, the benefits are exclusively associated with end-user applications.

The reduced budget ($10.6 million versus the original estimate of $22 million) required that some tough decisions be made. Given that the development of key datasets was crucial for building the foundation of the program, King County's reduced GIS development budget essentially required sacrificing the development of a number of end-user applications. Some shortcuts were taken in parcel data development, and funding for imagery acquisition was very limited.

In 1996, the KCGIS capital project management office was converted into a GIS operations and management office. GIS units sprang up in several county departments. By 1997, a growing number

CASE STUDY > > > >

of GIS end users could be identified; county staff members were using GIS software as a part of their business processes.

A major change to the structure and funding of the GIS program in King County occurred in 2002. A number of agency GIS operations and staff members were consolidated into the new KCGIS Center, which has responsibility for all GIS enterprise operations. The KCGIS Center is not supported directly from the general fund or from any special funds, but rather through an internal service fund (ISF).[1] It provides matrixed staff[2] and on-demand client services to county agencies and outside customers. Because the center receives funding only for services provided to clients, the awareness of the cost of GIS services in King County has always been very high. With the advent of the new center, the number and size of departmental and agency GIS units declined.

In 1997, there were about one hundred individual GIS end users in King County. By 2004, this number had grown to more than 500 county staff using GIS software or software with GIS capability. The center began providing a number of interactive web-mapping applications in 2003, and by 2007 web-mapping application use by county staff averaged more than 400 user sessions per business day.

Table 3.1 Agency GIS staff for agency budget and GIS user calculations

	GIS managers and leads	Professional GIS staff	GIS super users	GIS desktop users	GIS web application user sessions
1997	8.40	43.50	2.00	100.00	
1998	8.40	43.50	2.00	200.00	
1999	8.40	43.50	2.50	269.00	
2000	8.40	44.50	3.00	269.00	
2001	8.40	44.50	3.00	269.00	
2002	5.40	30.50	3.15	269.00	
2003	4.56	23.80	3.60	375.00	31,500
2004	4.95	23.39	2.85	534.00	63,848
2005	4.95	24.41	3.40	486.00	79,621
2006	4.95	24.05	3.20	466.00	89,636
2007	5.00	19.95	3.60	466.00	99,575
2008	5.00	22.45	3.30	466.00	106,310
2009	5.00	22.30	3.10	442.00	106,626
2010	5.00	20.15	4.00	432.60	94,409
2011	5.50	16.75	3.35	395.42	94,000

Note: While the number of GIS professionals has gone down over time, the number of GIS users throughout the county has generally increased, although the Great Recession of 2008 resulted in some decreases. Courtesy of King County (Washington) GIS Center.

CASE STUDY > > >

GIS consolidation in 2002 included a new GIS Technical Committee, responsible for providing technical and operational input to the KCGIS Center. As it started its work, the GIS Technical Committee identified a number of key issues to be addressed. One of these, commonly referred to as Issue 4, posed a question: What did KCGIS accomplish in relationship to the original 1992 GIS strategic plan and the later reduced-scope plan of 1993? The Issue 4 Report, completed in 2003, determined that the result of reduced funding was a deficiency in some of the KCGIS components. In particular, some key datasets, such as high-accuracy digital orthophotography, certain planimetric feature data, high-accuracy elevation data, and certain water and sewer data, had not been acquired. Also, the positional accuracy of the parcel data acquired did not meet the specifications of the original PlanGraphics report.

Nevertheless, KCGIS did go operational, and the King County Council considered the project to have been a success. The most telling finding of the Issue 4 Report concerned end-user applications. Of the 126 originally planned applications, only about 15 percent had been completed.

During the past ten years, most of the data deficiencies identified in the Issue 4 Report have been corrected through operational programs. Desktop GIS software and an extensive suite of web-mapping applications has put GIS tools into the hands of end users, which likely meets the business needs for some portion of the 126 applications that were not developed.

The benefits of KCGIS

The Issue 4 Report (and subsequent KCGIS annual plans) documents what was accomplished. But two unasked questions in 2003 were, "What did King County achieve from its investment in GIS?" and "Did King County get the expected return on its investment?" Although a small number of studies have attempted to quantify actual ROI achieved by a city or county GIS, these typically have been conducted by in-house staff or GIS consultants and have been limited in scope.

In 2009, New Zealand's national government published a report titled "Spatial Information in the New Zealand Economy: Realising Productivity Gains" (`http://www.geospatial.govt.nz/ productivityreport`), authored by ACIL Tasman (`http://www.aciltasman.com.au/`), an international economic consulting firm. The report demonstrated the benefit of having professional economists, rather than GIS proponents, conduct such a study. "Spatial Information in the New Zealand Economy" looked at the economic benefits of geospatial development in every segment of the New Zealand economy, not only within government agencies, but also for commerce, industry, agriculture, forestry, transport, fisheries, mining, and other fields. The study found that in 2008 geospatial technology added $1.2 billion in productivity-related benefits to the economy, or 0.6 percent of GDP. The report further determined that if impediments to the full use of geospatial technology were removed, the benefit to the economy of New Zealand would be significantly higher.

During the 2009 Urban and Regional Information Systems Association (URISA) Annual Conference in Anaheim, California, the "Spatial Information in the New Zealand Economy" report was discussed by a small number of individuals interested in the topic (`http://www.urisa.org`). This discussion led to an agreement between the KCGIS Center and the State of Oregon to jointly fund a narrow study by a professional financial or economic consultant of the benefit of twenty years of GIS development and use within King County. A request for proposals was issued, and a team headed by Dr. Richard O. Zerbe of the University of Washington's Evans School of Public Affairs was chosen. Dr. Zerbe's credentials include heading the University of Washington's Benefit-Cost Analysis Center, founding the Society for Benefit-Cost Analysis, and authoring more than 100 publications on this and related topics.

How does one determine the costs and benefits of GIS for a large county agency going back twenty years? For costs, the KCGIS has very good financial records for the original GIS capital project; for the GIS Project Management Office and its successor, the KCGIS Center; and for agency GIS staff and operations going back to 1991. Costs also needed to include the time and effort of the end users who put the GIS tools and applications to work. These were estimated based on the number of known GIS software end users going back to 1997 and the number of web-mapping application user sessions going back to 2003. The cumulative total of these costs from 1991 through 2011 is more than $215 million, including a total of $14.6 million in 2010.

The Zerbe methodology to determine benefits used was a "with versus without" research design. The basis of the research was to determine what would have happened if KCGIS applications had not been implemented, and how the county is better off having them. The Zerbe team's scope included an extensive literature review on both GIS in general and on the development and operation of KCGIS in particular. For the Zerbe research team, this review identified the types of expected productivity gains to look for.

The team developed an extensive questionnaire to assess the extent to which benefits were realized across different county business units as opposed to what users in the units would have done without GIS applications or tools to achieve the same results. A broadly distributed but more narrowly focused follow-up survey went to a much larger group of individual GIS users to refine the questionnaire results and improve the quality of data.

The team completed thirty highly structured face-to-face interviews, some lasting more than three hours. Based on analysis of the interview results, the team sent an online survey to approximately 500 targeted county employees who are known to use GIS; 175 survey responses were received from this group, representing a 35 percent response rate. The interview and survey data analysis resulted in a monetization of the benefits of using GIS by county business staff.

The final KCGIS ROI Report, published March 12, 2012, found that:

The use of GIS by the County has been hugely beneficial. An analysis of the survey responses indicate that overall the use of GIS—compared to not having the GIS technology—had a net benefit of approximately $180 million for the year 2010 alone. This estimate assumes that the quality and usefulness of GIS reports remains at the same level as pre-GIS. In reality, we expect that the value of GIS-produced outputs is almost certainly higher than comparable outputs . . . prior to the implementation of GIS Technology. Nevertheless, on the assumption that the marginal value of output has decreased (a linear downward sloping demand curve) we find a lower bound estimate of net benefits of $87 million per year in 2010.

Compared with 2010 costs of $14.6 million to maintain, operate, and use GIS within King County, the annual benefits received range from six to twelve times the annual costs.

CASE STUDY >

Results by department based on the more conservative downward sloping demand curve show that the largest benefits are concentrated in two county departments: Natural Resources ($54 million) and Transportation ($19 million). One department (Assessments) showed a small productivity benefit, but a negative benefit for efficiency.

An interesting observation from the compilation of costs for this study is the decline in the total number of GIS professional staff at the same time that the number of GIS users has been rising. In 1999, there were an equivalent 51.90 full-time employees (FTE) in departments and 22.25 FTE in the predecessor to the KCGIS Center. In 2002, after GIS consolidation, these numbers were 35.90 and 32.00 FTE, respectively. In 2011 the numbers had declined to 22.25 and 28.00 FTE, an overall reduction of 26 percent. This, in itself, represents significant efficiency gains as training, best practices, and improved coordination support growing GIS use by county end users.

A key question for King County is where the untapped potential remains for GIS use. Although GIS use has spread to forty-two departments, divisions, and offices within King County, there are still areas where it remains underutilized. The sense within KCGIS management is that GIS utilization is far less than 50 percent of the future potential. An $87 million benefit from using GIS represents 2 percent of King County's annual budget. The potential to double this benefit through full utilization of GIS is a significant opportunity for the county to continue to provide the services citizens and businesses need while controlling costs.

> **An $87 million benefit from using GIS represents 2 percent of King County's annual budget. The potential to double this benefit through full utilization of GIS is a significant opportunity for the county to continue to provide the services citizens and businesses need while controlling costs.**

Next steps

The final KCGIS ROI Report was released in March 2012. The Zerbe team has already started work on another GIS ROI study, this time for Multnomah County, Oregon. URISA, a professional membership association for GIS professionals, has initiated discussion with Dr. Zerbe to cooperate in applying the ROI methodology to other jurisdictions. How do King County's results compare to other similar-sized counties? What are the ranges of ROI results for medium- and large-sized cities? What is the ROI from use of public GIS data by citizens and businesses?

At one point KCGIS Center management asked itself: What if the findings showed that there was no ROI? Interest in this study is international and within the United States ranges from states to counties and cities. Although the results were positive, the KCGIS Center is interested in other similar studies to determine just how good—or bad—King County results will compare to other jurisdictions. All jurisdictions should be interested in determining their ROI and examining variations among peer agencies. This will then allow the GIS professional community to determine the characteristics of the agencies with the highest ROI so that individual GIS managers can adopt the recognized best practices, standards, and tools to improve their own agency's results.

CASE STUDY •

Considering the benefits of GIS and ROI: Moreno Valley's participation in the 2010 Local Update of Census Addresses (LUCA) program

Michael K. Heslin, GIS Administrator; and Bonnie Flickinger, Mayor, City of Moreno Valley

Level of government: City
State/province: California
Country: USA
Population: 193,365

In a tight economy, any decision to invest in new technology must receive careful consideration by elected officials. Government investments have to demonstrate improved efficiencies, cost savings, and, in many cases, an actual ROI.

Moreno Valley, situated 70 miles east of Los Angeles, has been labeled one of California's fastest-growing cities. With a population of more than 186,000 residents, it is the second most populous community in Riverside County. Its fast growth can be attributed to a wide range of housing options, including high-end executive homes, affordable single-family homes, and condominiums; a family-friendly lifestyle; good schools; and impressive quality-of-life amenities.

Like many other cities across the United States, Moreno Valley first acquired GIS technology to help manage its tremendous growth. The city began its GIS journey with desktop mapping software that was used by various departments. For the most part, the software was used for mapping and visualization of data, with its users working independently of the city as a whole.

The city eventually realized it needed a more strategic plan to deploy its GIS and in 2001 turned to its newly hired GIS administrator for help. The city's GIS group conducted interviews with various city divisions and performed an extensive GIS needs assessment. The GIS group also investigated how other local government agencies managed information. In the process, the group studied other enterprise implementations and instantly recognized the many benefits that were possible.

What resulted was a clear understanding that an enterprise GIS implementation was needed to streamline Moreno Valley's GIS processes and leverage the true analytic capabilities a GIS can provide. In addition, the city recognized the need for leveraging data managed independently within separate departments. An enterprise approach would allow various departments to use data managed outside their own department. Plus, the city wanted more powerful functionality.

The city opted to deploy an enterprise GIS for all city departments, including planning, public works, fire, law enforcement, parks and recreation, and economic development, and the public. As a result of this reorganization, the city can do more with fewer resources and do it in less time.

CASE STUDY > > >

The 2010 Census and the LUCA program

Based on California Department of Finance reporting, city officials knew that Moreno Valley's population had increased by approximately 30 percent since the 2000 US Census, from 144,600 in January 2000 to 188,500 in January 2010. With the 2010 Census looming, the city faced a significant challenge to verify its population increase in order to secure federal funding resources. City leaders determined participation in the US Census Bureau's Local Update Census Addresses (LUCA) program was imperative.

The Census Address List Improvement Act of 1994 (Public Law 103-430) authorizes the Census Bureau to provide the census address list for review and comment by tribal, state, and local government liaisons who agree to conditions of confidentiality. The LUCA program is an integral part of the census. The program uses the expertise of state and local governments to improve the accuracy and completeness of the address list used for administering the census. State and local governments can opt to contribute to a complete enumeration of their populations by reviewing and commenting on the list of housing unit and group quarters addresses that the US Census Bureau uses to deliver census questionnaires.

Option 1, the highest level of participation, allows government entities to review the entire census address list for their jurisdictional boundaries. The City of Moreno Valley received a $50,000 state grant for participating in the LUCA program at the option 1 level.

Using GIS for Moreno Valley's LUCA program

Using addresses currently on file, the city had a four-month window to analyze, compile, and submit findings on their accuracy and completeness. The GIS team developed a multistep process that used GIS to get the job done:

- First, the GIS team brought the census table into the city's system, so the existing census address locations could be spatially located on a map of the city. To achieve this, the census records were geocoded against a parcel database provided by Riverside County.
- Once the Census Bureau addresses were plotted on the map, the county data was also geocoded. This step helped determine where duplications or invalid addresses existed.
- The remaining parcels in the county database were categorized as either "residential" or "other." Overlaying the map with a city zoning data layer helped determine which addresses fell within residential areas or within areas that could have a residential component, such as commercial/residential. The records were flagged and copied into a master table.
- Multifamily complexes required field verification to determine the number of units and to attain the address for each building and individual apartment, townhouse, or condominium unit. This information was compiled into a separate database, and then added to the master table to be returned to the Census Bureau.
- The final step included a count of all the addresses within each census block. A summary was performed to determine the number of addresses in each block. Areas that had a different count than what the Census Bureau provided in its original data table had to be compiled into a new table and sent back for the Census Bureau's review by April 2008.

CASE STUDY > >

The Census Bureau reviewed and computer-matched each local address list file submitted by the city. The Census Bureau also sent staff into the field to conduct address canvassing to determine the validity of the city's submitted addresses.

The Moreno Valley LUCA study revealed an additional 10,382 housing units that needed to be added to the Census Bureau's master address list and 579 address corrections. The study ensured that the city received credit for 34,261 additional residents who otherwise would not have been counted in the 2010 Census. These additional residents will result in additional funding for projects such as building and improving schools, roads, hospitals, libraries, and senior centers. Additionally, significant amounts of state-generated funds are distributed on the basis of population data. Census data drives redistricting decisions and directly affects the distribution of more than $300 billion in federal funds each year.

Figure 3.1 Census Bureau staff are sent into the field to conduct address canvassing.
Courtesy of EdBockStock/Shutterstock.com.

Additional developments

During September 2009, the city submitted additional information regarding new housing construction that started after March 2009 and was on target to be completed by April 2010, the mailing date for the 2010 census.

In October 2009, the city received the findings from the Census Bureau's review of its submission and had thirty days to respond for the appeals process. After extensive research of the tables, it was discovered that a number of addresses were removed during the canvassing process. The deleted records were geocoded against the city parcel layer so that patterns of neighborhoods could be located where the deletions occurred. An analysis was conducted and, from the results, a true table of deleted addresses was created during the canvassing process.

A second data geocoding was performed; the inconsistencies in the results raised concerns and required field verification. City findings revealed areas where half of a cul-de-sac had been dropped out of the database or a section of homes in a tract was not counted. Two employees from the GIS team spent three days in the field confirming the validity of the addresses. Although a small percentage of addresses were found to be nonexistent or uninhabitable, there were a number of addresses that could be verified and documented.

The documentary evidence that the city submitted for each address included an exhibit map containing three-inch aerial orthophotography taken in June 2008 by Sanborn and 2009–10 property tax records obtained from the Property Information Center on the Riverside County Assessor/Clerk/Recorder public website. In the case where homes had been built since June 2008 and aerial imagery

CASE STUDY >

was not available, building permit information from the city's Building and Safety Division was acquired and included. GIS staff then submitted this evidence as part of the appeals process in November 2009. The city subsequently received formal notice that all the addresses submitted were accepted and included in the US Census master address list.

The ROI of GIS

The City of Moreno Valley has identified and used GIS technology to improve its business processes, infrastructure, services, information, and decision making. In the time that has passed between the 2000 and 2010 censuses, GIS has risen to become the city's flagship system. Today, city leaders and employees recognize the value and importance of the enterprise GIS, thereby taking the necessary actions to ensure that the system's needs are met and supported by management. Without the investment in GIS technology, the city would not have had access to the analytic power needed to document in the 2010 Census the scores of new residents who made the community their home.

"I would recommend to every jurisdiction . . . establish a GIS program. It will provide eye-opening data and information that will make your decisions that much smarter. Another important concept I want to put out there is that GIS enables you to get access to data that you didn't know existed."
Bonnie Flickinger, Mayor,
City of Moreno Valley

CASE STUDY •

City of Airdrie implements a secure, real-time, and virtually paperless online census

Esri Canada

Level of government: City
State/province: Alberta
Country: Canada
Population: 28,927

The City of Airdrie, Alberta, left behind its manual, paper-based method of collecting census data to embrace an online system that has increased productivity by 50 percent and reduced annual costs by almost 80 percent. This environmentally sound, completely secure, and almost entirely paperless

CASE STUDY > >

system serves as a model for neighboring municipalities looking to streamline and drastically improve the census data collection process.

Challenge

The city clerks, who are in charge of the annual census process, were frustrated with their legacy, paper-based process of collecting data. It involved manually creating census ballots, tracking completed addresses, and then processing both statistics and static, paper-based maps that were marked up with colored pencils.

This operation was time consuming and costly and was not conducive to maintaining data integrity. In response, the city clerks turned to the city's IT Department to request a web-based process that would improve the collection of demographic data across the City of Airdrie. This led to the creation of a virtually paperless online census.

Several key challenges arose in developing the paperless census. For example, in 2008 the ability to view a GIS web map containing live status information was introduced; however, the bandwidth available on each tablet fell short of fully supporting this functionality. Furthermore, the new process created a security challenge, because there was no way to authenticate the enumerators. But the team quickly found solutions to these challenges, and the online census was born.

Figure 3.2 The community mapping interface shows residences that have completed the census, residences that enumerators must process, and residences that enumerators must still visit. Courtesy of Esri Canada.

Solution

Development occurred through four stages, and the census has since evolved to a 99 percent electronic process. Enumerators use a ruggedized tablet PC supported by a wireless network card and a stylus pen to collect information. To overcome security concerns, a personal identification number (PIN) system

CASE STUDY >

was implemented that processes municipal addresses and creates eight-character identification numbers. PIN numbers are hand delivered to residents who are then given three weeks to fill out the online census, after which time enumerators go door to door to the outstanding addresses.

The tablet's wireless card equips each enumerator with GIS mapping capabilities. With ArcView and basemap data installed on each tablet, the bandwidth issue was resolved, and enumerators now have access to live maps that are fed to the tablets through the corporate network. To further enhance security, the network can only be accessed through fingerprint authentication.

A logic-based question-and-answer system was developed in 2008 to allow a variety of information to be collected about each person in a household rather than only capturing the number of people per household. This information is now fed into a database that allows customized reports to be generated, replacing legacy Microsoft Excel spreadsheet reporting.

> **"Moving to the online census system has greatly enhanced efficiency for enumerators, particularly with the addition of mapping components. Not having to double- and triple-check the scan sheet prior to delivering information to city clerks cuts their time in half."**
> Corey Halford, IT Data Services Team Leader, City of Airdrie, Alberta

Benefits

By 2008, 55 percent of residents participating in the census were using the online system, reducing the amount of field enumeration by over 50 percent. The web-based system allows Airdrie to conduct a census for only Can$1.42 per address compared to the national average of $5.00 to $7.00 per address. This creates an overall annual census budget of approximately $20,000 compared to similar-sized municipalities that operate on a budget in excess of $100,000.

The new system also provides guidance in regard to the growth of the community and enables city clerks to make changes to address information based on what is collected in the field, so that data is always current. The collected data is more secure than ever before since fewer people are involved in handling the information. Workflows are streamlined, and the overall amount of effort put into the preparation, collection, and reporting of census information has now been cut in half.

The city's success and innovation now serves as a model for neighboring municipalities. Airdrie was also awarded the URISA 2009 Exemplary Systems in Government (ESIG) award.

CASE STUDY •

Getting the job done

GIS technology enables the development of powerful new tools for completing work tasks. A review of current business processes and how things are accomplished in government will often highlight the potential for new efficiencies. The analytic capabilities of GIS make it possible to reconfigure and automate many of those business processes so that tasks can be completed more quickly and efficiently. Whether it's providing an integrating mechanism for managing a project as it moves through the various development processes in Mono County, California; improving emergency response times by developing a routing system for emergency vehicles in Lexington County, South Carolina; or developing and updating a ten-year capital plan in Niagara, Ontario, GIS enables governments to get the job done.

Improving efficiency and flexibility in the development process in Mono County, California

Nate Greenberg, GIS Coordinator, Mono County and Town of Mammoth Lakes, California; and Susan Kirk, BasicGov

Level of Government: County and town
State/province: California
Country: USA
Population: 14,202 (county) and 8,234 (town)

Mono County, California, has a wealth of natural beauty and environmental resources. Located near the eastern entrance to Yosemite National Park, the county draws hundreds of thousands of tourists each year, as does the county's largest incorporated community, the town of Mammoth Lakes, which is home to the Mammoth Mountain Ski Area. Although largely rural in character, the county and the town are subject to tremendous development pressures as a result of the local tourism industry. These pressures are further complicated by the fact that roughly 90 percent of land in the area is owned and protected by the federal government, leaving only about 7 percent in the hands of the private sector and available for development.

The volume of permit applications, code enforcement inspections, and other development activities are substantial, especially for rural jurisdictions with a small staff. The county and the town work closely together and share many resources, but even combined staffing levels are modest (see the accompanying table). The jurisdictions also have a strong commitment to smart growth and sustainable development that govern decisions regarding community planning and land use, but these commitments require compiling additional information to support decisions.

Table 3.2 Staffing levels for Mono County and the town of Mammoth Lakes*

Jurisdiction	Building	Planning	Finance	Code
Mono County	4	6	2	1
Mammoth Lakes	3	9		1

* Staffing levels reflect employees using BasicGov software.

CASE STUDY > > >

Additionally, the State of California has been hit especially hard by the economic downturn. As a result, jurisdictions across the state are looking at staffing levels and efficiency as they relate to development fees to determine where the tipping point is. Elected officials have had to consider how best to provide services and answer some difficult questions in the process. If a procedure takes an inordinate amount of time to complete, more than the actual monetary value of the associated fee, does the process need to be changed, or does the fee structure need to be reviewed? Both elected officials and staff are discussing performance measurements and looking at the timeline of projects going into and out of the system. "Are we meeting our commitment to a thirty-day turnaround? Or are we actually overworking projects? We've also discussed adding functionalities that would allow elected officials and perhaps the public to go into the system and generate reports or view a dashboard with simple charts and graphs," explains Nate Greenberg, GIS coordinator for the county and the town.

Greenberg goes on to say, "There is an extreme amount of pressure on all aspects of government to perform at a certain level. As we're squeezed tighter and tighter, both in terms of budget and staff, it can be challenging to meet those deadlines. So this goes both ways. Local governments need to uphold their end of the bargain with the public in terms of meeting deadlines, but if staff cannot meet those deadlines, we need to be able to track and analyze why delays may be occurring."

Around 2001, the county's Planning Division implemented a new work order management system for tracking progress on projects, but it wasn't integrated with any of the other county systems or workflows in the different divisions it was supposed to support. As a result, after four to five years, things began to fall apart under the weight of heavy workloads. Data was being duplicated, questions arose about data accuracy, and debates escalated about which sources were the most authoritative. The story was similar at the Town of Mammoth Lakes during this time, as staff had been working with an antiquated permitting system that was no longer supported and starting to break down.

Mono County has been building its GIS capacity for over a decade, while the Town of Mammoth Lakes has had a program for several years. The origins of the county's GIS program started in the Planning and Assessor divisions, where staff wanted the ability to do project-level mapping for planning purposes. In 2005, the county expanded its GIS program into an enterprise system and began to deploy a few web-based applications for queries on parcel data, ownership, and similar information. GIS users and stakeholders had a simple but robust environment to do what they needed and were able to move away from the high paper volume that is often characteristic of the development process.

In 2008, the town started to look for a unified strategy that covered not only construction permits, but also plan applications and building inspections that are associated with any project development and review process. The ability to have all the information needed for the development process in one location, together with the ability to easily track and monitor progress on projects at each stage of the development process, would help county and town staff determine where that balance is and improve service delivery.

After determining what features it needed in a solution, the town selected BasicGov, a suite of web-based applications designed for managing development projects. The town implemented four modules—permits, inspections, planning, and code enforcement—that marked the first time the respective departments were working in a unified platform. Staff members were able to exchange information back and forth more efficiently, as well as answer public inquiries about projects that

CASE STUDY > >

multiple people were working on. The issue of authoritative information was also resolved, because the system is updated each night with data from GIS and the tax databases.

Figure 3.3 The search functionality within the system provides users with the ability to locate and associate any information stored within the system on the map through a simple interface.
Courtesy of Mono County (California) GIS.

GIS now serves as the conduit for integrating six or more data and record management systems operated by different departments across both organizations.

Following in the town's success, the county also made the move to BasicGov in late 2008 and has realized many of the same benefits of the system. In many ways, the project spurred significant technology integration into the agency's business-support processes, because other departments that are only superficially associated with development and project review have jumped on board to use the system for business licensing and other related functions.

Through this process, the two agencies have further realized the benefit of collaboration and shared information, and as a result have refined their GIS strategy to make it more of their core information system. GIS now serves as the conduit for integrating six or more data and record management systems operated by different departments across both organizations. This internal system provides access to the joint GIS technology for front-counter personnel as well as departmental managers. Elected officials will also eventually have the ability to log on to see how quickly people are getting permits. It's all GIS-based data whether people are looking at a map or not. This makes sense, because almost all the work done by the jurisdictions is parcel based, and as long as other data elements contain an assessor parcel number (APN) or address, they can be

CASE STUDY >

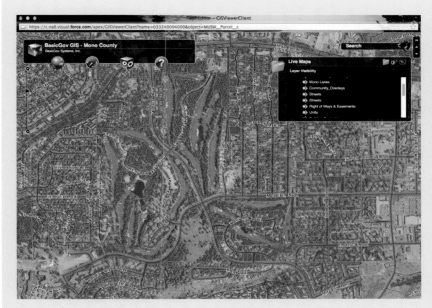

Figure 3.4 The BasicGov GIS Viewer inherits the county's GIS basemap and data, allowing users to interact with the data they use on a daily basis directly within the system.
Courtesy of Mono County (California) GIS.

connected—for example, ownership, valuation, and development constraints. The ultimate vision is for a public portal for the jurisdictions that allows citizens to go online and initiate simple permits, review projects, or discuss planning and building questions with county or town staff.

CASE STUDY •

Emergency management service (EMS) investment returns big for Lexington County, South Carolina

Brian Hood, Lexington County EMS Coordinator; Jack Maguire, Lexington County Planning and GIS Manager; and Tony Bradshaw, Bradshaw Consulting Services

Level of government: County
State/province: South Carolina
Country: USA
Population: 262,391

Lexington County is one of the fastest-growing counties in South Carolina, situated just outside the state's capital. The regional economy is thriving, attracting steady growth with its high-tech industries,

CASE STUDY > >

agriculture, and popular retail centers. Nearly a quarter million people make their homes within Lexington's 750 square miles.

Such population growth has increased demand for emergency services. Since 2006, the county has experienced a 6–7.5 percent annual increase in call volume for emergency services, which now runs about 30,000 calls per year. Normally with such a growth in demand, the county would need to add at least one new vehicle per year—a cost exceeding $3 million for an ambulance, crew, station, and other equipment—just to maintain previous performance. Before deciding to make such a substantial investment, Brian Hood, EMS coordinator for the county, opted to talk with Jack Maguire, Lexington County's planning and GIS manager, about what other options existed for maintaining a quality service.

Hood remembers the situation well. "Our vehicles were AVL [automatic vehicle location] equipped, and our response speed was respectable," he recalls. "But sometimes, the vehicle location wasn't as reliable as we wanted. It would lose track of a unit in the field for a short time, or they'd turn out to be in a different place than the system indicated."

The unreliable AVL system, in turn, caused a number of concerns among the EMS staff. "We have a very good crew of dispatch professionals, some with many years of experience and a real investment in the department's success," says Hood. "They couldn't trust the AVL, and they told us so. It hadn't caused a disaster yet, just the occasional short delay, but they wanted the tools they needed to do the best job possible. And we were all concerned that as our call rate continued to climb we'd just have more and more trouble."

Working with Maguire and his team, Hood and the EMS Department were able to leverage and improve the quality of existing GIS street data for locating addresses and improving route recommendations for emergency vehicles. These improvements included descriptive attributes for road segments, such as realistic speed limits; verifying overpasses and underpasses, as well as specifying travel directions of ramps; and validating emergency service number (ESN) areas. There were also procedural improvements for handling GIS data that included automatic validation of topological relationships and simplifying data updates coming from fifteen different municipal jurisdictions.

As part of the effort, the county invested in analytical software called the Mobile Area Vehicle Location Information System (MARVLIS), which is used to predict future demand and respond efficiently based on current resource availability and position. (MARVLIS was developed by Tony Bradshaw with the Bradshaw Consulting Service.) The new software offers CAD with highly intelligent routing, live graphical displays of current and required resources, and on-demand innovative analysis. When an emergency occurs, dispatchers can quickly locate the incident and track the location of response units on a GIS map. Vehicle location, status, speed, and direction are relayed to the CAD system every three to ninety seconds, depending on vehicle status.

Dispatchers can easily visualize current resources by status to make any adjustments to ensure their ability to meet the forecast demand and achieve or exceed compliance with response targets. First responders instantly receive incident information from the CAD system directly to their mobile computers, including the incident location displayed on an interactive map. Continuous data updates are also available while the vehicle is en route to the incident.

CASE STUDY >

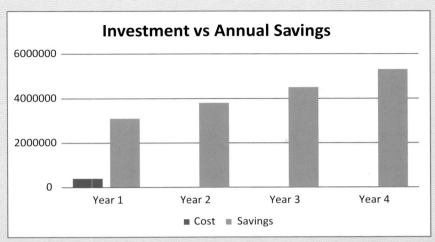

Figure 3.5 This chart demonstrates the savings Lexington County estimated it has saved as a result of implementing the MARVLIS system. Courtesy of Lexington County, South Carolina.

> ## "This is exactly what technology should do, provide better service at a reduced cost, and further leveraging existing county investments is a bonus. But the key is in developing appropriate partnerships."
> Brian Hood, EMS Coordinator, Lexington County

The new technology has helped improve service efficiency, which has resulted in improved response times even without any additional staff or vehicles. The only upfront investment that was required included the new software along with some communications hardware upgrades of roughly $400,000 in 2006. From 2006 to 2010, however, the county has saved millions of dollars while providing improved service. With the compounding effect of recurring costs for adding staff, the county estimates a cost savings of nearly $16 million resulting from the initial investment, an ROI of 3,900 percent. "This is exactly what technology should do, provide better service at a reduced cost," says Hood. "And further leveraging existing county investments is a bonus. But the key is in developing appropriate partnerships." The proof of success is in the results. When Hood took a skeptical county councilman in his vehicle to follow calls based on recommendations from the new system, it was clear he was convinced that the system was working as promised.

CASE STUDY •

Visualizing a ten-year capital plan in Niagara: Time savings, improved communication, and increased collaboration

Esri Canada

Level of government: City
State/province: Ontario
Country: Canada
Population: 427,421

For local governments to manage assets effectively and plan for sustainability, it is essential to develop a comprehensive multiyear capital plan. This plan should play an integral role in the budgeting process and be updated yearly. With a sound, multiyear plan in place, municipalities can promote sound infrastructure management, determine where investment is needed, reduce future operating costs, and prevent unforeseen infrastructure failures in the future.

The Niagara has developed a comprehensive 10-Year Capital Forecast that plays a central role in its budgeting process. The Capital Forecast identifies and prioritizes expected needs based on the region's growth management strategy, establishes project costs, estimates amounts of funding from various sources, and projects future annual costs. The Regional Public Works Department then regularly presents this complex information to regional councilors and budget stakeholders. To communicate

Figure 3.6 Niagara Connections combines interactive mapping and tabular information with visualization tools for dynamic presentations.

Courtesy of Esri Canada.

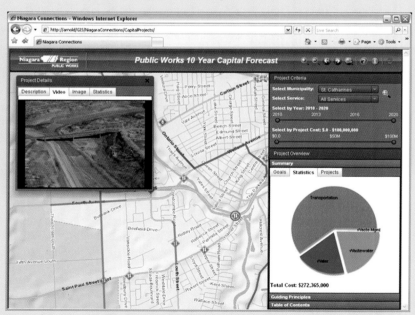

CASE STUDY > >

more effectively, the Regional Public Works Department approached GIS Services within the IT Department to develop a presentation-ready tool that would make it possible to clearly visualize the 10-Year Capital Forecast and associated financials.

In response, the team developed Niagara Connections, an interactive, custom application that brings together dynamically connected GIS maps, charts, graphs, photos, and video for the region's capital projects (figure 3.6). It serves as a key information tool for Niagara's capital planning and ensures that decisions are aligned with regional policy. The tool was built using the Adobe Flex application programming interface (API) and ArcGIS for Server technology, and merges Niagara's basemaps with aerial photos, road networks, parcel information, and infrastructure data. Assets are linked to videos and images that can be viewed through a web-based interface to assess their status. It can also be used to demonstrate how capital assets, including roads and bridges, may deteriorate over time.

A number of drop-down filters facilitate targeted access to information during budget review meetings and allow end users to specify search criteria for projects and associated content. This allows project managers, regional councilors, and financial personnel to get a visual snapshot of the capital assets under discussion, rather than rely on tabular data. By selecting a project on a map, a detail window opens that includes the description, costs, and associated pictures or video. For example, if a question arises regarding the status of capital spending in the city of St. Catharines, the user can select the city from an interactive list and drill down to view information such as the dollar amount spent in the area during a particular period of time and its relationship with other planned infrastructure.

As a useful tool for collaborative discussions, Niagara Connections has supplemented the traditional method of preparing for budget meetings, which is the creation of slide presentations to communicate the current status of capital projects across the region.

"We used to spend a considerable amount of time pulling information together from multiple tools for presentation at budget meetings," describes Tom Jamieson, manager of GIS Services for the Niagara Region. "Niagara Connections brings together different visualization methods, including charts, graphs, images, video, and dynamic tables, so that all information can be accessed from a single source."

The tool has also made it easier to adhere to the guiding principles that govern the region's 10-Year Capital Forecast and is used to communicate the rationale behind projects. The tool can be used to answer questions such as: Does it contribute to the asset's maintenance? Is the project intended to mitigate risk? Is it supporting growth? Will it help to ensure regulatory compliance? Is it an enhancement to an existing system?

> **"We now have a valuable visualization tool to assist staff in organizing and presenting details of the proposed ten-year capital program. This application will assist us in forecasting how, where, and when capital infrastructure funding will be implemented, to better serve Niagara residents."**
> Bob Steele, Associate Director, Niagara region

CASE STUDY >

Charts and graphs communicate this information by revealing the weighting that is assigned to the guiding principles for specific projects. For example, a bar graph can show that 40 percent of a project's intended goal is to support growth, whereas 60 percent is to promote sustainability. Pieces of data can then be selected, exported to a comma separated values (CSV) file, and printed. By effectively sharing this information with key stakeholders, the region's Public Works Department can gain faster approvals and buy-in for proposed projects or for repairing existing infrastructure.

"We now have a valuable visualization tool to assist staff in organizing and presenting details of the proposed 10-Year Capital Forecast to regional councilors and other key stakeholders," says Bob Steele, associate director of the Public Works Department. "This application will assist us in forecasting how, where, and when capital infrastructure funding will be implemented to better serve Niagara residents."

Functionality within Niagara Connections will subsequently be applied to other regional departments, and development is planned for an application that will support the region's community services. Niagara's IT Department is also looking to develop a public-use tool that will keep residents informed of the status of capital projects in their neighborhoods.

CASE STUDY •

Applying GIS to business problems

Challenges inevitably arise in the operations and management of government. GIS can be used to understand the nature of a business problem by providing a clear representation of a problem in a spatial context—for example, identifying where flood zones are located in relationship to a new housing development proposed for the community. It can also be used to address problems such as market analysis or site selection by allowing the user to set different parameters in order to select a best fit. In New York City, a site selection and marketing tool helps identify appropriate brownfield sites for redevelopment projects. The need to quickly identify and assist vulnerable individuals before and after an emergency event led to the development of a special GIS database in Broward County, Florida.

The need for SPEED: New York City's real estate and environmental GIS search engine promotes brownfield redevelopment

Daniel Walsh, PhD; Lee Ilan; and Shaminder Chawla, Mayor's Office of Environmental Remediation, City of New York, New York

Level of government: City
State/province: New York
Country: USA
Population: 8,175,133

CASE STUDY > > >

All cities have brownfields—properties with environmental contamination that remain vacant for decades because developers fear the risks, added costs, and uncertainty of environmental cleanup. These properties tend to cluster in low-income neighborhoods and represent lost opportunities for new jobs, housing, and other amenities; depress economic vitality and contribute to community blight; and increase municipal public health response obligations caused by contaminated land.

In order to address the brownfield problem, it is important for a municipality to first identify the location of its brownfield properties. The US Government Accountability Office estimates that as many as 425,000 brownfields exist throughout the United States. However, on a local scale, few municipalities have mapped brownfield sites or performed and reported rudimentary environmental analysis. As a result, effective marketing of these properties for cleanup and redevelopment is significantly impaired, and the debilitating brownfield cycle continues.

Identification and basic evaluation of brownfields can open the door to development by focusing developers' attention on available properties and enabling them to gauge their risks, such as determining the cost and length of time for cleanup. It can help municipalities focus their resources to provide financial and other incentives on brownfield properties with the greatest potential for redevelopment.

To promote redevelopment of brownfields in New York City, the Mayor's Office of Environmental Remediation (OER) sought to create an Internet-based GIS application that would perform as a real estate search engine and environmental research tool to allow developers and community planners to find vacant properties and assess the potential degree of contamination. Established in 2008, OER had established a variety of programs to promote cleanup and redevelopment of brownfields, including the nation's first brownfield cleanup program run by a municipality. However, the public-facing GIS search engine was needed to focus developers' attention on brownfields.

The GIS application, called SPEED (Searchable Property Environmental Electronic Database), was completed and launched in October 2010. SPEED enables the search of every real estate lot in New York City and provides basic information on each property, such as building size and area, construction date, and ownership. A variety of useful data layers have been added to overlay onto property searches, such as political districts and the location of schools, hospitals, truck routes, and public transportation hubs.

SPEED has been populated with a broad range of environmental data that is keyed to individual properties, including data from all federal, state, and city environmental programs. This data can be searched, and maps can be exported from the application. Other valuable layers have also been incorporated, including historical maps dating back to 1800 and aerial photos dating back to 1924. Users have the option of overlaying these maps and aerial photos as a background during property searches, or they can use the standard map showing tax lot, road, and shoreline outlines.

SPEED also provides detailed information on more than 3,150 vacant commercial and industrial properties in New York City. To develop this information, historical records, including fire insurance maps from seven time periods over a one hundred-year period, were studied, and historical land-use data pertinent to environmental contamination for each property was transferred into a tabular form. Historical land-use tables were then installed into SPEED and are available to users when these properties are explored in the application. This GIS data layer, called the Vacant Property Database (figure 3.8),

CASE STUDY > >

Figure 3.7 SPEED users can select different types of data from multiple databases to generate maps with the information they specifically need. Copyright 2012. The City of New York. Courtesy of Mayor's Office of Environmental Remediation.

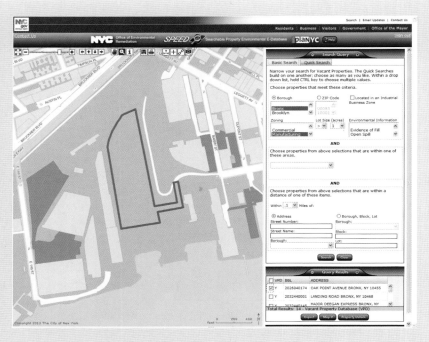

Figure 3.8 The Vacant Property Database layer has detailed historical information on more than 3,150 vacant commercial and industrial properties in New York City. Developers can use this information to assess the potential for environmental issues at sites around the city. Copyright 2012. The City of New York. Courtesy of Mayor's Office of Environmental Remediation.

CASE STUDY >

enables OER to focus developers' attention on vacant properties—those in greatest need of redevelopment—and provides information for developers to make early judgments on past land use and the likely environmental issues they may encounter.

Search queries can be performed on a wide variety of criteria, such as spatial characteristics (address, block, and lot number), physical characteristics (site size), and environmental characteristics (known petroleum spills, Superfund sites). All information available for individual properties in SPEED, including property information, environmental data from government databases, and land-use histories, can be exported in the form of a comprehensive report or as tables readable by standard software, such as Microsoft Excel.

SPEED is very popular. In its first year of operation, the site was visited more than 3.7 million times by more than 1.6 million different visitors, making it one of the most popular websites offered by the city. OER is in the process of canvassing users and will develop upgrades and release improved versions of SPEED in the future.

To explore SPEED, visit http://www.nyc.gov/speed.

CASE STUDY •

Locating vulnerable populations in Broward County, Florida

Ginny Hazen, Broward County Emergency Management Division; Carolyn Rodriguez, Broward County Human Services Department; Hillary Hinds, Broward County Enterprise Technology Services; Roberto Castillo, Broward County Enterprise Technology Services; Bob Humple, Broward County Emergency Management Division; and Tami Price, Broward County Emergency Management Division, Broward County, Florida

Level of government: County
State/province: Florida
Country: USA
Population: 1,748,066

In 2005, Hurricane Wilma, a category 2 storm, hit the state of Florida with gusts up to 120 miles per hour, causing widespread damage to critical infrastructure, including power lines and the traffic system, and compromising other public systems. In Broward County, Florida, the hurricane resulted in an extended sheltering of up to four weeks in some parts of the county with limited public services available. Ninety-eight percent of the county had no power for up to three weeks. Many county residents had opted to stay in their homes and ride the storm out rather than evacuate. Following the

CASE STUDY > >

storm, elderly and disabled residents were left in severely damaged mobile home parks and in high-rise condominiums without electricity, individuals in wheelchairs had no elevator service, and the county had limited means for assisting many of its most vulnerable citizens. At the same time, the storm also destroyed landmarks, ripped away street signs, and damaged traffic lights, all of which made it difficult to locate and reach citizens needing assistance.

Figure 3.9 In 2005, hurricane damage left emergency workers unable to identify streets throughout much of Broward County, Florida. Courtesy of Broward County Board of County Commissioners.

According to Chuck Lanza, director of Broward County's Emergency Management Division, "The Vulnerable Population Registry is another well-conceived program that gives the county and the municipalities the ability to preidentify people requiring additional assistance following a major event. With an updated list in hand we can contact, reassure, and, in a worst-case scenario, deliver sustenance and, in some situations, lifesaving support to vulnerable persons in our community."

Broward County's difficult experience reaching its most vulnerable citizens after Wilma led three county commissioners to push for the development of an online registry for the county's vulnerable populations in 2007. The purpose of the system is to provide the county with a knowledge base of where vulnerable citizens live, what health conditions or limitations they might have, and other critical information first responders and other organizations, such as the Salvation Army and Red Cross, might need if those citizens opt to remain at home during an emergency event. The web-based Vulnerable Population Registry application uses a GIS service to geocode registrants' addresses and adds latitude and longitude coordinates to the database. The GIS also determines the map grid number that corresponds to the county's first responder fire grid map and the jurisdiction of the location to determine the responsible agency. Having these detailed coordinates, in addition to street addresses, enables rescue personnel to use GPS technology to find a particular location even if landmarks and

CASE STUDY >

street signs are missing as the result of an emergency event. Working with the thirty-one municipalities located in the county, Broward County developed and serves as host for the online registry and is responsible for verifying that the GIS data included in the registry is correct. The municipalities have control over the data contained therein; they can update, add, or delete their registered citizens' information and sort the data for their own reports and other uses.

Some jurisdictions make greater use of the data than others. Several cities have produced vulnerable-population maps from the GIS data provided by the registry for Citizen Corps response teams and first responders to use to go door to door following an event and check on people to see if they need assistance. Other municipalities have grouped registrants by need or restriction—for example, those in wheelchairs or those who require oxygen—which the municipality uses to prepare its rapid impact assessments. The municipality can easily analyze what populations might need in the way of special accommodations in the event of evacuation due to any disaster, including storms, hazardous spills, or terrorism events.

The GIS team supporting the registry is part of the county's Emergency Operations Center, and it maintains multiple GIS layer maps that are used during planning, response, mitigation, and recovery. The ability to use GIS to geocode locations is a key strategy in the county's disaster recovery plan. In the aftermath of Hurricane Wilma, the county served nearly 10,000 people—providing food, water, and ice door to door—in the four weeks of the extended evacuation, before the registry was developed. The registry now enables the county to group data by category to create a snapshot of the types of vulnerabilities that exist. For example, the county is in the process of cross-referencing the vulnerable population database with its Special Needs Registry in order to avoid duplicate or unneeded calls or visits when individuals appear in both registries (Special Needs Registry residents who opt to stay home need to be contacted as part of the Vulnerable Population Registry follow-up efforts).

As of November 2011, the Vulnerable Population Registry had 2,400 individuals listed in its database. Although the number isn't large compared to the approximately 18,000 people who have registered for paratransit service in the county, the system does allow the county to have a closer connection with registrants, who can be reached by phone, visited in person, or contacted by e-mail based on the information they provide. An outreach effort via a multimunicipality user group is being developed to increase the number of registrants.

CASE STUDY •

GIS tied to workflow and business processes

Many governments have interrelated business processes that require two or more departments or agencies to work together. Planning, zoning, and code enforcement, for example, routinely work together to see a development project from start to finish. Using a common GIS framework creates an opportunity to connect the workflow and business processes of the individual departments so projects can be passed back and forth electronically as needed and can tie together most activities of the organization.[3] Linking all the various steps in the departments' required business processes means that a constituent need only submit initial background material once. The potential for introducing new errors and duplication of effort can virtually be eliminated. Furthermore, a complete record of all actions taken for a site is developed as a result.

Fairfax County, Virginia, has developed a GIS application that enables staff to track and report updates to the county's comprehensive plan. In Delaware, Ohio, GIS provided a common framework for one integrated system to tie information together and manage all its planning, zoning, and development processes and realize new efficiencies to keep workflows running smoothly. A GIS-based assessment tool that helps identify the suitability of brownfield properties for redevelopment purposes aids the renewal of Wauwatosa, Wisconsin.

Tracking Comprehensive Plan amendments in Fairfax County, Virginia

Indrani Sistla, Department of Planning and Zoning; and Thomas Conry, GIS manager, Fairfax County, Virginia

Level of government: County
State/province: Virginia
Country: USA
Population: 1,037,605

In Fairfax County, Virginia, which is located just outside Washington, DC, the county's Department of Planning and Zoning (DPZ) provides advice and assistance on land use, development review, and zoning issues to the county's Board of Supervisors, which makes decisions and sets policy on such issues. The county's Board of Supervisors and other advisory bodies, such as the Planning Commission and the Board of Zoning Appeals, are required by Virginia state law to use the Comprehensive Plan as a guide for decision making about the natural and built environments. The DPZ's work involves extensive geographic/land-use analysis, and the use of GIS is strongly encouraged. The DPZ is one of the major users of the Fairfax County GIS and also contributes a large amount of data to the system.

Over the past few years, Fairfax County has developed a suite of GIS applications to streamline and automate certain work activities and to increase the DMZ's overall efficiency. The use of these applications requires little or no GIS skills and has helped expand the benefits of using GIS to a wider range of DPZ employees. These applications have become part of the DPZ information system. Examples include:

- Property Owner Notification System. Automates the process of notifying affected property owners in case of land development applications.
- Comprehensive Plan Amendment Tracking System (CPATS). Integrates, streamlines, and automates various aspects of Comprehensive Plan amendment processing.
- Comprehensive Plan Potential Assessment Application (CPPAA). Captures and provides a snapshot of the Fairfax County Comprehensive Plan's development potential for any geographic area at any given point in time.

CASE STUDY > >

- Parcel Researcher Application. Serves as a one-stop application that queries various enterprise databases to provide land-use information at a parcel level. In addition, this application provides a mapping tool that the user can use with little or no GIS skills to create a variety of maps.

Comprehensive Plan Amendment Tracking System (CPATS)

One of the DPZ's three primary divisions, the Planning Division (PD), has responsibility for maintaining the county's Comprehensive Plan. Virginia state law requires that the Comprehensive Plan be used by the county's Board of Supervisors and other advisory bodies, such as the Planning Commission and the Board of Zoning Appeals, as a guide for decision making about the natural and built environments. It is also a guide for county staff and the public to use in the planning process.

Figure 3.10 GIS aids Fairfax County in tracking changes to the Comprehensive Plan.
Photo courtesy of Esri.

The Code of Virginia mandates that the Comprehensive Plan be reviewed at least once every five years. Because of the dynamic growth experienced by the county over the past thirty years, Fairfax County's plan has been evaluated much more frequently. Proposed amendments to the plan are submitted to a periodic public review process that includes public hearings before the Planning Commission and the Board of Supervisors. The Board of Supervisors must vote to adopt an amendment in order to change the plan.

PD personnel process all suggested and required amendments to the plan's text and map. The number of nominations to amend the plan in a given year can vary from 5 to over 150. Although the Fairfax County Planning Commission and the DPZ are the primary agencies involved, the process involves input from various other county agencies.

The Board of Supervisors relies heavily on DPZ staff reports to keep informed of the relevant amendments and nominations and pertinent details related to them. In the past, there was no one

CASE STUDY >

system, apart from a few Microsoft Word documents, that tracked the status of the plan amendments and nominations. Moreover, the DPZ planners reviewing these amendments and nominations did not have any query tools and had to rely on manual lookup of various county databases for their research when a question arose.

The CPATS application streamlined and automated the plan amendment data input, update, and query processes. Using CPATS, land-use planners can:

- Input details such as nominator information; current and proposed plan text; task force, staff, and Planning Commission recommendations; and board actions
- Capture the subject area information and create locator maps
- Query the plan geography information and zoning information for the subject area
- Quantify the development potential of the proposed amendments/nominations and build "what-if" scenarios
- Update and track the status of the amendments/nominations
- Create customized reports (e.g., status reports, staff reports, and so on)
- Create notification letters to send to property owners affected by the proposed plan amendments/ nominations
- Quantify the change in the development potential as a result of the adopted plan amendments in a given year

CPATS is an internal application that is primarily used by DPZ personnel to produce staff reports and maps for review by the Planning Commission and the Board of Supervisors. Future plans call for the system to go online and enable businesses and residents to submit materials for or to comment on the Comprehensive Plan electronically.

CASE STUDY •

Streamlining the permitting process in Delaware, Ohio

David M. Efland, AICP, Director of Planning and Community Development, City of Delaware, Ohio; and Matt Harman, Project Manager, Azteca Systems

Level of government: City
State/province: Ohio
Country: USA
Population: 34,753

Located along the Olentangy River about twenty miles north of Columbus in central Ohio, the City of Delaware is home to Ohio Wesleyan University. Delaware serves as the county seat for Delaware

CASE STUDY > > >

County, the fastest-growing county in the state. Despite being on the cutting edge of growth and development, the city found itself in 2005 playing catch up in the technology arena in managing the systems that govern growth. The city had lots of ad hoc systems in place, but it needed one integrated system to tie information together and manage all its planning, zoning, and development processes. With a small staff, the city also wanted to realize new efficiencies to keep workflows running smoothly. The following table lists all the applications, permit types, and cases implemented in each department.

Table 3.3 City of Delaware applications and permits

Department	Applications and permits
Building Division	6 commercial permits 17 residential permits 1 contractor registration/licensing 4 miscellaneous
Planning and Zoning Division	17 developments (final development plan, certificate of approvals, etc.) 4 predevelopments (annexation review, concept plan, etc.) 8 subdivisions (final subdivision plan, public way vacation, etc.) 12 zoning permits (conditional use permits, sign permits, variances, etc.) 7 housing and economic development grants
Code Enforcement	3 code enforcement case types consisting of dozens of code violations
Department of Engineering Services	1 land development construction process 2 right-of-way permits/violations

The city had a robust GIS in place at the time, but it was underutilized. Delaware wanted to access the wealth of data it had available in its GIS and to link that data to the numerous development and growth management processes that resided across several departments. The decision to use geographical data as the common element among all the various planning, zoning, and permitting systems was a logical choice and moved Delaware from a mostly paper-based permitting system to a new GIS-centric community development and management software application, Cityworks Server PLL, developed by Azteca Systems Inc. (Note the evolution of management systems in the figure that follows.)

Figure 3.11 Evolution of management systems in Delaware, Ohio.

The transition from a paper-based system to the more technologically advanced permitting system required the implementation of several change management strategies. Team members, who ranged in age from twenty to sixty, were accustomed to the current systems and were comfortable using them. The implementation process was challenging, mostly because it forced the city for the first time to write down, document, and confront its development processes. This review work became a key component in the implementation, often leading to changes in how processes flowed.

Although moving to the new system had its challenges, it provided several new benefits, such as the ability to generate monthly and annual reports for tracking workloads and monitoring progress on individual service requests. Most important, the new system produces maps that can be taken to elected officials to talk about city decisions, departmental budgets, and resource allocation issues.

With the new system, the city can start a project in the preliminary stages, such as a concept plan review, preliminary plan, or zoning change, and use the GIS to monitor it through all the various phases, as well as to track the associated fees. The ability to cross-reference projects has proved useful. For example, when a developer applies to subdivide a property, team members can review the site to determine whether any code enforcement actions have been taken on that same property and clear up those matters before work begins on a project. It is also easier for staff to record and reference future projects associated with a particular site, such as a planned bike path through a new development. Finally, property developments and changes through time (across multiple years) can be documented and accessed on a property-by-property basis.

Having the new system in place also allows for better coordination on projects with allied departments, including police, fire, public works, and engineering. For example, if the fire chief has comments on a project, his e-mail can be saved as a PDF and attached directly to the case number for the project in the system. Future plans for the system call for making the software available to different departments.

The city may also move the system online to allow constituents to apply for permits, enabling individuals to submit the necessary information directly using self-service forms. Even without moving the system to the web, the processing speed for permits has increased exponentially. Under the old system, doing pay-in (processing cash receipts for deposit) for a building permit took about an hour to complete, whereas under the new system the same task takes literally one minute. The quality of the data in the system is much more accurate as well, because it is entered only once, minimizing the human error associated with the previous systems.

The ability to produce maps has been useful for explaining to council members where development is taking place around the city as well as showing where code enforcement actions are taking place. Team members have used the system to help citizens better understand how code enforcement operates in the city. During a recent Delaware Citizens Academy class, a code enforcement map was color-coded to break down the type of actions underway for particular properties: orange for mowing violations, purple for trash and debris, and red for all other violations. Seeing the color-coded maps explains in a way that words cannot where problems are found around the city and demonstrates visually the sheer amount of work performed by city staff.

Other jurisdictions considering implementing a similar system should be aware that a long-term commitment must be made to this type of technology to achieve the greatest efficiencies. It is not a one-off purchase that can solve all problems. It is necessary to work with the staff before, during, and after implementation, and then continue to listen and hear their comments, concerns, and feedback

CASE STUDY >

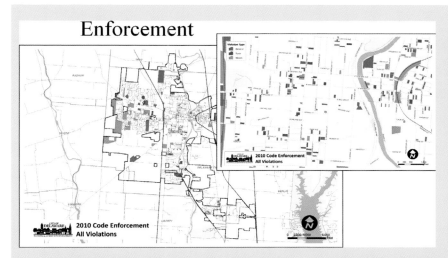

Enforcement

Figure 3.12 The City of Delaware used GIS maps to help Delaware Citizens Academy participants better understand code enforcement actions underway. Courtesy of City of Delaware, Ohio.

after the system has been in place for a while. Constant building of communications and flexibility between staff members ensures the best long-term results.

CASE STUDY •

Using GIS data for identifying and cataloging brownfield sites in Wauwatosa, Wisconsin

Nancy Welch, Director of Community Development, City of Wauwatosa, Wisconsin, and Principal Urban Planner, NLW Consulting

Level of government: City
State/province: Wisconsin
Country: USA
Population: 46,396

The US Environmental Protection Agency (EPA) awarded the City of Wauwatosa, Wisconsin, two Communitywide Brownfields Assessment Grants in 2009 with funding received through the American Recovery and Reinvestment Act of 2009. Implementation of the grants required the city to identify and catalog brownfield properties for the purpose of prioritizing sites for assessment. To facilitate this process, the city created a custom GIS application database to serve as a common platform for data collection and management. Working with Symbiont from West Allis, Wisconsin, the city launched a dynamic brownfields GIS database that combined historical property use documentation

CASE STUDY > > > >

with contemporary information to create a comprehensive look at existing and historical land-use patterns. The GIS database provided a basis for identifying redevelopment opportunities, possible liabilities, and potential environmental impacts on the community. The database also serves as a model for other municipalities looking for tools to aid with their brownfield redevelopment work.

The Wauwatosa brownfields GIS database has proven to be a valuable source of information in identifying and mapping out a strategy for future redevelopment projects and best use of funds. Pairing the city's GIS system with planning initiatives produced a high rate of success in using grant funds to facilitate redevelopment of high-priority projects. To date, the city has successfully leveraged $10.50 in private, local, and state redevelopment funds for every dollar of grant funds expended. Having the tools to take a proactive approach to potential environmental contamination has given investors and developers more confidence in moving forward with challenging redevelopment projects. It has made it easier for the city to identify key projects and prioritize available funding for their redevelopment. The investment has also provided necessary stimulus for projects during difficult economic times, resulting in critical growth of the city's tax base.

Figure 3.13 This screen capture illustrates how the city directory search feature works. Courtesy of City of Wauwatosa, Wisconsin.

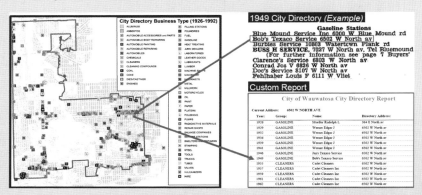

To date, the city has successfully leveraged $10.50 in private, local, and state redevelopment funds for every dollar of grant funds expended.

The foundation for the custom GIS database came from a collection of twenty-two city and county basemap layers that identified physical and other municipal features in the city—for example, parcels, buildings, roads, and zoning boundaries—by overlaying these layers over current aerial photographs. By allowing existing layers to predefine the projection and extent of the custom brownfields GIS database, future datasets could be built and seamlessly integrated between generators and users. Using the basemap parcel dataset, other relevant databases and records from federal and state environmental regulatory agencies were imported into the database, allowing for analysis across multiple agency databases. For example, regulatory agency datasets included the Wisconsin Department of Safety

CASE STUDY > > >

and Professional Services' underground and aboveground storage tanks database, the Wisconsin Department of Natural Resources' (WDNR) Bureau for Remediation and Redevelopment Tracking System (BRRTS), and the EPA's Facility Registry System database. To increase data access, hyperlinks to specific regulatory records were created for each record in Wauwatosa's new database.

One of the major lessons learned in the development of the database was the importance of leveraging local resources. The city worked with the Wauwatosa Historical Society and the Milwaukee County Historical Society to create high-resolution, full-color scans of deteriorating historical plat maps. Staff scanned and imported the plat maps, and then georeferenced them into the database, providing the city with continuous documentation of property ownership and land use from the mid-1800s through the mid-twentieth century. The city also provided the high-resolution scans of the individual maps to the Wauwatosa Historical Society, preserving a fragile resource and allowing the society to reprint the maps as needed for future research projects. In a similar fashion, the city suffered a major loss when its collection of historical Sanborn Fire Insurance Maps was destroyed by fire several decades ago. As a result, the city lacked an overall comprehensive resource documenting site-specific property histories and land uses. To rebuild this critical data source, the city obtained high-resolution full-color scans of the historical Sanborn Fire Insurance Maps published in 1910 and 1927 from the American Geographical Society Library located at the University of Wisconsin-Milwaukee. Staff again scanned, imported, and georeferenced pages of the individual Sanborn maps for use in the new database. The resulting seamless mosaic provides a valuable tool in identifying properties with the potential for environmental liabilities from previous operations.

In continuing to investigate and leverage local resources, city staff met with the director of the Wauwatosa Public Library and discovered that the library had implemented a preservation grant in the early 1990s allowing it to scan its entire collection of city directories dating back to 1926. The resulting page scans were consolidated into three separate databases, which were no longer accessible due to incompatibility with the current versions of Microsoft Access. Because the printed directories had become very fragile, general public access was limited, though demand for use remained high. The library had archived the material but lacked the right vehicle to make the information accessible. Working with a local programmer, the old databases were disassembled and the scanned pages converted to a searchable digital format. A web-based database program was developed and is hosted by the library (http://wauwatosalibrary.org/tosadirectory/) to provide open searchable access to all Wauwatosa City Directories published between 1926 and 1992. (Open access also provides a significant benefit to genealogy researchers trying to prepare a history of their home or family.) Digital access to the city directory records allowed staff to create a unique GIS database of property history by searching to identify historical uses that could have environmental implications, such as gas stations and dry cleaners. The resulting GIS database identified 790 unique businesses, 67 unique business types, and 348 unique parcels with historical uses of potential environmental liability. In many cases, the city directories identified businesses that had not been in operation for decades and revealed some surprises in terms of sites with potential environmental liabilities from past uses.

The resulting custom brownfields GIS database also provides a dynamic tool for inventorying properties. Although the Wauwatosa brownfields GIS database continues to be updated as new records are identified, it currently contains records from eighty-six unique federal, state, local, and regional data types and sources and has helped to identify potential environmental liabilities at nearly 1,400 unique properties that appear to meet the EPA's definition of a brownfield property. By serving as a common data analysis platform, the database serves as a tremendous asset in performing environmental due diligence investigations. In one case, staff used the database to identify a high-priority potential redevelopment site as a former gas station, even though there had been no available records with that information and subsequent development had removed the usual visual clues. Sanborn map coverage of the site illustrated the approximate location of the former gasoline tanks, which allowed for the identification of the most likely source for legacy environmental liabilities. Having this information available made the subsequent phase II environmental site assessment more focused, and the property moved more rapidly to redevelopment and regulatory closure.

At another high-priority redevelopment site, the database helped identify clues of previous and adjacent land uses. Combining that information with WDNR records helped spot a recurring pattern of elevated arsenic concentrations in the soil and groundwater throughout the entire redevelopment

Figure 3.14 This map shows how historical data can be applied to a single site analysis. Courtesy of City of Wauwatosa, Wisconsin.

CASE STUDY >

corridor. This trend bolstered the argument made for closure of the site because arsenic appeared to be a naturally occurring constituent found throughout the corridor, and identifying and treating it as a "source" of pollution was impractical. Identifying this naturally recurring element will also benefit other future redevelopment projects within the corridor that are likely to experience similar elevated levels.

Significant redevelopment of several large former industrial properties occurred in the 1970s and 1980s when legacy environmental impacts were not addressed through due diligence investigations. Several of these properties continue to sit vacant as a result of the recent economic recession. As Wauwatosa is completely developed, redevelopment of these large former industrial properties is paramount to promoting any large-scale economic redevelopment in the city. However, the environmental liabilities associated with the previous industrial use of the properties are a significant barrier to redevelopment. Developers and lending agencies are reluctant to pursue projects in former manufacturing areas due to fear of potential unknown environmental liabilities. In many cases, because redevelopment in the latter parts of the twentieth century essentially erased all visual evidence of previous industrial site use, records contained in the brownfields GIS database serve as one of the few remaining records of previous site operations. The database assists in identifying potential sources of contamination and providing information that allows for a more proactive approach to redeveloping these sites. By showing historical impacts on the site, developers are more willing to pursue the next stages in assessment and move on to any necessary remediation and redevelopment of the site.

The City of Wauwatosa continues to expand and update the brownfields GIS database as funding allows. Future updates are likely to include mapping the horizontal extents of known plumes of residual soil and groundwater impacts. Such mapping will identify properties that may be affected by migrating plumes originating from offsite properties. Because lending agencies are hesitant to provide financing without completing some form of environmental assessment, this mapping will help to prevent delays on redevelopment projects, ensuring that the proposal moves forward smoothly. As funding allows, the brownfields GIS database will be published online to allow for transparent access to community members, stakeholders, and redevelopers.

CASE STUDY •

Integrated GIS

Integrating GIS with other software programs—such as asset management, work order management, and constituent relationship management (CRM) software—adds value by providing a common operating platform for comparing diverse data types. A CRM system alone can provide important data on the number and type of citizen services requests received. Integrated with GIS, however, government officials can use CRM data to identify which neighborhoods are placing service requests and what type of requests are being submitted, as Hartford, Connecticut, has done. Having this type of information available helps managers spot possible trends and respond appropriately to neighborhood challenges. In Quebec City, Quebec, citizens have access to an interactive web-based map that allows them to collect a wide variety of different types of data and information on properties throughout the city from one source. Corpus Christi, Texas, has a jointly held work order and asset management system with integrated GIS that is used by sixteen of the city's departments.

Adding value to 311/CRM data in Hartford, Connecticut

Brett Flodine, GISP, GIS Project Leader, Metro Hartford Information Services; and
Andrew Jaffee, Director, Emergency Services and Telecommunications, City of Hartford,
Connecticut

Level of government: City
State/province: Connecticut
Country: USA
Population: 124,775

In 2006, the City of Hartford, Connecticut, opened a 311 call center as a centralized resource for information and to receive nonemergency requests for city services from residents. Central to the operation of the call center is a customer relationship management (CRM) software application that allows center employees to catalog and maintain a huge knowledge base of information on city programs and services, as well as record and process all incoming calls. The system ensures that the city responds to requests for service in a timely and efficient manner, and it also provides city officials with a wealth of new information about the services residents want most.

When city residents call into the center, agents collect information about where the service request is located. This spatial information is a link to the city's GIS program, which maintains and updates more than 38,000 address points for the city. This link ensures that valid addresses are recorded in a standardized format and geocoded for different types of GIS analysis.

For the mayor and city council, the data derived from Hartford's 311/CRM system, combined with GIS, is useful for working with constituents and making decisions on policy matters.

For the mayor and city council, the data derived from Hartford's 311/CRM system, combined with GIS, is useful for working with constituents and making decisions on policy matters. The city has seventeen established neighborhood associations that meet on a monthly basis. Using the address points from the GIS to sort out calls received, the 311 manager is able to generate neighborhood-based reports that detail what types of calls come in from which neighborhoods and how those calls are addressed.

When a city council member is scheduled to attend a neighborhood association meeting, he or she might look at the neighborhood reports and see that the Barry Square neighborhood had X number of calls to Environmental Health regarding pest problems and that Public Works–Sanitation had

CASE STUDY > > >

Y number of calls for bulk waste pickup during the same time period. This information gives the elected official the opportunity to bring in staff from Environmental Health and Public Works–Sanitation to the meeting and suggest that the neighborhood schedule a designated neighborhood cleanup day.

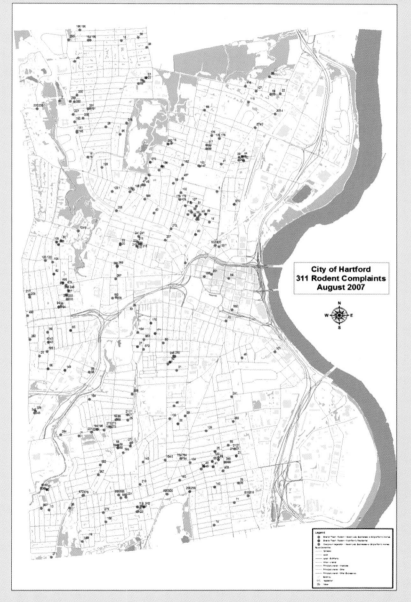

Figure 3.15 This map was used by housing code inspectors to identify target areas in the city.
Courtesy of City of Hartford, Connecticut.

The GIS team has also developed an interactive web-based 311 case map that enables elected officials and citizens to look up online which 311 cases are open and which ones are closed around the city. Simply by highlighting a point on the map, users can look up the case identification number, the location of the case, when the case was opened, which department is responsible for responding, and a brief

Figure 3.16 This map was used by the mayor's office to determine whether the snow and ice complaints being called in to 311 were for a specific area in the city. Courtesy of City of Hartford, Connecticut.

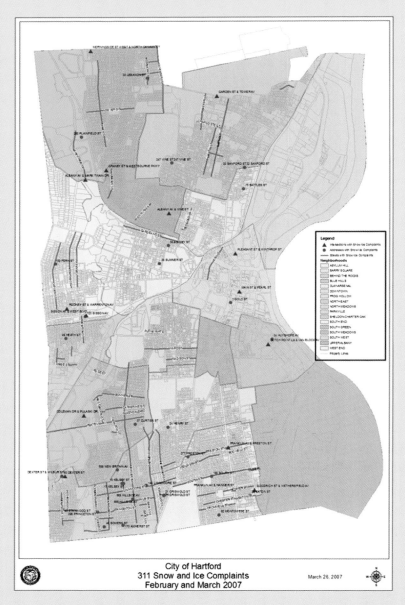

City of Hartford
311 Snow and Ice Complaints
February and March 2007

March 26, 2007

CASE STUDY >

description of the case. The map allows everyone to easily look up case numbers, find out the status of a case, and get a broad overview of what's happening around the city.

Finally, the city has used the 311/CRM data and GIS applications to analyze specific concerns as they arise. For example, in the midst of the blizzards of 2007, the GIS team demonstrated that snow removal service was being provided equitably among the different neighborhoods in the city by analyzing the incoming 311 calls for snow removal (figure 3.16). Likewise, the GIS team has used 311/CRM data to identify "hot spots" around the city with pest control issues.

CASE STUDY •

Putting Quebec City on the map

Esri Canada

Level of government: City
State/province: Quebec
Country: Canada
Population: 525,376

In 2002, thirteen cities merged to create what is now the unified Quebec City. This was one of many mergers that swept across the province and was based on the concept that larger municipalities would be more efficient and better positioned to compete with other Canadian cities. After the merger, Quebec City developed an interactive map that offered public access to cartographic data and information on properties located within the newly formed city. However, it became evident that the application lacked compatibility with popular operating systems and browsers, and the Geomatics Department was tasked with developing a more robust, compatible interactive map.

The city's main goal was to develop a web-based map that would offer easy access to an abundance of high-quality data, above and beyond what many other commercial applications could provide. It incorporated a range of large-scale cartographic data that included parks, fire hydrants, cycling paths, and administrative zones, along with residential, commercial, and

> **"The new and improved web map has greatly reduced service calls to the city and allows [the] public or organizations to freely exchange information. Data is updated much more frequently and served up to the public through a modern, fast, and easy-to-use tool."**
> Denis Dufour, Section Manager, City of Quebec

CASE STUDY >

public buildings. It also integrated information on major events occurring throughout the city. This data is updated on a nightly basis and provides a valuable resource for taxpayers who want to keep informed about their surrounding community. They can evaluate a property, find the best routes to local schools and hospitals, access garbage collection schedules, or research an upcoming event in their area. It is also referenced by professionals, including notaries, land surveyors, lawyers, real estate agents, insurance companies, and bankers, who need quick and easy access to accurate property information.

The city selected the ArcGIS API for Microsoft Silverlight to build the interactive web-based map. This developer tool allows users to create rich Internet and desktop applications that consume ArcGIS for Server as well as other mapping, geocoding, and geoprocessing services. The city selected the Silverlight API because it satisfied its main objective of creating a web-based application that offered superior compatibility, speed, and ease of use.

Quebec's web map offers a wealth of navigational tools that make it incredibly intuitive to use. In addition to being able to scroll through or pan the map to change the scale, users can rotate the map, return to their previous view, zoom in and out and switch between cartographic and orthophoto views of the city. The Silverlight API allowed developers to exploit the transparency of data layers so that the user can merge cartography with orthophotos and adjust the degree of transparency. This provides a detailed, realistic view of the city. Users can research addresses, roads, intersections, and buildings, and then apply a comprehensive toolset to take measurements, bookmark pages, or draw points of interest on the map.

Figure 3.17 Buildings are color-coded to distinguish commercial, residential, and industrial buildings, along with schools, hospitals, and churches.
Courtesy of Esri Canada and City of Quebec.

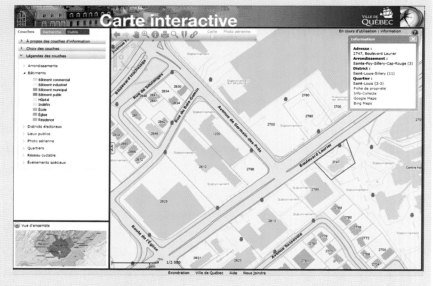

As a next step, the city plans to expand on the success of the application by developing a more complex, internal-facing web-based map that can be leveraged by city staff. This application will be used for land planning and development, vehicle tracking, snow removal, infrastructure maintenance, street lighting, and a variety of other engineering projects. Visit the interactive map at http://carte.ville.quebec.qc.ca/carteinteractive.

CASE STUDY •

Work management and GIS: Identifying where the work is in Corpus Christi, Texas

Michael Armstrong, Chief Information Officer, City of Corpus Christi, Texas

Level of government: City
State/province: Texas
Country: USA
Population: 305,215

The old real estate adage—location, location, location—also applies to local government service delivery. A significant portion of service delivery involves identifying where work needs to be done in the community, and then sending the appropriate work crew out to do the job. In Corpus Christi, Texas, this is especially true because the municipality provides water, wastewater, utility, and storm water services in addition to more traditional city services such as parks, traffic, and other public works functions.

The city had developed a robust GIS program, but it wasn't connected to any form of work order management system or CRM system that would allow for the easy capture of spatial data for analysis. However, city leaders realized that nearly 90 percent of the service requests and work orders being received by the city were associated with a physical location. In order to better understand what was happening in neighborhoods throughout the city, city leaders wanted to be able to look at a map and see where things were happening.

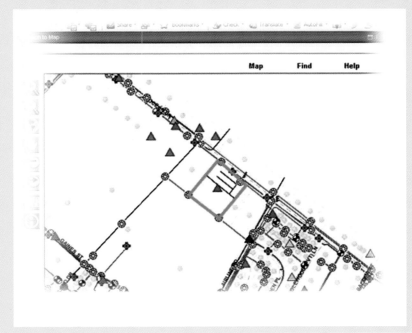

Figure 3.18 This map shows how field crews can use GIS to identify the locations of different types of service requests in a neighborhood. Courtesy City of Corpus Christi, Texas.

CASE STUDY > > >

When the city began researching work order management systems, it determined that integration with its GIS program was paramount. Ultimately, in 2002, the city opted to implement IBM's Maximo software as the standard work order management software for sixteen departments that required such a system. One of the reasons was that the application had full GIS integration, which helps the city easily identify duplicate service requests and thus avoid sending work crews out to do the same job twice.

In 2003, the city also adapted the software for use as a CRM application in its Customer Service Center. When a citizen calls the center with a service request, agents collect address data in a standardized format so that it can be mapped. Based on the service level agreement (SLA) for the request (i.e., how long it generally takes to perform the service) and the priority level assigned to the service, managers can review a map of all requests received and determine how best to route work crews.

Figure 3.19 Citizens' service requests can be made online through the Customer Service Center. Courtesy of City of Corpus Christi, Texas.

The city went a step further in 2009 and began working in a mobile environment allowing work crews to access work orders and file reports on laptops and other mobile devices while in the field. If a work crew is out working in a neighborhood when a new service request is received, the crew can address the matter immediately rather than making a second trip to the neighborhood.

Citizens can also assist with identifying where work is needed around the city. An online request form allows individuals to report problems twenty-four hours a day, seven days a week. In 2010, the city introduced a new mobile application for citizens called CCMobile. Using a smartphone application, citizens can capture the GPS coordinates of the location where a service request needs to be filled. A commuter can report the location of a pothole or a neighborhood resident can take a picture of graffiti in the area and submit it to the city to be filled.

The decision to introduce both the online self-service form and the smartphone application represents a strategic decision to engage young people and to keep the next generation involved with the

CASE STUDY > >

community. "We like to be on the leading edge and try to stay on top of trends in the area as well as the country," explains Michael Armstrong, the city's CIO. But the decision also has financial implications. The city estimates that service requests received via a traditional phone call cost about $4.50 per transaction, whereas those generated by the online request form and mobile application cost about $0.50 per transaction. The goal is to generate 1,000 service requests per month via the mobile application.

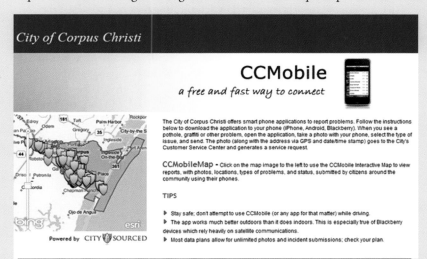

Figure 3.20 The smartphone application is designed to engage young people. Courtesy of City of Corpus Christi, Texas.

No matter how the data comes through in the various methods offered by the city, it adds considerable value in helping to achieve new efficiencies:

- Geographic analysis. This function helps the city look for patterns in reports. For example, if the city begins to receive a large number of dirty water complaints coming from a specific location, it can send a work crew out to investigate.

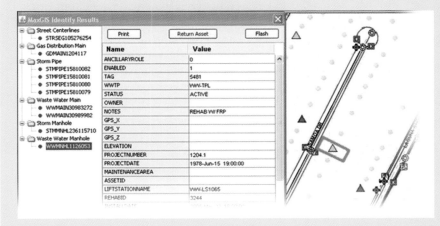

Figure 3.21 This map provides details on a work order. Courtesy of City of Corpus Christi, Texas.

- Operational reports. Each department receives a daily operational report. For example, the Water Department has a morning report that includes requests received overnight. Managers use the report to look at the requirements for the day. What might be high-priority tasks? Has a service-level agreement been breached? Based on information in the report, managers structure the workday. In the summer of 2011, the city had trouble with water main breaks due to the high summer temperatures. The operational reports were vital in determining how best to adjust the work schedule and add crews to repair the breaks.
- Statistical analysis. This analysis provides the city with important business intelligence—for example, usage data from automated water meters. The city can monitor the amount of water it is producing and compare it to what it is selling. The reports help the city determine whether a water leak might be in the system. Water, in particular, is a revenue issue for the city, so it can't afford to wait for someone to report an issue. Reviewing incident and service requests can provide early indicators where work is needed that can be compared with work crew schedules. The city is in the process of making this information public so residents can know where construction projects are planned.
- Cost and time tracking. One report that has been particularly useful is cost and time tracking. The city has been able to develop precise information on what amount of resources it takes to perform a particular service. This gives the city a significant advantage in its ability to understand and predict what costs are going to be, including determining what the labor-hour requirements are likely to be on any given project.
- Balanced scorecard data and performance metrics. The city adopted the balanced scorecard as its performance management system in order to align daily management decisions with its broader corporate strategy, support the budget process, and provide meaningful, actionable feedback to managers and employees. The Maximo system allows the city to pull performance data from the system for consideration in determining leading and lagging indicators in the balanced scorecard.

The ability to connect geospatial data to performance metrics has been extremely valuable in providing departments useful tools for scheduling work crews. It also gives Corpus Christi the ability to do some predictive analytics (e.g., a spike in water leak reports in a geographic area may indicate that serious infrastructure problems exist).

Integration has been the key to making the system work in Corpus Christi. All the departments requiring some form of work order management use the same system, which, in turn, has been linked to the city's GIS and other relevant software packages. Having one system in place that is tied to the city's GIS program greatly improves the ability of Corpus Christi's leaders to look across departments and simplifies technical assistance support services required from personnel in the IT Department. The system also allows for on-the-spot updates for field reporting, so the city has nearly real-time data to review in emergency situations.

A recent upgrade to CCMobile has provided additional capabilities for this application, including the ability to submit reports from mobile devices that do not have cameras. Users also can now attach video and audio files to provide work crews additional information. In addition, people who submit reports to the system can enable "push" status updates back to their mobile devices so that they don't have to log in to a website to check the status of a work order.

CASE STUDY •

Performance measurement and accountability

There is an old adage that what gets measured gets done; an ancillary lesson that can be drawn from this saying is that what gets done also gets reviewed. The need for greater transparency and accountability in government operations has never been higher than it is now. The news media, citizen watchdog groups, and constituents themselves want to know how policy decisions are being made, where their tax dollars are being spent, and what the results of those expenditures are. GIS can help elected officials show citizens the full context of, and mitigating circumstances around, decisions that must be made as well as demonstrate the results from the investment of taxpayer dollars. GIS technology helped the State of Utah open up the process it used for establishing redistricting jurisdictional boundaries. In Rancho Cucamonga, California, the city designed a new mobile application to make greater use of its GIS data and deliver city services more efficiently. Finally, the New York State Liquor Authority found that GIS not only helped open up the state's permitting process so community groups could see where applications were sought, but also significantly increased the efficiency of staff enforcing the permitting process.

Opening up the redistricting process in the State of Utah

Based on an interview with John Cannon and Chris McClelland, with the Office of Legislative Research and General Counsel, State of Utah

Level of government: State
State/province: Utah
Country: USA
Population: 2,763,885

Redistricting is the system by which electoral boundaries, based on population shifts, are drawn every ten years after the US Census has been conducted. The process of redistricting can be highly political. Aware of the public's sometimes skeptical view of politics, legislative leaders in the state of Utah sought to open up the process in their state and make the system more transparent and accountable to the citizens of Utah.

The Utah State Legislature formed the 2011 Redistricting Committee in April 2011 to oversee the redistricting effort. Working with the Office of Legislative Research and General Counsel, legislative leaders determined that they wanted to engage the public in mapping possible boundaries for the new congressional and legislative districts. The 2011 redistricting effort was especially important as the US Census determined that Utah's population had grown 23.8 percent from 2000 to 2010, making Utah the third fastest growing state in the country. As a result, Utah received a fourth congressional seat. In all, the state needed to create four congressional districts, twenty-nine state senate districts, seventy-five state house districts, and fifteen state school board districts.

The Redistricting Committee opted to contract for an online mapping tool that individuals could use to create their own redistricting plans. Any person could go online and register to use the application to draw up a plan for suggested boundaries for the new districts. During the six-month process,

CASE STUDY > >

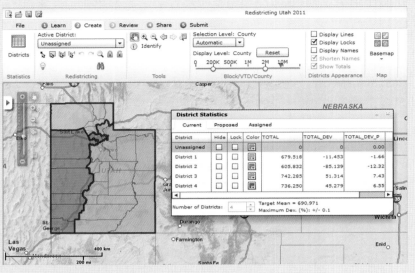

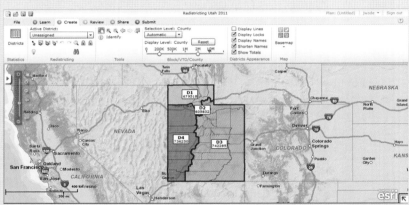

Figure 3.22 Two examples of maps created as part of the State of Utah's redistricting effort.

Courtesy of State of Utah.

well over 1,000 people registered to use the online mapping application, and approximately 400 maps were drawn and submitted online for consideration.

The state also developed a website that was harmonized with the online mapping tool, allowing the maps to be shared in two ways. First they were made available through the online mapping tool itself, and then images of all the maps created online were transferred as images to the website. The online mapping application provided a powerful tool for creating possible district boundaries, and the dedicated website enhanced communication about and distribution of the proposed maps.

In addition to the eleven meetings held at the state capitol, the Redistricting Committee held seventeen public hearings throughout Utah—many more than had been held for past redistricting efforts. The hearings gave citizens an opportunity to discuss redistricting plans. At the hearings, individuals who had submitted maps online were invited to present their plans to the group. At many of the public hearings at least one or two individuals made presentations on maps they had created. And, in fact,

CASE STUDY >

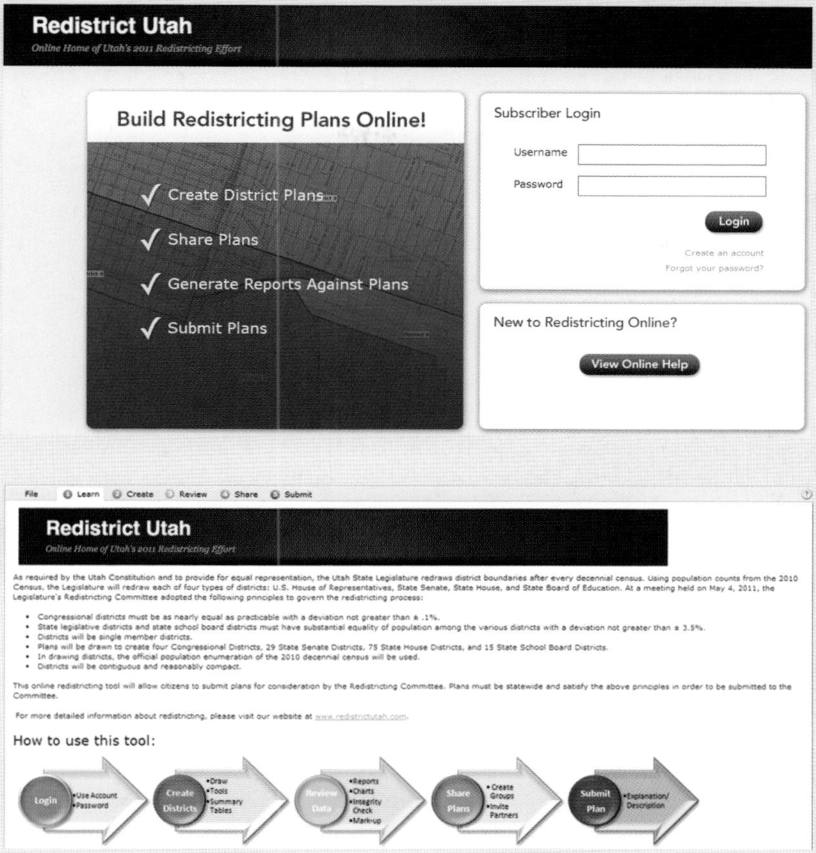

Figure 3.23 Accessing Utah's redistricting effort online. Courtesy of State of Utah.

as a result of this participation, the underlying basemap adopted for the school board districts proved to be a map created by a citizen. Some adjustments were made to the map before it was passed, but the new districts were largely developed from the citizen's submission.

The media followed the redistricting effort routinely and reported on the Redistricting Committee's work on a regular basis. One reporter, it turns out, got very involved in the story. District boundaries for the US House of Representatives were of high interest given the new congressional seat the state received. Beginning with over one hundred different maps, the Redistricting Committee selected six possible maps as finalists before voting for the redistricting plan. One of those six finalists was a map created by a local reporter when he went online to research how the mapping tool worked.

There were some legislators who went online to use the mapping tool themselves, but the Office of Legislative Research and General Counsel purchased the necessary hardware and software in order to produce maps in-house for legislative members, and, more often, legislators would work with staff to create maps. Interoperability between the online mapping tool and the in-house GIS technology provided important functionality for adaptation of maps created online but required fine-tuning using the in-house system.

CASE STUDY •

Using GIS to promote city services in Rancho Cucamonga

Ingrid Bruce, GIS/Special Districts Manager; and Solomon Nimako, GIS Fire Analyst, City of Rancho Cucamonga

Level of government: City
State/province: California
Country: USA
Population: 165,269

Mobile devices—laptops, smartphones, and tablets—have dominated the computer technology market in recent years. Garter Inc. (2011)[4] predicts that these technologies will represent more than 90 percent of new net growth for computer devices over the next four years. These communication technologies provide a unique opportunity for local governments to interact and engage with their citizens.

Figure 3.24 Residents can use the RC2GO application to report a problem using their smartphone. Courtesy of City of Rancho Cucamonga, California, Administrative Services Department.

In the city of Rancho Cucamonga, California, Mayor L. Dennis Michael and the city council observed this trend and wanted to take advantage of the new technology to expand how city services were being delivered to citizens. Mobile applications developed for local governments were being introduced on a routine basis, and making use of the technology seemed a prudent venture. The mayor and council directed then-Assistant City Manager John Gillison (now city manager) to develop a mobile application for the city.

Given the trend toward increased emphasis on efficiency, accountability, and effectiveness over the last decade, Gillison determined that building in a level of performance accountability was crucial for the design of the new application. He points out, "Voters want to ensure that their hard-earned taxes go as far as possible with as little waste as possible. Likewise, chief executive officers want to ensure they are optimizing the use of scarce resources, making decisions based on solid analytics and proven data, and running their agency at the highest levels possible. Elected officials and governing boards want to show the general public that their agency is running at maximum effectiveness,

CASE STUDY > > > >

making use of all available resources, and properly accounting for tax dollars received." As a result, the city closely tracks how the application is used by citizens to determine which features are most frequently used as well as what types of service requests are being received through the application.

GIS technology offered the city the ability to combine its data collection systems with maps in a meaningful visual representation. Although GIS started in public safety, including police and fire, the technology quickly spread to all departments, resulting in a wealth of available city data. Given the significant amount of city data available, it made sense to tap into this resource in developing the new mobile application.

Gillison pulled together a cross-departmental team of city employees to discuss how such an application should function. The team worked with CyberTech Systems and Software Inc. to ensure the final delivery of the application. There were numerous reporting applications already on the market at that time, but the team determined that the city needed more than just a reporting application. The city wanted to have an application that people could potentially use every day, not just when they saw something that needed to be done. The application needed to help people learn more about their community and the city they lived in. Several audiences were defined during this process, including current residents, realtors and developers, potential citizens, and visitors. The final product needed to be useful for multiple audiences.

Figure 3.25 The RC2GO application can be used to search for a specific property. Courtesy of City of Rancho Cucamonga, California, Administrative Services Department.

CASE STUDY > > >

The city maintains a multitude of GIS data layers. Using these data layers to give constituents easy access to location information for various community services gives new value to the data layers. In considering how to design the application and make greater use of the city's extensive GIS data, the team determined that all the services residents have web access to should also be available in a mobile environment. Not only would the city receive information from residents via a reporting function, but it would also provide information on available services. The intention is to promote the community to its constituents. Toward that end, the city tapped into its business license database and used it to provide information on shopping and dining opportunities as well as community attractions. Wi-Fi locations throughout the city can be accessed, as can the locations of automated external defibrillator (AED) devices for medical emergencies. Even the locations of charge stations for electric vehicles can be found through the application.

Figure 3.26 The RC2GO application can be used to find shopping opportunities within the city, among many other uses. Courtesy of City of Rancho Cucamonga, California, Administrative Services Department.

Since its launch in mid-February 2012, the RC2GO application has been downloaded nearly 2,000 times by roughly 1 percent of the city's total population of 165,269. The public outreach campaign for the application itself has been a lesson in citizen engagement and outreach. Mayor Michael officially launched the application during his annual address to the city. From that point on, Francine Palmer, a marketing manager for the city, has led a wide-ranging strategy to ensure that residents

CASE STUDY > >

know about the application's availability. Banner ads for the application have a position of prominence on the city's website. Ads have also been incorporated into other city promotional materials, such as posters for National Fitness Month and the Recreation Department's quarterly newsletter, *The Grapevine*. Printed bookmarks with a QR code to the application's download site have been developed as giveaways. The city has partnered with numerous community attractions and facilities to get the word out. For example, the city shared costs with the Rancho Cucamonga Community and Arts Foundation to print a custom chocolate bar wrapper for a promotional giveaway that promoted the application as well as the foundation's Chocolate and Wine Festival. Public service announcements (PSAs) have been made at RC Quakes (a minor-league affiliate of the LA Dodgers) games, and ads have been run in the Lewis Family Playhouse (performing arts center) playbill. The city also secured ad placement on digital display boards located on a major cross street and high-traffic area within the city and on the I-15 freeway.

The city has developed an aggressive social media campaign featuring links to the application. Three versions of Facebook ads have been developed, and announcements on Twitter have been sent out. The city has also worked with local attractions, such as Victoria Gardens, to run announcements about the application launch on their Facebook sites. (Victoria Gardens' Facebook site has more than 26,000 followers.)

The application makes use of a number of existing and diverse GIS data layers. For example, GIS data layers that contain information from the city's business license program have been used to create lookup functions for shopping and dining opportunities. Likewise, GIS data layers can help constituents find the location of Wi-Fi hot spots and charging stations for electric vehicles. Because the application uses GIS as its background, updates have been easy. For example, if a phone number for a department changes, the change is made in the city's GIS, and then pushed out to the application rather than made directly to the application. The city is currently working on testing a second version of the application that will feature a number of enhancements based on feedback received from citizens and city personnel. One of the new features will involve a push notification function that allows the city to send out emergency communications via the application in the event of flooding or a fire or some other disaster. Another new feature is a healthy-living link that will enable the user to look up trail locations in the city and plot out rest stops along the trails. The city will also introduce turn-by-turn directions to any shop, restaurant, or city amenity within the application. This newer version will also include a Construction Projects Alert (CPA) feature that will show all major construction projects and provide details about each project.

Development of the RC2GO application took nearly a year, which included securing the necessary hardware and licensing as well as application design. The popularity of RC2GO with citizens indicates that the city was successful in its goal of developing an application that is beneficial to everyone.

As Rancho Cucamonga Mayor L. Dennis Michael notes, "We first began utilizing GIS when I was fire chief to determine station location, routes of travel, analyze response time, and improve emergency response. Now, as mayor of Rancho Cucamonga, I have been able to see the evolution of GIS over time, and its use is enterprise-wide throughout our city. As a mayor, I want to know that all public funds received are being utilized with maximum impact. GIS allows our city manager and executive team to do just that, and I can't imagine how we functioned without it."

CASE STUDY >

By tapping into its GIS program to develop the RC2GO application, the City of Rancho Cucamonga has drawn new value from an existing resource and, in the process, developed a new city service that will provide value to constituents on a regular basis as well as provide greater accountability of how public dollars are being invested.

Opening up the liquor license process in the State of New York

Based on an interview with Joshua Carr, Deputy Commissioner, New York State Liquor Authority

Level of government: State
State/province : New York
Country: USA
Population: 19,378,104

In 2009, a major reorganization occurred in the executive management of the New York State Liquor Authority (SLA) following several audits by the New York State Attorney General's Office. The audits uncovered issues of mismanagement and attempts by outside parties to influence employees within the SLA. Among the most serious concerns, the Attorney General's Office found that applicants for liquor licenses had attempted to bribe license examiners and that the agency had virtually no internal controls for preventing fraud. The findings from these investigations established the need for new leadership at the SLA with a broad mandate for change. The need for greater transparency and accountability in operations was apparent.

The new team brought a consolidated management approach to working within three designated geographic zones within the state—Albany, New York, and Buffalo. For example, the team made a critical decision early on to centralize the intake function for accepting liquor license applications and engaged a bank to provide lockbox services for applications. Incoming applications and accompanying checks are no longer handled directly by SLA staff, but scanned and processed by the bank. The paperwork associated with applications goes from the bank directly to the SLA's Albany office, and from there the applications are distributed to all three zones. This change has helped tighten workload management and eliminated the potential for any impropriety.

Outsourcing these functions also permitted SLA examiners to spend more time focused on their core mission of reviewing applications, which includes determining the appropriateness and suitability of locations for establishments holding liquor licenses. The idea of building a GIS application arose in conjunction with discussions about how to make the application process more open, in addition to easing overall demands on the SLA's enforcement and licensing staff.

CASE STUDY > > > >

Completed liquor license applications provide a tremendous amount of data, but without access to other relevant data—proximity to other licenses and the location of places of worship, public schools, police district boundaries, and other points of interest—the value was limited. The launching of the SLA's new Liquor Authority Mapping Project (LAMP) enables the authority to capture the application data and use it to search, analyze, and visualize licensing data with respect to relevant geographic data. In addition, LAMP provides licensees, attorneys, applicants, community boards, and other interested parties easy and immediate access to a whole host of information that previously required filing a formal Freedom of Information Law (FOIL) request. The LAMP project is unique because license locations, proximity reporting, and historical violations are available for the first time to citizens of the state of New York in dynamic maps. Use of the GIS application has opened up access to government data while saving staff time and resources.

Figure 3.27 Opening welcome message for the LAMP GIS application. Courtesy of New York State Liquor Authority.

Additionally, one of the many analytic tools available through a GIS solution is the ability to establish buffer zones. Whether used for establishing an appropriate distance for development in a sensitive watershed or creating space between conflicting zoning uses in a community, a proximity analysis (aka buffering) helps identify places at risk of impact in a location. New York's Alcoholic Beverage Control (ABC) law has two key provisions with a geographic or spatial element that are ideally suited for using the buffering tool. The 200-foot rule prohibits the issuance of a full on-premises license or liquor store license for any establishment located within 200 feet of a school, church, synagogue, or other place of worship. The 500-foot rule contains certain restrictions on the approval of full on-premises liquor licenses if the location is within a 500-foot radius of three or more existing licenses.

Ordinarily, an application for an on-premises liquor license must be approved unless the SLA finds that there is good cause not to issue the license. However, with applications falling under the 500-foot rule, the presumption is reversed, and the SLA must grant the license only if it is in the public interest to do so. Consequently, it is vitally important for the SLA to determine whether an application falls under either rule. All on-premise license applicants must notify the community board (CB) or the municipality thirty days prior to applying to the SLA, allowing time for CBs and the municipality to provide the SLA with recommendations. Although these recommendations are not binding on the SLA, the SLA strongly weighs the opinions of CBs and local governments when deciding whether to issue a license.

CASE STUDY > > >

The law requires that the distance must be measured from the point of entry in one establishment to the point of entry of the next establishment, or from the school, church, synagogue, or other place of worship. The density of development in New York City in particular makes it important for the SLA to enforce these laws with a high degree of precision. Given the sheer volume of applications the SLA receives on an annual basis—nearly 70,000 applications statewide and 24,000 for New York City alone—SLA staff previously had limited methods of verifying whether these distance requirements were being met. The SLA routinely had to rely on the applicant to provide the distances, and at times the data provided on applications was inaccurate.

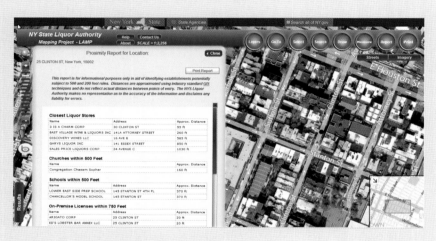

Figure 3.28 The LAMP application can be used to quickly determine the proximity of a proposed location for a license to other relevant geographic data, such as other licenses, churches, and schools. Courtesy of New York State Liquor Authority.

With the new GIS application, users can look up establishments with an active license or pending application in a particular area, locate schools and churches in proximity to licensed or potentially licensed premises, determine whether an application may be subject to the 500-foot rule, identify police precinct boundaries, and learn about an establishment's adjudicated disciplinary history. The program also offers the SLA the operational tools needed to examine applications and streamline the review process, while keeping location and status information transparent. Implementing the LAMP application has benefited SLA in three critical areas: enforcement, monitoring, and customer service.

On the enforcement front, LAMP enables SLA staff to quickly determine which license applications may need to be measured more closely. This has led to sharp reductions in the need for investigators to go into the field to physically measure distances, saving valuable staff time. From a monitoring standpoint, LAMP allows the SLA as well as members of the public to track compliance with ABC laws for establishments with existing liquor licenses. Disciplinary information on an establishment at a given location can easily be looked up and reviewed using the system. It is important to note that only adjudicated findings are available on the map; pending cases are not listed.

The ability to track and update relevant data regarding pending applications has also improved customer service. Prior to the implementation of LAMP, the ability to track an application for a

CASE STUDY > >

Figure 3.29 The application can be used to quickly determine the status of pending applications or the disciplinary history of existing licenses. Courtesy of New York State Liquor Authority.

license and to answer questions on its status was virtually impossible. LAMP allows licensing staff to tie relevant application status information to the applicant's address location record, allowing the applicant and the public to retrieve status information online, limiting the need to call the SLA for verification.

The SLA invested $75,000 in the development of LAMP. Although a formal ROI study has not been conducted, the authority has realized considerable benefits from the application. For example, the process of verifying the locations for applications has been reduced from a fifteen- to twenty-minute process to a one- to two-minute process. Another important by-product has been the economic development benefits of the new system. The liquor industry is very competitive, and liquor wholesalers have begun using the site to look up pending licenses and make calls on businesses in the process of applying for a liquor license. Although LAMP was not designed with this particular benefit in mind, it has definitely had a positive impact on the industry.

In subsequent phases of LAMP, the authority hopes to integrate social media functions into the GIS application. For example, citizens would be able to locate pending liquor license applications in their neighborhood on a map and comment on the suitability of the proposed location. The SLA also wants to create a richer data infrastructure in future phases. For example, the SLA is exploring development of a mobile application that would allow enforcement officers to look up the location of an establishment on smartphones or tablets while they are out in the field and review background information. The SLA anticipates that regulatory agencies involved with licensing and permitting in other states might be interested in adapting the LAMP application for their own uses.

Through the development and release of the LAMP application, the authority has learned about the limitations of its data. The number of records involved and the cleanliness of the data posed substantial challenges in preparing LAMP for release. For example, the addressing system in Queens, which has the largest area of New York City's five boroughs and is the second-largest in population, was a challenge. The Queens Borough began as a series of small towns, each with its own unique addressing system. As a result, a street address can have two sets of assigned numbers—for example, 104–04 Ditmars Boulevard.

CASE STUDY >

The LAMP application has transformed how the SLA uses information and enhanced the management of agency data. The SLA is much more tuned in to how it can effectively convey large amounts of geographic information to industry stakeholders as well as the greater public as a result. With its focus on providing greater transparency in its operations, the SLA has used GIS to take a leap forward in meeting these goals.

CASE STUDY •

The right tools for the job

Until a tool is invented, people often don't realize how much they needed it. New tools can increase productivity exponentially and make individuals wonder how they ever got along before the tool was invented. Such is the case with a multitude of GIS applications that have been developed and are being developed day in and day out. When the East Central Florida Regional Planning Council introduced the Central Florida GIS Initiative, the effort shortened the development and implementation time needed on a wide variety of projects in the region. In Carson, California, the number of serious traffic accidents led community leaders to use GIS to take a serious look at traffic patterns in the city and the settings where accidents were occurring in order to remediate problems. A mobile office initiative in the Province of Alberta allowed its Sustainable Resource Development (SRD) staff to have more field time rather than spending time in the office updating paperwork.

Responding to the needs for a regional GIS in central Florida

Claudia Paskauskas, MCSD, GISP, 6 Sigma Green Belt, PMP, GIS Manager, East Central Florida Regional Planning Council, Altamonte Springs, Florida

Level of government: Regional
State/province: Florida
Country: USA
Population: 3,172,380

The places where people live, work, and play are not defined by geographical boundaries. People cross such boundaries every day when they commute to work, shop for groceries, go to see a game, or need to use a public service such as a hospital. The reality is that development projects in one community routinely impact other communities in a region. The District 5 Region of the Florida Department of Transportation (FDOT) first recognized the need for a regional approach to GIS in 2001 and approached the East Central Florida Regional Planning Council about initiating a regional effort, known as the Central Florida GIS Initiative, which would provide available local GIS data for the

CASE STUDY > > > >

entire community. Since its creation, the CFGIS program has brought the central Florida GIS community together to promote education, networking, knowledge-base sharing, and development of data guidelines. The program functions as the central coordinating body to promote GIS data sharing in the region and maintains a data repository with interactive mapping functionality. It has also served as a catalyst for forming valuable partnerships between jurisdictions and government entities throughout central Florida.

Prior to the development of the CFGIS, there was little collaboration or data sharing occurring among jurisdictions and other government entities in the region. What data sharing did happen took place on a limited project-by-project basis, and the planning and implementation of regional projects occurred at a very slow pace. Participation in the CFGIS was informal and voluntary at first, but when FDOT joined the program as its major funding partner and began to offer its GIS data to the group, jurisdictions and other government entities began to follow suit. Although there was some friction initially, good communication skills combined with persistence on the part of CFGIS leaders helped educate stakeholders, and the value of collaboration soon became self-evident. The group collaborated to minimize duplication of efforts to search for, collect, and standardize data. As a result, the scope of work for several projects across the region shrank, saving valuable tax dollars. The CFGIS program is now used by thousands of people in central Florida every day, with its website averaging 3.7 hits per second. Most of the website demand is generated by shared interactive mapping tools, GIS data downloads, and information on GIS professional education opportunities.

One of the first projects undertaken by CFGIS was the development of a regional land-use classification system. All the jurisdictions have their own independent land-use classification systems, and as a result 1,700 or more definitions for different land uses existed across nine counties in the region. In order to better identify and plan for locating possible transportation corridors and other transportation projects, FDOT needed to have some type of standardized system that could recognize similar land uses across jurisdictional boundaries. CFGIS, working closely with 106 jurisdictions, created a crosswalk classification among the different systems that allowed each jurisdiction to maintain the integrity of its individual system while at the same time making better planning possible throughout the region. The project was fully endorsed by FDOT, and several jurisdictions now use the regional land classification in their planning processes.

The regional land-use classification effort was followed by a massive two-year regional visioning and planning effort, called How Shall We Grow?, that involved 750 elected officials from seven counties and ninety-three jurisdictions along with about 20,000 citizens and several partners in the region. The effort looked at emergency management, transportation, and growth management initiatives across the region. Of particular concern was the fact that land development in the region was outpacing population growth, with the population in the region expected to double from 3.5 million to 7.2 million by 2050. The effort created a shared vision for what the central Florida region should look like in 2050, resulting in a regional compact and policy framework that identifies specific policies suggested for implementation.

CFGIS was instrumental in developing a series of vision maps that showed what the impact of different urban designs would have on the region. Beginning with a map of what the central Florida region looked like in 2006, additional maps representing various hypothetical scenarios showed what

Figure 3.30 Urban growth in the east central Florida region has increased significantly every decade since 1950. Courtesy of East Central Florida Regional Planning Council.

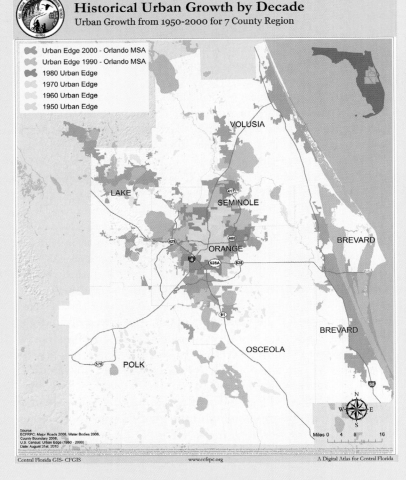

Historical Urban Growth by Decade
Urban Growth from 1950-2000 for 7 County Region

- Urban Edge 2000 - Orlando MSA
- Urban Edge 1990 - Orlando MSA
- 1980 Urban Edge
- 1970 Urban Edge
- 1960 Urban Edge
- 1950 Urban Edge

VOLUSIA

LAKE

SEMINOLE

ORANGE

BREVARD

BREVARD

OSCEOLA

POLK

Source:
ECFRPC: Major Roads 2008, Water Bodies 2006,
County Boundary 2008,
U.S. Census: Urban Edge (1950 - 2000)
Date: August 31st, 2010

Miles 0 4 8 16

Central Florida GIS- CFGIS   www.ecfrpc.org   A Digital Atlas for Central Florida

the region would look like in 2050 if (1) current development patterns remained in place and (2) a unified vision with supporting policies were adopted. CFGIS led the technical portion of the How Shall We Grow? project, helping in the data collection, offering technical expertise during the dozens of community workshops, collaborating in the fine-tuning of each proposed scenario, and creating scorecards that allowed participants to pick and choose how to best create the future desired by the central Florida region. The How Shall We Grow? project won several awards at the local, state, and national levels for its coordination, innovative approach, and best use of technology.

One regional project stemming from the How Shall We Grow? effort is the Central Florida 2060 Plan, also known as the Strategic Regional Policy Plan. This plan allowed the region to take a step closer to the development of the SunRail commuter line. The new transit project will substantially

CASE STUDY > >

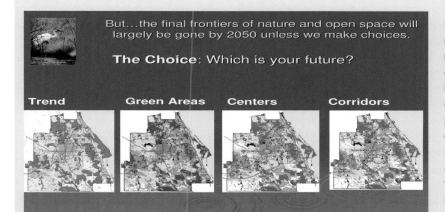

But...the final frontiers of nature and open space will largely be gone by 2050 unless we make choices.

The Choice: Which is your future?

Trend   Green Areas   Centers   Corridors

Figure 3.31 These maps show four possible scenarios for growth in the east central Florida region based on the adoption of different development policies. Courtesy of East Central Florida Regional Planning Council, myregion. org, Florida Department of Transportation, District 5, Sun Data.

change the transportation profile of the region, offering greater connectivity to move people around the region. Again, CFGIS has contributed to the project by developing maps to help determine where the planned sixteen station stops should be located and what kind of development should be encouraged to grow up around the stations. A grant from the US Department of Housing and Urban Development (HUD) is allowing for continued analysis of the impacts the commuter line will have on the region for six of the twelve SunRail stations.

Finally, the East Central Florida Regional Planning Council plays an important role in emergency management planning. CFGIS has recruited a number of emergency management entities to join a GIS collaboration focused on this pivotal topic. The goal is to create a one-stop resource shop and a data repository. The emergency management portal on the CFGIS website enables the emergency management community to easily exchange reports and data. As part of the emergency management efforts, the Regional Planning Council has promoted greater coordination and collaboration among counties in the region when refreshing their emergency management and evacuation plans.

The State of Florida has deemed that a single methodology—Statewide All Hazards and Hurricane Evacuation—will be used throughout Florida in order to ensure a coordinated response. The new methodology is heavily GIS oriented and requires great cross-jurisdictional collaboration for data sharing. Because the central Florida jurisdictions had already established working relationships as a result of the CFGIS program, they were able to significantly cut the amount of time needed for data collection and data sharing. From 2006 to 2011, all the east central Florida jurisdictions successfully refreshed their respective plans. The Statewide All Hazards and Hurricane Evacuation project methodology has since been widely recognized for excellence, winning several awards at the state and national levels.

CFGIS recently invited regional leaders and partners to examine how the initiative could continue to provide the right tools its members need. Through the compilation of a series of face-to-face interviews with key stakeholders, the program goals were revisited with the idea of better attending to the GIS community's needs. To that end, CFGIS developed an online survey for its membership, targeting policy makers and executive managers, to assess where the initiative was at that moment and to identify what steps were necessary to move toward the future. The focus of the survey was largely

CASE STUDY >

on understanding expectations and how CFGIS could best support the current GIS activities, business objectives, and requirements of its membership. Results from the survey were used to develop an action plan for moving forward. The action plan analyzed the program from conceptual, marketing, and operational standpoints. Since then, the CFGIS team has been implementing the action plan recommendations. Immediate recommendations led to a structural change in the program, culminating in the development of a new website, http://www.cfgis.org, which offers additional tools oriented to the decision making, citizen, and professional GIS community.

After more than ten years of existence, the CFGIS program continues to dynamically reexamine its goals. CFGIS is the result of some well-defined goals in its early stages as well as a lot of education and persistence by its champions. The initiative will continue to add value to the GIS community, decision makers, and partners by promoting education, collaboration, data sharing, and support to decision making in central Florida.

CASE STUDY •

Traffic safety: How GIS is improving the safety of streets in the city of Carson, California

Barry Waite, Director, Economic Development, City of Carson, California

Level of government: City
State/province: California
Country: USA
Population: 91,714

"We have a great opportunity to make a difference. Now that we know just where and what type of improvements we can do, we can be smart about investing to keep people safe. This is a great example of how Carson's use of GIS is making our community better."
Jim Dear, Mayor, City of Carson, California.

Like much of Southern California, Carson has a substantial commuter population with a considerable number of people driving into the city to work each day. About 60,000 people commute into Carson from surrounding communities for work. There are also approximately 14,000 students who attend nearby California State University-Dominguez Hills, and just south of the city are the Port of Los Angeles and the Port of Long Beach, which generate significant volumes of truck traffic through the city. The result is a heavily used road network with significant risks for collisions between vehicles and between vehicles and pedestrians.

CASE STUDY > > >

The costs of traffic accidents are manifold. First and foremost, there is the human suffering associated with injury and the grief in the event of a fatality. The true cost of a human life lost cannot be calculated. For accidents involving only property damage, the expenses can easily cost thousands of dollars for those involved. Add in the cost of traffic disruptions for drivers trying to make their way through the area, and the total expense further escalates. For commercial haulers, wait time in traffic delays can be painfully expensive.

With a goal of making its city streets as safe as possible and keeping traffic flowing smoothly, Carson community leaders used GIS technology to learn where and how collisions were occurring throughout the community. The city provided the resulting product to the University of California-Berkeley's Institute of Transportation Studies Technology Transfer Program for additional study and recommendations, which have resulted in a number of safety improvements to the city's highway and street system.

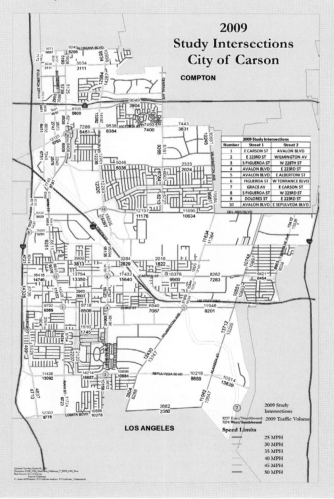

Figure 3.32 A map of traffic volumes helped the city identify intersections to study. Courtesy of City of Carson (California) Geographic Services.

GIS identifies study locations

For Carson council member Mike Gipson, traffic safety is particularly important. Several years ago, his son was killed by a hit-and-run driver. "For me, it's personal," Gipson explains. "Like every city, safety is our top priority. We owe it to our citizens to be proactive." His council colleagues agree. Council member Lula Davis-Holmes adds, "There is no limit to the value of a human life. If we can direct our resources to prevent an accident, then an ounce of prevention is worth a pound of cure. We need to be smart in how we spend our money to have the most impact."

In 2009, which is the most recent year for available data, Carson had 953 reported collisions. The vast majority of the accidents occurred at intersections. There were two fatalities, both alcohol related. There were 196 injury collisions, with 336 people injured. Pedestrians were involved in fifteen of the accidents. As with most communities, resources for improving intersections are limited. The city needed a way to focus its available resources where they would have the greatest impact.

The California Highway Patrol collects collision data through its Statewide Integrated Traffic Records System (SWITRS). Looking at the data tables can be overwhelming. The printed report for a single year can be inches thick. It is virtually impossible to identify clusters of collisions or recognize any patterns among the collisions in such a tabular format. Presentation of the information in this format

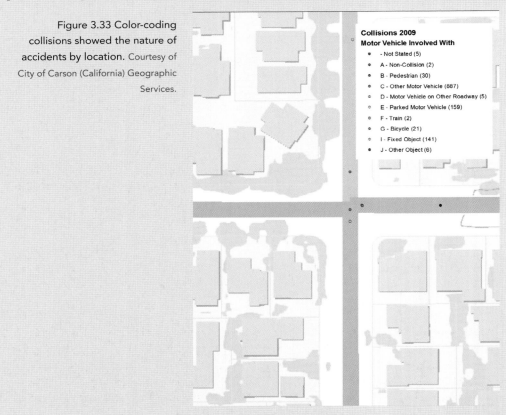

Figure 3.33 Color-coding collisions showed the nature of accidents by location. Courtesy of City of Carson (California) Geographic Services.

Collisions 2009
Motor Vehicle Involved With
-   - Not Stated (5)
-   A - Non-Collision (2)
-   B - Pedestrian (30)
-   C - Other Motor Vehicle (887)
-   D - Motor Vehicle on Other Roadway (5)
-   E - Parked Motor Vehicle (159)
-   F - Train (2)
-   G - Bicycle (21)
-   I - Fixed Object (141)
-   J - Other Object (6)

CASE STUDY >

to the public or the city council is useless. There is no good way to interpret the data and answer key questions. Are accidents associated with particular turns or a given time of day? Do they involve passenger vehicles or trucks? Were pedestrians injured? Where did fatalities occur and under what conditions?

GIS technology presents the data in a usable format. The city's Traffic Engineering Division worked with GIS staff to plot each SWITRS collision report to identify areas in need of further study. City staff culled through the data to make sure each point was as close as possible to the police report. The process took two days.

As the city's GIS administrator, Alex Rocco, describes it, "Once we had the data in a usable format, it was obvious that some intersections had more than their fair share of accidents. We picked the top ten problematic intersections. That gave the Traffic Engineering Division the clues they needed to focus on the right places and identify changes at each location to reduce collisions."

At that point, the Traffic Engineering Division started to develop solutions for the most problematic areas. There were immediate steps for each area, including:

- Monitoring school areas to identify locations with heavy pedestrian crossings at uncontrolled intersections. One result? The city installed new traffic signals with pedestrian countdown signs at two intersections.
- At another intersection, the city installed radar speed feedback signs and flashing school area warning signs.
- In cooperation with the Los Angeles County Sheriff's Department, particular intersections receive special patrols at hours when accidents have typically occurred.

Richard Garland has been the city's traffic engineer for fourteen years. He has seen the power of GIS grow as a tool for him. "GIS has evolved into an important data management tool for the Traffic Engineering Division. The technology provides the opportunity to clearly identify the high-collision locations throughout the city. We can formulate relationships between collision statistics and traffic volumes so that resources can more effectively be focused on problem locations."

The University of California-Berkeley's Institute of Transportation Studies Technology Transfer Program helps cities address safety hot spots. Funded by a grant from the California Office of Traffic Safety, the program can be a lifesaver. The institute describes its service as follows:

The primary objective of a traffic safety evaluation is to improve traffic safety in a city or county. Improved local enforcement and engineering practices and programs can reduce traffic collisions that cause injury, death, and property damage. To achieve these objectives, Tech Transfer provides free traffic safety evaluations, in which evaluators will review your city or county's traffic safety conditions, programs, and needs, and suggest new strategies to improve local traffic safety.

Based on the city's GIS analysis of collision sites throughout the community, the Traffic Engineering Division asked the institute to conduct an evaluation for Carson. The institute was surprised by the quality of information the city had already developed with GIS. It served as a springboard for focusing the evaluation and addressing key variables such as time of day or type of accident. Thanks to the work already completed by Carson's GIS team, the institute agreed to conduct the evaluation free of charge. Upon completion of the study, Carson leaders hoped to further reduce accidents in their community.

CASE STUDY •

The Mobile Office Initiative: Trailblazing changes in Alberta's resource management

Esri Canada

Level of government: Province
State/province: Alberta
Country: Canada
Population: 3,290,350

The province of Alberta is one of Canada's most vibrant economies. Despite the downturn in the global financial market, the province's economy grew by more than 3 percent in 2011 and represents nearly one-fifth of the country's Can$1.72 trillion gross domestic product. According to the Alberta Economic Development Authority, energy remains the key economic driver, supported by other sectors, such as forestry, agriculture, and agri-foods.

Striking a balance between resource extraction and preserving the earth's finite resource base has become a priority for most jurisdictions. Alberta Sustainable Resource Development (SRD) is the government branch that strives to manage these competing interests across the province. The agency consists of three divisions: forests, fish, and wildlife. SRD is focused on finding the right balance between economic development by industry and other interests, including the health of watersheds, grazing opportunities, prosperous fish and wildlife populations, recreation availability, and the maintenance of some land for its intrinsic value.

Alberta's growing economy created a significant increase in the number of requests for development and resource extraction submitted to SRD. The result was increased workload for SRD staff—which led to a need for greater efficiencies in day-to-day work. Upon further analysis, SRD realized the solution was for staff to spend more time in the field; however, staff members still had to be able to access their office work. The solution was to equip staff with the tools they needed to have remote access to real-time data. This led to the Mobile Office Initiative.

Supporting the Lands and Range Division

The Lands and Range Division of SRD is responsible for land-use planning and management in the province. It conducts field inspections to determine the best places for various types of land use, including industrial development, oil and gas exploration, sand and gravel harvesting, livestock grazing, and public recreational use. Alberta currently has Can$120 billion worth of oil sands projects at various stages of development, and it is expected that this industry will continue to fuel the province's economic growth.

Previously, staff would spend time conducting research and planning for inspections. They looked up existing information about the land using paper archives and enterprise GIS and printed area maps using their desktop computers. To ensure that they had all the information needed to conduct the

CASE STUDY > > >

inspection, they brought the relevant paper files with them to the site. With each staff conducting up to eight inspections per day, and with the need to do more, it became impossible to collect the required information in a timely manner.

After completing their field work, staff would return to the office to manually update the data and respond to clients regarding the inspections by phone or e-mail. This resulted in field staff spending about two days a week in the office doing paperwork, rather than being in the field.

Going mobile

In 2007, some areas within SRD launched the Mobile Office Initiative. They deployed ruggedized notebooks installed with ArcPad, which enabled the Lands Division staff to collect and update field data automatically to their enterprise GIS. They also used ArcGIS for Desktop to edit and analyze geographic information and maps. The notebooks were equipped with wireless connectivity using NetMotion Wireless, secure virtual private network (VPN) access, Bluetooth capability, and built-in GPS functionality. With the click of a button, staff in the field were able to retrieve more than 200 sets of data.

Figure 3.34 The Mobile Office Initiative allows staff to be in the field more and at their desks less. Courtesy of Esri Canada.

SRD began the pilot project with only five notebooks, but field staff began to realize efficiencies associated with retrieving, updating, and analyzing information almost immediately. It allowed them to increase the quality and quantity of decisions, such as where to drill oil wells, build utility corridors,

CASE STUDY > >

and harvest forests. They were able to provide immediate feedback to clients, enhancing customer service. As a result, more ruggedized laptops were deployed to more than 300 SRD staff within eighteen months.

"Industry used to have better technology and data than government," says Evert Smith, a land management specialist with SRD. "With our Mobile Office Initiative, we've significantly improved the province's capability to provide quick and reliable information that companies need to secure business opportunities while at the same time preserving our natural resources."

The Mobile Office Initiative's interconnectedness has eliminated the time lag between actual data collection and system updating, increasing the accuracy and number of inspection reports completed. According to Smith, with staff spending more time in the field, productivity has increased by approximately 30 percent.

Supporting the Forestry Division

The Mobile Office Initiative has allowed SRD to become more agile in delivering services. This is especially critical to wildfire management. Previously, the SRD's Forests Division needed numerous staff to conduct area mapping in support of wildfire response activities. Now, fire staff can go immediately to the site without taking any paper files or maps. Through their mobile solution, they can analyze the area using online maps to calculate the length of hose needed and create a perimeter guard to effectively contain the fire.

Communication between the field and the office has significantly improved. Fire personnel previously had to fly out to assess the wildfires and relay information by radio so that senior staff in the office could make decisions. Now, they can send aerial images of the fires so that the appropriate resources can be promptly dispatched to the site.

The amplified GPS functionality also enhances staff safety. When rangers get stuck in rough terrain, they can take a snapshot of their location and e-mail it to the dispatch center so they can receive assistance.

Supporting law enforcement

The mobile solution also helps enforce laws against illegal hunting and angling. With direct access to their corporate databases, officers from the Fish and Wildlife Division can easily verify hunting and fishing licenses on the spot. They can pull up information on past infractions and warnings, identify repeat offenders, and take the necessary corrective action. They can also enter occurrence information remotely, as well as receive and act on e-mail notifications about calls from the public regarding potential offenders.

"GIS is an important component of the mobile office. It keeps our field and office operations connected and enables us to maintain an up-to-date source of information. The efficiencies gained by using the solution allow the province and industry to save thousands of dollars in field surveys. In addition to better client satisfaction, it also increases job satisfaction for our staff because they're now able to do work they used to do at their desks right in the field, where they should be," remarks Smith.

CASE STUDY >

Figure 3.35 Field staff have ready access to maps and other resources needed for their jobs through the Mobile Office Initiative. Courtesy of Esri Canada.

Due to the program's success, SRD received the Premier's Award of Excellence in 2009 for superior client service and business excellence. In 2011, it received a technology leadership award from the Alberta Science and Technology Leadership Foundation.

The agency plans to expand the program to support other business areas across the province. It is also looking to deploy the solution on other mobile devices, such as tablet computers. To further enhance the system, it plans to add more datasets, including remotely sensed imagery; support live video streaming; and integrate the system with other provincial information systems.

"GIS is an important component of the mobile office. It keeps our field and office operations connected and enables us to maintain an up-to-date source of information. The efficiencies gained by using the solution allow the province and industry to save thousands of dollars in field surveys. In addition to better client satisfaction, it also increases job satisfaction for our staff because they're now able to do work they used to do at their desks right in the field, where they should be."

Evert Smith, Land Management Specialist, Alberta SRD

CASE STUDY •

GIS is changing

Just as the computer industry has changed (and continues to change) over the years, GIS technology has followed suit. And as the technology has changed and advanced, so has the structure of how GIS programs are managed and maintained. Organizationally, GIS technology has moved from largely being a support service offered to an entire organization to having an overall coordinating function for a largely self-service application that can be operated by many users. As a result, GIS professionals spend less time building data layers and more time focused on analysis and collaboration. In addition to coordinating GIS activities within an organization, GIS professionals educate and advise users on the technology rather than producing deliverables for others. The evolution of GIS programs in a midsize city (Cape Girardeau, Missouri), a rural county (Newton County, Georgia), and a regional GIS alliance (eCityGov Alliance in Washington) demonstrate how governments have adapted to this changing technology.

Working toward greater GIS access in Cape Girardeau, Missouri

Anamika Anand, GIS Coordinator, City of Cape Girardeau

Level of government: City
State/province: Missouri
Country: USA
Population: 37,941

Cape Girardeau serves as a regional hub in southeast Missouri. As home to a university and two major medical complexes, the small city's population swells to nearly 100,000 during the workday. As a result, the city has experienced considerable growth in the past few decades and has had to work through many annexation decisions, zoning challenges, and permitting issues. The city began its GIS program in the mid-1980s as part of an update to its comprehensive plan. What began as a need for a map showing elevation levels throughout the city grew into a comprehensive online GIS program that produces maps for elected officials, citizens, real estate professionals and developers, and a host of other stakeholders, including city employees. Over the course of fifteen years, the city built a very well-developed GIS database. By 2010, city leaders determined that they wanted to make better use of the resource. At the same time, service departments were asking for greater access to GIS software and data.

The long-term vision for GIS in Cape Girardeau is to make the technology available to everyone within the organization as well as improve city–citizen interactions via cloud-based GIS technology.

CASE STUDY > >

Cape Girardeau leaders made the decision to upgrade and move the city's GIS program to an enterprise "cloud-based" system. Cloud-based systems make an application available on the Internet rather than requiring software and hardware be purchased and stored on-site. A cloud-based system made sense given the city's small GIS support team of one full-time person and a second part-time person. An in-house system would have required hiring more IT support staff for maintenance, whereas a cloud-based system provides that support as part of the vendor's contract with the client. The increased availability and affordability of laptop computers and smartphones also makes it easier for work crews to use the GIS system in the field. Ultimately though, the investment decision came about as the result of the right person in a decision-making position who had a vision of GIS and what the technology could do to increase staff efficiency and productivity.

The new system increases staff access to the GIS database. As long as Internet access is available, a city employee can work with the GIS database from nearly anywhere outside the office. Not even a laptop computer is needed. New smartphone applications allow users to link to the database and make modifications in the field, enabling the city to provide up-to-the-minute data to the public. The long-term vision for GIS in Cape Girardeau is to make the technology available to everyone within the organization as well as improve city–citizen interactions via cloud-based GIS technology. Cape Girardeau will use the software to strengthen and support this fast-growing community by educating city employees on how GIS works and how to apply the program to their particular field.

Anamika Anand, GIS coordinator for the city, explains, "Our model is to provide GIS for everyone. Because we have a well-developed GIS database—it has fifteen years of input into the GIS program—we've established a lot of GIS information that we want to share with departments to make work more efficient and a little easier for them. Right now, we have a GPS unit for about five people who work out in the field. Once the cloud is installed and good to go, I will be doing a lot of training."

Figure 3.36 The city's training lab is critical for expanding Cape Girardeau's GIS program. Courtesy of City of Cape Girardeau, Missouri.

CASE STUDY >

Cape Girardeau's GIS program operates as a centralized service for the city, but with such a small GIS support team the program is working to establish GIS experts in each department to expand its access. The departmental GIS experts essentially wear two hats, doing their regular jobs and serving as in-house liaisons with GIS responsibilities included as part of their job description. These liaisons work with the GIS program staff to develop appropriate applications for their respective departments.

The GIS team sees that moving to a cloud-based GIS application will open new opportunities for data verification and collection. For departments with field crews, such as Public Works and Water, GPS units will be provided for inventorying the utility assets throughout the community. When field crews go out to do repairs, they gather GPS coordinates that can be used to update the city's GIS datasets with more accurate information. This enables the city to better track, for example, when pipe diameters or materials change.

Currently, approximately 75 percent of the city departments are using GIS.

The following table shows the planned rollout of mobile GIS for the city. Currently, approximately 75 percent of city departments are using GIS. City employees are excited about the access to GIS data, but the need to provide continuing training has proved to be a challenge for the city's small GIS department.

Table 3.4 Planned rollout of mobile GIS

Phase 1	• Public Works • Water
Phase 2	• Police • Fire
Phase 3	• Customer Service • Inspections

The intention is to get GPS units into city cars and connected to laptops so that the GIS address database can be updated and accessed by employees in the field.

The new information is used primarily for asset management purposes, but the GIS team has begun doing more modeling work. For example, water and storm water modeling can help better manage future growth and development. Modeling enables the city to better determine what size pipes should be used to support a new subdivision or determine the best height for a new water tank.

Having a well-developed GIS program has realized significant savings for the city, particularly when working with consultants, who charged less to develop needed engineering models based on the easy availability of needed data. Having the models available has proved to be particularly useful for elected officials in helping them determine what level of investment is needed in public infrastructure.

CASE STUDY •

Information is key in Newton County, Georgia

Kathy Morgan, Chair, County Commission; Lynn Parham, GIS Manager; and Ernie Smith, GIS Coordinator, Newton County, Georgia

Level of government: County
State/province: Georgia
Country: USA
Population: 99,958

In 1997, the GIS program in Newton County began with a handshake, an understanding, and one staff person working in the Tax Assessors' Office. Three partners—Newton County, the City of Covington, and the Newton Water Authority—agreed to share expenses to start the program following a mandate from the Georgia Environmental Protection Division to document the city's sewer and storm water infrastructure. From this informal beginning, the program has grown to nine full-time employees and nearly thirty users of mapping applications as of 2011. Along the way, the handshake and understanding turned into a letter of agreement in 2006 and then a memorandum of understanding (MOU) in 2008. And for this small rural county, GIS and the information it produces have become key to how business is done.

Kathy Morgan, chair of the Newton County Commission, says that she uses the county's GIS on nearly a daily basis for her work. "One thing that happens is that if you really dig in and use GIS, it becomes part of your day-to-day business model, and the more you want to use it. You see how it can advance your community. Even if you're a small rural county or a county with limited funds, GIS is actually a cost saver. It will help you make your decisions on a daily basis," she says.

"Information is key. The time savings alone makes it worth the investment."

Kathy Morgan, Chair, Newton County Commission

Morgan pointed out that Newton County has always been a community that works together. The MOU simply documented the practices that were already taking place among the three main partners in the GIS program. However, because the program had grown so significantly, the MOU helped define how the need for making decisions on staffing, facilities, data structure, protocols, and best practices would be guided in the future. The need for better coordination and collaboration also led to hiring Lynn Parham as the GIS manager for the enterprise. Parham works with stakeholders in the three organizations and serves as a neutral party who can manage all the competing priorities. Her position serves as a clearinghouse for all map and project requests, as well as a connection between

CASE STUDY > > >

departments, staff, and the public. Although she is a county employee, her salary is paid by both the county and the city. She also works with elected officials following a protocol that requires requests to go through the mayor and city manager, the county commissioner and county manager, and the director of the Newton County Water and Sewer Authority.

Ernie Smith, the county's GIS coordinator, inherited the program in 2000 when a coworker who had been running the program left to take another position. "I could barely spell GIS and didn't really know anything about the program at all," says Smith. Following his attendance at a training seminar in Charlotte, however, Smith reports that "I had the 'Oh! Aha!' moment." As his own interest in GIS developed, he took advantage of every opportunity to showcase what the technology could do for elected officials and department heads. "Initially we had to approach department heads about helping them. Now they come to us. They think more in GIS terms, and they see Newton County more clearly," Smith says.

"The cost of developing a GIS program has changed dramatically since I first took over," says Smith. "In 1999, the GIS program was the single largest capital expenditure outside of the county's public works capital improvement plan. But that's not the case at all these days, and the value of what we get out of the program is enormous. Not too many months ago, our county manager asked for a document and had an analytic response within the hour. His comment was, 'This would have taken days if we didn't have GIS. I honestly don't know how we did it before.'"

Two departments in particular—the District Attorney's Office and the City of Covington's finance coordinator—have become strong advocates for the GIS program. The District Attorney's Office has used GIS to win several murder and robbery cases. In one particular instance, the district attorney was able to demonstrate that the defendant was not at the locations he claimed to be by using GIS maps to show where he was when he made cell phone calls throughout the night. The financial coordinator routinely uses GIS to prepare the problem analysis component of proposals. Additionally, the Newton County Board of Commissioners routinely uses maps, analyses, and data during its monthly board meetings to assist with important decision making. For example, the Tax Assessors' Office has been

Figure 3.37 One of the most frequently used applications in Newton County is the county's sex offender application, which allows citizens to go online to determine the location of sites that are prohibited to sex offenders. Courtesy of Newton County (Georgia) GIS.

CASE STUDY > >

providing updates and using GIS to show foreclosure trends in the county. "You'll find that you get to a place with GIS where your work is seen as producing more value than what it costs," explains Parham.

Another example of this kind of ROI occurred in 2009 when unprecedented flooding took place in the county. Staff from FEMA came to meetings with county officials with stacks of paper maps that were ten years old. The county pulled up its own GIS floodplain maps on a projector; the county's maps were accurate to within two feet of the floodplain model. FEMA staff quickly requested access to the Newton County maps, which greatly aided coordination of the disaster response and recovery efforts throughout the community.

The GIS program has enabled the county to have a high degree of confidence in the accuracy of its maps. One result of that confidence, Morgan says, is that Newton County has saved tens of thousands of consulting dollars by requiring all outside contractors to use county maps rather than producing their own

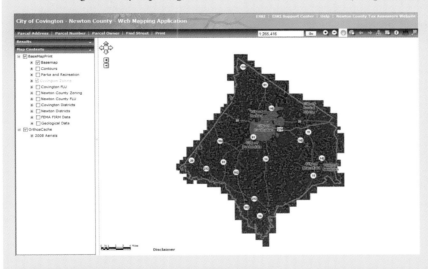

Figure 3.38 Accessing Newton County's web-mapping application.
Courtesy of Newton County (Georgia) GIS.

CASE STUDY >

for projects. She estimates that the county has saved anywhere from 20 to 50 percent in consulting fees on projects. The time savings from having information immediately available is also significant, says Morgan.

Morgan routinely uses the GIS program to pinpoint the location of property owners, property lines, and elevations. She also reviews it for engineering plans and planning and zoning for facilities. When department directors come to meet with her, her first two questions are: "Have you been to GIS?" and "Do you have a map?" She felt the need for GIS technology so strongly that she brought the program into the county's new Department for Development Services when she took office in 2009 in order to integrate GIS more tightly with the county's planning and zoning processes. Although the program has a new organizational home, it continues to provide support and service to the county, the City of Covington, and the water authority.

The GIS program also provided critical support during development of the county's 2050 development plan. The long-term plan is intended to guide the development of the county through the next forty years, during which time the county anticipates growing by 400 percent. Every decision regarding the plan was based on statistical and geographic analysis, with the GIS team preparing maps covering everything from critical environmental issues to analysis for the location of fire stations, libraries, and schools to the impact of development on existing infrastructure. For the first time in the county's history, GIS provided the backbone structure for the plan. The commissioners have also used GIS data to develop community overlay districts to provide greater guidance on how development should occur in specially designated areas of the county.

GIS in Newton County did not happen overnight, but over time it has changed the way the county does business. Smith sums up the change by saying, "Find a way to do it. You must do it. The biggest mistake you can make is not having GIS services; the only thing you can't recover from is not having GIS."

CASE STUDY •

The evolution of a regional GIS program: eCityGov Alliance, Washington

John Backman, Executive Director, eCityGov Alliance; and Emily Arteche, Senior Planner, City of Sammamish, Washington, and Chair, NWMaps.net Business Committee

Level of government: Regional
State/province: Washington
Country: USA
Population: 1,524,111

Starting in 2002, the eCityGov Alliance, an interlocal agency, formed as a regional collaboration of local governments in the Puget Sound region of the State of Washington. The alliance is a unique

CASE STUDY > > >

e-government initiative with a mission to provide shared-service web portals for local government agencies. The group has grown from nine local government members to forty-six member agencies with seven shared-service web portals. Although GIS itself is not the primary focus of the group's web portals, several of the web portals incorporate regional GIS services and data.

The eCityGov Alliance launched its first GIS-based service, NWMaps.net, in 2004, and the group has learned many lessons since then about working collectively to implement and support a regional GIS portal. The first iteration of NWMaps.net focused on leveraging existing GIS datasets to create a portal that constituents could use to view GIS spatial data and access property information. Due to technical and staff capacity limitations at the time, NWMaps.net provided the GIS data and interface on a city-by-city basis rather than a region-wide map. Despite the limitations, NWMaps.net offered a rich set of GIS and property data available through a single, easy-to-use site. Member cities benefited in that the shared service provided a very cost-effective solution to providing online GIS services.

By 2008, the NWMaps.net business and technical committees had begun planning and budgeting for a major redesign of the portal. The committee members, representing twelve cities, were faced with the rather difficult task of articulating a new vision for the portal and turning that vision into reality. Getting organized was difficult. The group had to decide who was going to do what and what elements were needed to create a good product. The Business Committee established the overall direction of the redesign including defining the mission, goals, objectives, and identification of customer needs.

The Technical Committee, made up of GIS staff from the participating cities, included GIS analysts, GIS developers, and GIS coordinators/administrators. This group did much of the

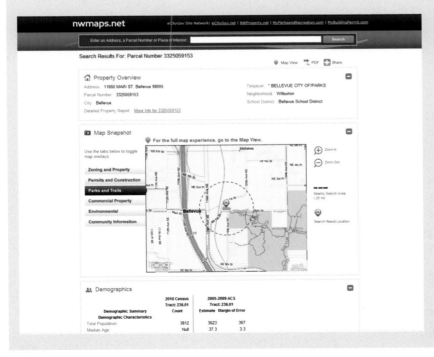

Figure 3.39 NWMaps.net has been redesigned to add new value for users in the region. Courtesy of John Backman, executive director, eCityGov Alliance, and Emily Arteche, senior planner, City of Sammamish, chair of NWmaps.net Business Team.

CASE STUDY > >

heavy lifting by defining the scope of work, including design requirements and site function-alities, gathering and standardizing spatial datasets, refining regional data schemes; uploading and aggregating individual cities' datasets, and generally supporting the project development and implementation.

Through this process, the two committees began to come together on a vision for the new site design. The vision was to create a one-stop GIS information portal built on a mapping platform to allow users to look for and retrieve the information in a more intuitive manner. Xiaoning Jiang, GIS administrator, City of Kirkland, and co-chair of the Technical Committee, explained that the com-mittees envisioned a gateway information portal that focused more on the information citizens might be seeking rather than a more complex GIS-centric service.

Using a use case methodology, the Alliance project manager led the committees through a series of meetings to collect and refine user stories that, in turn, were used to define the scope of work for the project. Ultimately the group documented fifty-three user stories for use in its RFP and development process. From the user stories, the business committee developed six themes. Each of the themes had a number of associated spatial layers and datasets intended to address specific sets of user stories. The selected themes are highlighted in the screen capture.

Figure 3.40 Themes of the eCityGov Alliance web portal. Courtesy of John Backman, executive director, eCityGov Alliance.

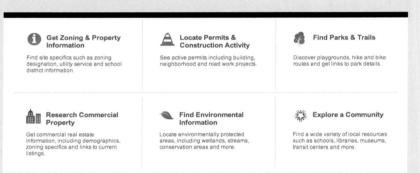

The intent was to make it easy for average citizens to locate the information they need. For example, a homeowner seeking information about his or her property can quickly retrieve a variety of govern-ment data associated with the parcel. The homeowner doesn't care that the city provides the zoning, comprehensive plan, and neighborhood data or that the tax assessment information comes from the county. The integration of the needed datasets occurs behind the scenes.

The system goes beyond reporting on zoning, permits, and other traditional uses of GIS technol-ogy. "It provides a lot more information than our first version," says Emily Arteche, a senior planner with the City of Sammamish, Washington, and chair of the NWMaps.net Business Committee. Residents and business owners can use the system to determine where bus stops are located in the community or determine what permitted development is underway or scheduled in the community or in the neighborhood. The new technology enables data, such as active building permits, to be dis-played on a map. As a result, citizens can quickly see all the activity in an area as opposed to just seeing a public notice posted on-site or mailed to their home.

CASE STUDY >

In addition to introducing themes to help the user navigate the portal, the committees made use of web-based technology to design a system that will provide seamless site navigation by allowing the user to navigate and search the entire region rather than limiting the user to only one city at a time. The new technology also allows GIS staff in each of the different cities to manage and maintain their own spatial layers and datasets.

Another feature that has been introduced with the new version of NWMaps.net is live integration of data provided by other websites and agencies. Data includes:

- Available commercial property from NWProperty.net and the Commercial Brokers Association
- Parks from MyParksandRecreation.com
- Active building permits from MyBuildingPermit.com
- Tax assessments from the King and Snohomish County Assessors
- Demographics from a commercial service

Not only does the additional data enrich NWMaps.net, but because the data is retrieved through live interfaces and hyperlinks, it is always up to date, and no additional data maintenance is required.

Staff members leverage existing datasets to build GIS layers and data themes whenever possible, but they have also learned about the absolute importance of establishing data standards and the need to have tight control over data used in the system. Creating the system has been one "giant integration," according to John Backman, executive director for the eCityGov Alliance.

The NWMaps.net collaboration spun off another successful regional collaboration. One of the newest data layers is the result of the group successfully coordinating its first regional orthophotography flight in 2009. (Such flights provide accurate mapping details that simple aerial photography does not. An orthophotograph corrects and adjusts for contours in the earth's surface. As a result, the scale is uniform and doesn't reflect any distortions due to the curvature of the earth.) Again, the collaborative effort paid off with the participating cities recognizing savings of 20 percent or more over the cost of individual RFPs for orthophotography flights. An even larger regional flight was planned in 2012.

The participating cities in the alliance include Shoreline, Kenmore, Bothell, Woodinville, Kirkland, Bellevue, Mercer Island, Renton, Tukwila, Issaquah, Sammamish, and Snoqualmie. The cities range in size from Snoqualmie (population 9,850) to Bellevue (population 122,900). Because the alliance uses a shared-service funding model, it sets rates in proportion to the size of the city, which makes the services affordable for even the smallest cities. For larger cities, the alliance shared-service model saves cities between 40 and 60 percent over the cost of providing the service alone. "It would be impossible for smaller cities to have and maintain a system of NWMaps' caliber on their own. The alliance shared-service model treats all communities equally, so it bridges what would otherwise be a digital divide between large and small cities," notes Backman.

Alliance members advise other jurisdictions interested in pursuing a regional collaboration to make the establishment of formal governance and funding structure a top priority. Informal collaboration and funding arrangements could quickly disintegrate in the face of disagreements or funding issues. The eCityGov Alliance was formed under the Washington State Interlocal Cooperation Act, which allows municipal corporations to form independent interlocal agencies. Under the act, one of the member cities may serve as the host for the interlocal agency. In the case of the alliance, the City of Bellevue serves as the information technology host and fiscal agent for the group. The alliance, through its member fees, pays the city for the full cost of the hosting services. The alliance is governed by an executive board made up of the chief executive officer (city manager, city administrator, or mayor) of the ten interlocal partner member cities.[5] Other alliance members may join individual services as subscriber members.

Additional information on NWMaps.net and the eCityGov Alliance is available at `http://www.eCityGov.net`.

Three-dimensional GIS

Three-dimensional (3D) GIS is an extraordinarily powerful tool that helps government leaders better understand the context of their decisions on a given location. Traditional maps show *where* a decision will have an impact. Three-dimensional GIS also demonstrates *how* a decision will have an impact. This new technology is especially useful for contemplating the impact of a new development on the existing environment. Indeed, as the following Fairfax County, Virginia, case study illustrates, one of the most popular uses for 3D GIS is for planning and development purposes.

Designing the future with Virtual Fairfax

Thomas Conry, GIS Manager, Fairfax County, Virginia

Level of government: County
State/province: Virginia
Country: USA
Population: 1,037,605

In 2010, Fairfax County introduced a new web-based mapping and 3D visualization tool, Virtual Fairfax (VF), for use by the general public, particularly individuals who are interested in or impacted by development in the region. The county is subject to intense development pressures as a result of its proximity to Washington, DC, and the phenomenal growth the entire region has experienced over the last three decades. (Fairfax County's population has increased 81 percent in the past thirty years.) VF can easily be used by anyone with Internet access. Data layers, such as address points, parcels, and metro routes and station locations, can be added with the click of a button.

Having the processes and tools required to better visualize development impacts, build consensus for ideas, and minimize contention provides significant benefits. The Land Use Information Accessibility Advisory Group, appointed by the elected Fairfax County Board of Supervisors, anticipated the need for the 3D information and display tools early on. The members of the advisory group

CASE STUDY > >

Figure 3.41 Reston, Virginia, looking northwest. Parcel outlines and address points are turned on. Links to other property information databases are shown.
Courtesy of Fairfax County, Virginia.

CASE STUDY >

were involved in county land development issues and identified a series of guiding principles and recommendations, which were adopted by the county supervisors, to improve understanding of impact and citizen involvement in the land planning and development process. VF specifically addresses several of their principles and recommendations.

VF enables users to fluidly navigate the county and surrounding jurisdictions, view buildings in key county areas in 3D, determine terrain and building elevations, and evaluate the shadow impact of buildings. Nearly 50 percent of all existing commercial space in Fairfax County is currently modeled in VF. Additionally, users can add their own 3D building models to the Fairfax landscape to view their impact, print maps/views, create links to or snapshots of a specific location that can be e-mailed, and turn on parcel outlines and road information. VF contains direct links to key county land information systems containing assessment information, nearby zoning, and building activity, as well as school districts, elected officials, parks, and calls for police service.

Released in June 2010, the application averages more than 350 sessions per workday, with peaks of close to 1,000. Its visualizations are being used in county reports, and discussions are underway with county agencies to enable viewing of proposed development in Tysons Corner, an important Fairfax County business district. Traditional two-dimensional (2D) applications do not give an accurate representation of what the resulting 3D environment will look like. VF provides that key element in an interactive tool.

Figure 3.42 Tyson's Corner, Virginia, looking southeast at 9 a.m. March 6, 2011. Intensity Development Zones around the stations for the new Metro line are illustrated. Note shadows cast by buildings. Courtesy of Fairfax County, Virginia.

Endnotes

1 All ISFs in King County are expected to develop rates that are "fair, equitable, and directly relate to the type and volume of services provided."

2 "Matrixed staff" are KCGIS Center employees who are assigned to work directly and exclusively for end-user agencies for a defined time period. For KCGIS, staff provides the functional and professional supervision while the end-user departments make work assignments and manage assigned projects.

3 Rebecca Somers, "Developing GIS Management Strategies for an Organization." *Journal of Housing Research* 9, no. 1 (1988): 157–78.

4 Gartner Inc. Media Release, "Top Predictions for IT Organizations and Users for 2011 and Beyond." http://www.gartner.com/newsroom/id/1480514.

5 The Alliance Partner member cities are Kenmore, Bothell, Woodinville, Kirkland, Bellevue, Mercer Island, Renton, Issaquah, Sammamish, and Snoqualmie.

Part 4. Building a strong GIS program

Takeaways:
- GIS technology represents a long-term commitment to change how a government does business.
- A strong GIS program will result in the development of a wealth of new applications for nearly every government department and agency.
- The ROI of GIS technology will only grow over time.

Unlike many other software applications, which can simply be installed on a computer and put to use, implementing a GIS application requires government agencies and departments to approach the technology as a program. Establishing a GIS program is not just a matter of investing in the necessary equipment and software; it also requires the organization to make a long-term commitment to change how it does business. It represents a pledge to use data to guide decision making and improve the efficiency of government operations. It makes the business of government more accountable and transparent, and thus encourages greater trust from citizens. Elected officials should understand that in championing a GIS program they will change the way government does business.

To achieve the greatest value possible with GIS technology, organizations must develop a vision of what they want this new program to do. They need to determine who will be involved in its implementation and in what role(s). They need to decide how the new program will be managed and establish standards for developing products with it. Building a strong GIS program requires collaboration and coordination, both internally among users of the program and externally with numerous producers of GIS data.

The real worth of a strong GIS program is that it will become more valuable over the years as new data layers are built and added to the system. These data layers enable the development of highly customized applications that respond to the specific needs and requirements of the users. GIS technology has been used to develop thousands of applications for nearly every program and service offered by government. As a result, the ROI of GIS technology will only grow over time.

Developing a vision

The first step in developing a vision of what GIS technology can do for a government is to see live demonstrations of what can be done with the technology and learn from others how they are using it. Time and again, GIS professionals report that once people have seen for themselves what GIS technology can do and the questions it can help answer, the proverbial light bulbs turn on and people start coming up with their own ideas of how they can use the technology.

From there, developing a vision is a matter of harnessing people's energy and assessing what the government's needs are. In Boone County, Missouri, a GIS visioning workshop brought area stakeholders together to identify needs and develop a consensus of what priorities should be undertaken.

GIS visioning workshop and strategic plan in Boone County, Missouri

Karen Miller, County Commissioner; and Jason Warzinik, GISP, GIS Manager, Boone County, Missouri

Level of government: County
State/province: Missouri
Country: USA
Population: 162,642

> **"By sitting down and going through the process to get everybody's buy-in and feedback, you know you're headed in the right direction for everybody."**
> Jason Warzinik, GIS Manager,
> Boone County

A strong GIS program does not simply happen on its own. It requires discussion and planning about the current needs and future direction desired by the government entities running the program. Creative thinking early on about potential uses for the technology will result in cost savings and increased efficiencies.

GIS visioning workshop

In 2009, members of the Boone County GIS Consortium opted to hold a GIS visioning workshop. The consortium, which was formed in 1993 to conduct a needs assessment for GIS, consists of Boone County, the City of Columbia, and the rural electric cooperative. The decision to conduct a needs assessment was sparked by the county assessor's proposal to convert the county's parcel maps into digital form. A needs assessment study provided information on potential costs and proposed a governance structure for a regional GIS consortium.

Boone County serves as the main coordinating body for the consortium and provides staff support for the group. The work of the consortium is overseen by two committees: a policy committee and

CASE STUDY > > >

a technical committee. Both committees include representatives from all the consortium members. The policy committee is composed of directors and elected officials who determine the consortium's agenda and can commit resources for its work. The technical committee includes the analysts and programmers who work with the technology. Generally, the technical committee brings forward its recommendations for ideas and projects to the policy committee for approval and authorization to proceed.

Members of the consortium have interagency cooperative agreements that are signed off by the county commission, city council, or board of trustees. Funding for the consortium's work comes from allocations set aside from members. The consortium's initial goal was to fund the assessor's parcel map conversion, which was completed in 2003. In early 2004, the county started putting GIS maps on the Internet through the assessor's website.

Following the completion of the assessor map conversion, much of the consortium's work involved sharing datasets. Proponents of the workshop suggested that more could be done. In addition to bringing current partners in the consortium together, invitations were extended to other vested stakeholders, including the university, the engineering community, the Police Department, the Fire Department, and other users of the GIS, such as the Collector's Office.

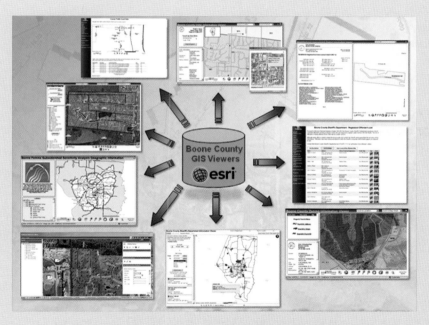

Figure 4.1 Boone County has developed task-focused web-based mapping applications to provide the general public and staff cost-effective and timely access to the county's GIS. Courtesy of Boone County, Missouri.

As County Commissioner Karen Miller explains, "We did the workshop because we wanted to see where our next steps should be. We identified what our shortcomings were and defined the strength of each of our consortium members because whoever's data it was, they owned the data. It was good to just get caught up on what layers were out there."

CASE STUDY > >

> **"We're using GIS even more regionally. From my perspective, there's nothing better than to not worry about whose territory it is. You've got a solution and you've got a better system, why should you care if you're not the one delivering it as long as it's being delivered?"**
>
> Karen Miller, Commissioner, Boone County

During the course of the workshop, the group determined that a vital data layer for the region—master address points—was not finished. Due to the lack of a central coordinating team, the city had not created and uploaded new points in the data layer as new addresses were brought online. As a result, current data for points (addresses) in the city did not exist. As the discussion progressed, it became evident that the addressing issue wasn't just one person saying that a data layer was critical, but rather the collective group recognizing a problem and agreeing it needed to be fixed. When it came time to have technical people devote time to the project, the policy makers had already bought into the decision. They knew there was a problem because of the discussion during the workshop, so securing staff resources to fix it wasn't an issue.

Asked about the benefits of the GIS visioning workshop for elected officials, Jason Warzinik, coordinator for the consortium, says, "I think it really opened their eyes to the actual utility of GIS. We're pretty blessed with some progressive officials. They understand GIS and its value, but they did not understand the possible day-to-day uses, so one afternoon [of the visioning workshop] was set aside for technical presentations on how GIS is being used daily within the consortium. It put concrete examples of GIS and how it's being used in front of them. It was pretty interesting to see how all the light bulbs started turning on about how we could bring together the data pretty quickly on their policy issues or different projects they might be working on for the community."

> **"I think it really opened eyes to the actual utility of GIS."**
>
> Jason Warzinik, GIS Manager, Boone County

Participants in the workshop also learned to think about the geographical aspects of problems. Focus groups brainstormed about projects that would be beneficial to all members of the consortium, which led to several new requests for GIS data layers and applications.

Strategic plan

The next major project for the group is the development of a five-year strategic plan. Although the process for developing the plan has not been formally laid out, it will be prepared in-house without a consultant. The technical committee will likely take the lead in the plan's creation, identifying priorities and strategies for how to address those priorities. At that point, the plan and its priorities will be taken to the policy committee for discussion and approval. One item that may be discussed in depth is the possibility of extending the consortium to other entities in the region. Warzinik explains, "We're

CASE STUDY >

kind of at a point where we do what we do well, but is there more that people want out of the consortium? I think it's very important that we know where we're going, so we can put steps in place to get there. If you're just going along day by day and you really don't have any goals to shoot for, by sitting down and going through the process to get everybody's buy-in and feedback you know you're headed in the right direction for everybody."

Building a solid foundation: Data

GIS technology, with its ability to analyze significant volumes of spatial data, has been at the forefront of data analytics for decades. Data analytics—the study of large sets of raw data to gather critical business intelligence—enables organizations to identify critical process improvements and help plan for future operations. The common operating framework provided by GIS technology enables the analysis of significant volumes of data.

Using data analytics to improve business processes is still a relatively new concept for governments despite the large volume of data they routinely gather. Given the current fiscal retrenchment governments everywhere are undergoing, the need to provide better and cheaper service will drive more governments to consider new ways to use the vast amounts of data they already collect.

A strong GIS program, by its very nature, requires a strong data foundation. Developing base layers of GIS data, such as land parcels and street lines, is the first step. Although a government can develop data layers on its own, it can also access other needed data layers by working with regional GIS user groups, as the GIS Infrastructure Group in Washington County, Oregon, did.

Building a solid data foundation through the GIS Infrastructure Group (GIG), Washington County, Oregon

Preston Beck, GIS Coordinator and IT Project Manager, Financial and Information Services, City of Tigard; Jay Leroux, IS Manager, City of Hillsboro; and Nels Mickaelson, GIS Coordinator, Washington County, Oregon

Level of government: County
State/province: Oregon
Country: USA
Population: 529,710

In Washington County, Oregon, GIS professionals from agencies and jurisdictions began meeting informally in the mid-1990s to share data and ideas. Initially, the group had no ability to make recommendations on budgetary decisions or any authority to allocate resources toward projects; however, it made considerable progress on its own in basic data sharing, improving regional datasets, and establishing data-sharing agreements. The formalized GIS Infrastructure Group (GIG) came about as the result of an affiliation with a regional network infrastructure organization—Washington County Broadband User Group (BUG)—that worked to establish a central ArcSDE server, provided courtesy of Washington County. GIS data could be posted and made available for distribution to other BUG members through the server.

Through a series of focused meetings, occurring over several years, the group gradually began developing a conceptual structure for functioning as a centralized, countywide entity benefiting BUG members and partner agencies under the existing BUG intergovernmental agreement. Using the existing umbrella of the BUG structure, including its executive council and budget authority, provided an operating framework for GIG that moved the group's agenda forward quickly. Launching an independent effort to become its own governing entity would have required individual GIS representatives to seek approval from each jurisdiction's city council or agency's governing board, an undertaking that could potentially have taken years. The GIG conceptual structure went through several iterations to establish goals, structure, and operations, as well as identify member benefits and secure buy-in from decision makers.

By the end of 2009, the BUG Governing Board approved a final charter establishing the GIS Infrastructure Group. The charter stated that the activities of GIG would largely be identified and prioritized by the board. Membership consists of county, city, and special district GIS coordinators, GIS specialists, and their management. The general purpose of GIG is to help coordinate, plan, and execute GIS activities within the region represented by GIG participants and, specifically, among BUG agencies and partners.

Data sharing

Even before becoming formally organized, the group's initial efforts focused on pooling resources and staff to develop key datasets, such as tax lots, street centerlines, and jurisdictional boundaries. Sharing

Figure 4.2 The organization structure for Washington County's GIG. Courtesy of GIS Infrastructure Group (GIG), a committee of the Broadband User Group (BUG), Washington County, Oregon.

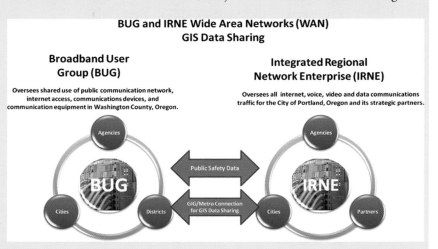

CASE STUDY > > >

data provided the individual jurisdictions and agencies with more layers for developing new GIS applications while sharing the responsibility of maintaining those layers. For example, the county maintains parcel data through the assessor's office while the cities and towns shared their street address data. The group developed key data layers and adopted maintenance procedures for keeping the data up to date.

Numerous data layers and associated tables are currently posted by Washington County. Most county data is countywide in its coverage (e.g., parcel basemap) and is usable for most GIG members. The basic framework consists of data maintained for county business purposes such as addresses, boundaries, elections, emergency operations, environmental concerns, facilities, health, and, permits, places, urban reserves, streets, survey, tax lots, transportation, and water.

In 2010, the group initiated a formal effort, the Data Framework Project, to establish what it needed to share. Data sharing is a two-step process:

1. Identify priority layers that group members would benefit from by centrally posting the data into a framework.
2. Develop data models that consolidate layers into a single model that is then made available for distribution.

For example, one effort involved creating a single layer of fire hydrants using a common data model that incorporates each member's separately maintained hydrant layers.

With these key layers in place, individual agencies and jurisdictions were able to focus on integrating GIS with their respective business processes. Subsequent meetings centered around general information sharing regarding what each jurisdiction was doing in terms of software, application development, and projects and an overall desire to coordinate activities to achieve efficiencies, avoid duplication of effort, and improve the movement of large GIS datasets.

Challenges in sharing data

Although the benefits of sharing data and resources have proved beneficial for all involved in GIG, concerns exist that data might be distributed outside GIG membership without the appropriate permission. One of the biggest challenges for data sharing has been establishing ground rules for what can be done with the data, especially when a third party is involved. Other concerns include the possibility of data being resold without the data owner's permission and privacy issues with sharing data.

GIG is currently working on a data-sharing agreement among its members. A subcommittee has developed a draft MOU to establish an interim agreement so that a minimum set of guidelines is available as soon as possible.

Working together as a region on GIS

One of GIG's first projects was to establish network connectivity and subsequent automated data sharing with the METRO regional government. (METRO is a regional governmental agency representing the Oregon side of the greater Portland area. Washington County represents just one of the urban jurisdictions located within the region.) For years, GIG agencies have individually shared and

CASE STUDY > >

exchanged data on a quarterly basis with METRO for individual business needs through a variety of ad hoc manual processes.

With the formal launch of GIG, the group has an opportunity to streamline and automate the data transfer between METRO and GIG members, thereby increasing the frequency and timeliness of updates, centralizing the upload and distribution of that data, increasing the security and reliability of the data, and standardizing the data maintenance processes for multiple jurisdictions via a coordinated planned effort.

This effort requires coordination from the City of Portland, the Portland area users group METRO, and BUG (both GIG and BUG's operations team). This project was approved by the BUG executive board for fiscal year 2011–12. The first effort of its kind in the Portland Metropolitan region, it will help bring regional GIS systems closer together while simultaneously coordinating the Washington County portion of the region with localized municipal level datasets and updating METRO with appropriate regional datasets in a central warehouse for the region.

Looking to the future

While still relatively new as a coordinating body, GIG envisions improving data sharing among its members and partner agencies. It is in everyone's best interest to increase the pool of information available for GIG members and avoid unnecessary duplication of effort. This is particularly true for some of the smaller jurisdictions, as is the case within GIG where several small cities lack GIS staff or have limited budgets to invest in mapping activities. One of the hopes of GIG is that with the pooling of resources and ideas the smaller cities will be able to garner mapping capabilities within their organizations. For example, it is hoped that simple web editing tools could be developed and deployed using the newer ArcGIS for Server technology to allow the smaller cities to make edits to countywide datasets (such as address points), streamlining some of the redundant workflow that currently exists.

Although information silos do still exist among the local, regional, and state governments, the Portland Metro area, known for its planning of growth, has made great strides in planning and coordinating data sharing among its various agencies. Plans call for creating a sustainable hub-and-spoke system of information in the state that GIG will tap when available. GIG also hopes to use new web services coming from various state agencies to enable better flow of information for emergency management purposes. Most of the technology required exists; the real challenge is creating consensus and agreements of all involved.

Finding common ground and identifying real benefits for participants was crucial for the creation and long-term success of GIG. For example, an obvious benefit was centralizing datasets on a GIS server and eliminating the need for transferring data via media or file transfer protocol (FTP). In terms of common ground, most everyone can agree on currency of data. With their data-sharing efforts, the group has been able to greatly improve access to the most updated GIS data. A few jurisdictions have taken this idea a step further and tapped into the county's parcel data by creating automated scripts that extract data from a defined geographic area within the city boundary once a week. The automation not only assures data quality, but has proved to be a great time saver.

CASE STUDY >

Finally, an illuminating effect of the collaboration of this group of individuals in GIG is the collective skills that everyone brings with them. There is an immense amount of knowledge, talents, and capabilities. GIG is finding there is a lot of potential among its own membership to tackle some very complex issues.

Devising an implementation plan

Any time an organization decides to make a fundamental shift in the way it does business, the development of an implementation plan can make the difference between a smooth transition to the new system or one that will serve as a cautionary tale that lives on for years to come. Good implementation plans consider not only how the new technology will be implemented, but also the people and processes that will be affected by the change. Implementation plans, therefore, should take into account the culture of the organization and whether it is one that embraces change and adapts quickly to new ways of doing business or if change comes in more incremental stages as people's comfort levels with new technology evolve as they see its benefits.

Leadership from elected officials can greatly influence the success of an implementation plan. People tend to adopt the attitudes of those they work with. They will more readily embrace change when they see leaders excited about the new technology and the benefits it will bring the organization. Boise, Idaho, found that by developing a change-management strategy when it restructured the city's GIS programs city employees accepted the new structure more willingly. In Novi, Michigan, the city's transition from an in-house server arrangement to a cloud-based program was aided by an implementation plan that made for a smooth transition.

Consolidating and integrating GIS into the business of Boise, Idaho: Ushering in a culture change

Jim Hetherington and Garry Beatty, Information and Technology Department, City of Boise, Idaho

Level of government: City
State/province: Idaho
Country: USA
Population: 205,671

Boise began its GIS program in the mid-1980s, initially entering into an agreement with a local company to develop and maintain a GIS basemap on a subscription basis. Although housed in the Public Works Department, GIS team members operated as an enterprise system serving all city departments and supporting service requests as they were made.

CASE STUDY > > >

When people who are not formally trained in GIS begin working with the technology, education is critical, as Boise has learned.

As the technology grew in popularity and new applications became apparent, the GIS team could not fulfill all the service requests it received. At the same time, several departments gained access to the city's base GIS data using new, easier-to-use software for mapmaking purposes. As the software became more robust and allowed editing capabilities, other departments began creating their own datasets but often did so without following any standards, such as creating metadata to describe the data available or taking into consideration other possible uses. These actions resulted in mission-critical datasets sometimes existing only on an employee's hard drive without any backup, and often without anyone else's knowledge that the data even existed. Frequently, employees doing this work were untrained in GIS or had limited knowledge on the basic use of the software. This resulted in substandard datasets that were incapable of supporting enterprise analysis for other purposes besides the specific ones for which they were created.

As part of a citywide IT strategic plan in 2006, Boise leaders opted to move the GIS team into the IT Department to support the city's GIS infrastructure and develop a full-fledged enterprise GIS. This move enabled the city to consolidate its GIS assets in a central location and implement a series of new policies regarding the development of datasets. Most GIS datasets that are considered enterprise or mission critical now reside in a central geodatabase with fully documented metadata that identifies the data and any constraints associated with it.

As the GIS team discovered, however, changing the culture of GIS from a department to an enterprise resource can be difficult and time consuming. It required both the adoption of deliberate change-management strategies and the support of a well-respected top-level champion pushing for the change. Team members approached the task with enthusiasm yet caution.

The GIS team began the process with a comprehensive GIS user needs assessment that identified more than 200 business processes city employees believed could be improved by incorporating GIS. The needs assessment fed into the development of a GIS strategic business plan to help communicate departmental needs to city leaders and staff for a better understanding of priorities within the GIS team. The new plan identifies enterprise GIS needs as they relate to departmental projects and also outlines costs and scheduling priorities required to move GIS forward in Boise.

Since GIS has been consolidated into the IT Department, all IT project proposals and business cases are reviewed by GIS team members to determine if there is a good fit. If integration opportunities exist, GIS team members comment on the project and frequently use the opportunity to educate their peers in other departments about the technology. Education has become critical in supporting how Boise approaches GIS and incorporates the technology into business processes. Without GIS professionals reviewing proposed projects, many slipped through without realizing the opportunities for integration. As GIS staff has continued the education push, departmental staff now consult with team members prior to the proposal stage because they are much more aware of GIS capabilities and opportunities.

CASE STUDY > >

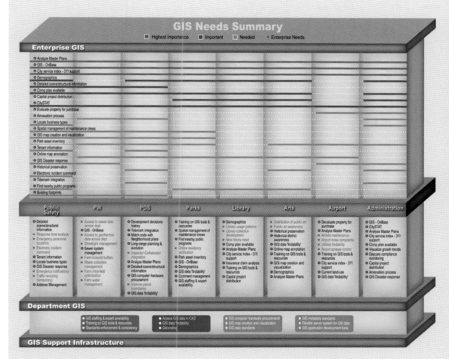

Figure 4.3 Summation of the technical or infrastructure needs, the "top ten" needs as provided by each department, and the enterprise needs. A scoring process was used to derive enterprise rankings of each department's identified "top ten" needs. From this, enterprise rankings were derived from a scoring process. Courtesy of City of Boise (Idaho) GIS Services.

The GIS team added GIS online mapping to the Boise website in the early 2000s. The online mapping site became a catalyst for further integrating GIS into daily processes and business decisions. Although in most cases GIS is not programmatically integrated with departmental software and business processes, the information is at all city employees' fingertips.

Shortly following the GIS move to the IT Department, the GIS team and application development staff worked together to create a public-facing web application that allows parents to locate after-school activities for their children based on their location and child's interests. The application uses GIS functionality in the background, displaying a list of sites based on the criteria set by the parent. Essentially the site enforces rules set by the parents. This site helps community leaders understand how GIS can be used to enforce business rules within city applications, all in the background using geospatial data.

As GIS technology has evolved, it has become easier to use and more accessible. Improved integration with business processes and procedures can realize significant cost savings as well as greater efficiencies. However, when people who are not formally trained in GIS begin working with the technology, education is critical, as Boise has learned. When employees and the public are encouraged to make use of GIS directly rather than simply request a service, systems need to be in place to support new users. The new project review system adopted by Boise encourages departments to think globally and look for other potential citywide uses of data that they need for their own projects. Likewise, the

CASE STUDY >

Figure 4.4 The After3
web application uses
GIS functionality in the
background, displaying
a list of activity sites
based on the criteria set
by the parent. The site
serves as an example of
how GIS can be used to
enforce business rules in
the background within
seemingly non-GIS
applications. Courtesy of
City of Boise (Idaho) GIS
Services.

GIS team's use of informal education on an as-needed, ad hoc basis helps their peers expand the depth of their own knowledge of the technology, enabling them to do their own jobs better.

When consolidating GIS into a single department, governments need to decide up front what kind of consolidation model best fits the organization. A dispersed model consolidates only the foundation of GIS, for example, server(s), software, applications, and major programming. Subject-matter experts continue working for the departments on GIS data creation and maintenance. The full consolidation model brings all GIS, including data creation and maintenance, together. "Our experience has shown that full consolidation will work best for Boise as we [IT/GIS Department] currently have no control over departmental training budgets and could likely balance workloads more efficiently," says Jim Hetherington, GIS manager.

CASE STUDY •

Moving Novi's online mapping service to the cloud

Christopher Blough, MPA, PMP, City GIS Manager, City of Novi, Michigan

Level of government: City
State/province: **Michigan**
Country: USA
Population: 55,224

Like many local governments across the country, the city of Novi, Michigan, started its GIS program in a single department, Public Services, to support public utility and environmental service applications. In 2004, city leaders moved GIS service delivery to the Department of Information Technology to ensure that resources and services had a citywide enterprise focus. Maintaining a citywide system enables Novi to share GIS applications that are designed and maintained for all departments and service areas. Taking this approach has prevented Novi from creating program silos that could result in applications not readily usable by multiple departments. The city also wanted to prevent inefficiencies resulting from departments independently procuring GIS software and resources, maintaining duplicate sets of data restricted to single department applications, and isolating staff talent that could not be leveraged across the entire organization. The city's GIS manager and CIO evaluate GIS project activities to determine the best fit within the city's IT project portfolio and support the annual goals set forth by the city council.

Since its inception, Novi's GIS program has grown in popularity with council members as well as the public. City council members use a multitude of GIS applications to help set policy and make decisions. Council members routinely review map exhibits and narrative support on complex topics in support of their agenda. The following table details the most frequently used GIS applications by Novi's city council members.

Table 4.1 GIS applications used most often by Novi, Michigan, city council members

Elected official activity or resource	Examples and descriptions
Grant application exhibits for parks and recreation improvements	Recent grant applications for land acquisitions involved a significant amount of research and justification through a competitive award selection process.
Private development project status maps	The Community Development Department uses a composite map to track the status of projects through the public review process phases: plan submitted, plan approved, project under development, and project completed.

(continued)

CASE STUDY > > > > >

Elected official activity or resource	Examples and descriptions
Utility and street acceptance actions	Many private residential and commercial developments construct their roads and utilities according to city standards. City council formally reviews each project to determine whether the city will assume maintenance responsibility for the infrastructure.
Zoning changes/Zoning Board of Appeals variance requests	Any zoning changes require a map publication to be advertised to the community and city council consideration to approve amendments to the city's Code of Ordinances. Michigan law requires property owners/occupants within 300 feet to be notified of zoning changes or zoning variance subject issues.
FEMA National Flood Insurance Program support and awareness	Novi actively participates in the National Flood Insurance Program Community Rating System. FEMA provides online map resources and educational outreach. Novi residents receive premium discounts if they elect to carry flood insurance.
Internet-mapping portal	This online, interactive resource provides 24/7 convenience for residents and businesses. It is frequently updated to reflect multiple themes of information, and more than fifty map layers of information service both internal (staff) and external (public) needs. Residents can create their own maps and locate properties, assessments, parks/trails, flood hazard areas, businesses, voting districts, road construction, ordinance restrictions, and more. It provides the public with on-demand access to timely, relevant, and accurate information.
Local, regional, international economic development opportunities reference	Novi is actively pursuing economic development activities to promote business growth and expansion in the city. Locations of more than forty major businesses have been featured over the past eight years.
Capital improvement plan activity locations	Capital improvement funding for infrastructure is identified as part of the five-year CIP planning process.
City street map updates and city transportation funding revenues	The city's public roads and new additions are identified and reported annually to the state, allowing the city to qualify for its fair share of state gas tax revenues. An accurate representation of the public road network is maintained using GIS to calculate the centerline mileage of roads as they are accepted by city council.

(continued)

CASE STUDY > > > >

Elected official activity or resource	Examples and descriptions
Public safety town hall meetings	Locations of fire and police incidents are geocoded for elected officials and citizens so they appreciate where demand for emergency services originates.
Parade and festival event planning	Special events and festivals require exhibits used by the city to pre-position staff and resources to manage traffic and event details.
City property and facility locations	The city owns and operates nine major facilities, nineteen sanitary lift stations, two water booster stations, eleven parks, and 1,569 acres that are identified each year within the city's budget document.
City utility system maintenance and management	The city's water, sewer, and storm water utilities are mapped and identified for operations and management activities.
Fire and police response districts and services sharing opportunities	The city's police and fire response districts are represented to elected officials and community members. Opportunities for sharing emergency services coverage are communicated to elected leaders for shared services proposals.
Special boards and standing committee activities	The city appoints leaders to the Library Board, Historical Commission, Planning Commission, and Recreation Commission who rely on map resources for their program activities, including master plan updates, nonmotorized trail planning, and historic sites inventory, using hard-copy and interactive map resources.
Winter street maintenance and service-level cost analysis	Winter plowing routes are reviewed and mapped to ensure that snow removal is efficient and responsive to community service-level expectations. Lane mileage is calculated to measure salt/brine materials distributed per lane mile to establish baseline measures and promote greater efficiencies.
Defending property tax assessment appeals at the Michigan Tax Tribunal	In 2010, the city defended more than 660 property tax assessment appeals at the State of Michigan Tax Tribunal. All these cases required the assessor to depict property sales of comparable value for owners appealing their assessed values, which required map exhibits and analyses. Property taxes represent more than 56 percent of General Fund revenue for city operations. The greater amount of fact-based, property sales information available, the more successful the city is in defending its assessments, which protects its primary means of revenue generation.

(continued)

CASE STUDY > > >

Elected official activity or resource	Examples and descriptions
Road construction and detour announcements	The city communicates road construction activities affecting major interstate, county, and city thoroughfares to promote community awareness of construction schedules and detours.
Reverse E-911 notification system updates	Public safety is a community priority, and the reverse 911 system can contact more than 50,000 residential and business landline phone subscribers in the city in the event of an emergency. GIS is used to accurately position (geocode) these phone subscribers every six months. The city has successfully achieved a geocoding accuracy rate of over 99 percent of its wireline subscribers, ensuring the greatest coverage possible in the event of a notification callout process.

For the public, the city's Internet Mapping Portal (`http://maps.cityofnovi.org`) is an online map information resource providing convenience and accessibility twenty-four hours a day, seven days a week (see the following table). Residents can access the online service via a standard Internet connection. City employees also use the resource to access commonly requested information.

Table 4.2 Available information on Novi's Internet Mapping Portal*

Local assessing records	Property boundaries	Right-of-ways
Structure-level address locations	Future land use/zoning	Wetland areas
Regulated woodlands/green infrastructure	Road weight regulations	School district service areas/ elementary attendance areas
Subdivision and condominium areas	Voting precincts/polling places	Parks and Recreation facilities/ lands
Road construction projects	FEMA flood hazard areas	FEMA floodways
Nonmotorized routes (trails, sidewalks, pathways)	Recent private development projects	Business locations/ZIP Code boundaries
Aerial photo history 1949–2010	Community historical sites	City benchmark locations
City water utility	City sanitary utility	City stormwater utility

*Information not typically available using commercially-based map resource providers.

CASE STUDY > >

Novi's Internet map offerings have consistently ranked among the city's top five most frequently visited online services. Public demand for the service has grown consistently since 2006. Although the service continued to increase in popularity, behind the scenes the city experienced many challenges to keeping the data accurate and timely. One of the most pressing challenges involved the vendor retained to provide the city with support for its GIS mapping application. The vendor was contracted to perform scheduled updates four times a year. Any updates made outside of its prescheduled cycle cost more than the city's budget allowed. This severely limited the city's ability to update the data as needed.

Continued demand for the mapping service motivated the city to find a new solution that would allow GIS staff to perform on-demand updates. In 2010, Novi made a decision to invest in a second generation of its Internet mapping application and began to research possible solutions. One option was to bring the service in-house and run the online offerings using the city's internal network. Because the city's Internet offerings are made through an externally hosted service agreement, the costs for configuring an internal secure network were considerable and additional staff hours would have been needed to provide additional network support.

The other option Novi explored was moving to a cloud service. Although cloud technology is very new, the city could essentially lease exclusive space through the service and pay for only the computing capacity it used. The cloud alternative differs from the traditional approach by offering computing infrastructure through an online service provider versus purchasing data server hardware and software for use on site. Essentially, this new approach frees up GIS staff to concentrate on using GIS data for analysis purposes or building new applications rather than maintaining on-site server software and hardware.

Novi's decision to take this unique approach provided increased flexibility and new options for the city to display its map-related information. With the new service, the city can independently manage

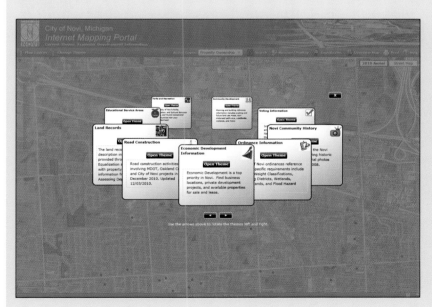

Figure 4.5 The City of Novi organizes its interactive, online map content into themes of information representing different types of geographic data associated with commonly requested community detail. Courtesy of City of Novi IT/GIS Department. All Rights Reserved.

CASE STUDY >

and update its online mapping resources as necessary. In converting to a cloud solution, the city avoids capitalizing the server hardware costs over multiple years, no longer needs to depreciate the costs of the server, and does not incur increased overhead required for IT staff to maintain additional network and sever resources. It pays only for the service availability and server activity actually used. In return, the vendor guarantees service availability and offers security controls that the city has the option of configuring directly. It also enables the city to remain within its current budget for maintaining online map services.

Figure 4.6 The Economic Development theme portrays locations of existing business locations and landownership information for both investors who are seeking business opportunities and consumers who are in search of goods and services. Courtesy of City of Novi IT/GIS Department. All Rights Reserved.

Citizens are increasingly concerned about the cost of government while at the same time have high expectations for service. They care less about who delivers the service and more that the services are there when they need them. Novi's first venture into cloud computing allows the city to continue providing a popular service while controlling costs. Although an initial investment was required to move to a cloud solution, the city anticipates a significant ROI as measured by the quality, availability, and timeliness of the information available for its citizens.

GIS resources and applications must be aligned with advancing the organization's strategic goals, just like every other public investment. The success of any project initiative should always begin with a clear business case and measures that demonstrate incremental progress that are reviewed and recognized by a community's elected and appointed leaders. The opportunities are endless, but the shared vision of the destination needs to be maintained, thereby demonstrating how GIS resources are building recognized business value. Even when budget pressures are foremost on elected leaders' minds, new opportunities can make economic sense.

CASE STUDY •

Sustainable applications

In this era of cutbacks and cost reductions, governments are more closely examining how they do business. The desire to control costs while still providing quality services has resulted in a greater emphasis on sustainability: Do the benefits of a program equal or exceed the cost of running the program? Can this program operate without increasing costs over time? GIS technology has been used to analyze the sustainability of practices in various fields—agriculture, tourism, development, and land-use planning, to name a few. But GIS technology can also demonstrate how it can be sustainable or can foster greater sustainability when integrated with other technologies. Salina, Kansas, has worked to ensure the sustainability of its GIS program by making it largely self-service. In San Marcos, Texas, GIS technology has helped deploy and manage the city's public utilities smart meter effort.

Moving to self-help GIS services in Salina, Kansas

Keith Ganzenmuller, GIS Supervisor; and Mike Fraser, Director, Department of Public Works, City of Salina, Kansas

Level of government: City
State/province: Kansas
Country: USA
Population: 47,707

The GIS program in Salina, Kansas, began in the early 1990s in partnership with Saline County, with the first full-time GIS employee hired in 1995. In the beginning, the county needed to have parcel data, and the city wanted to map things such as streets, zoning boundaries, and city limits. This was before the spread of widespread desktop computing, and the city and county had just a few dedicated computers to run GIS software.

The history of GIS in Salina runs parallel to the history of computing; as technology has changed, the GIS program has changed and grown with it. The program has gone from a single computer in the early days to being available on a dozen desktop computers and fifty mobile units, with a number of non-GIS employees using the system. Staff have also installed GIS computers and projectors in conference rooms to allow for the real-time use of GIS during meetings, which has spawned interest in GIS outside of the Planning and Engineering Departments.

> **"To do more with less you have to make GIS a self-service concept as much as possible. Make it easy for people to access the information they need on a routine basis. Take the time to develop tools, templates, and web pages that allow people to help themselves."**
> Keith Ganzenmuller, GIS Supervisor, City of Salina, Kansas

CASE STUDY > > > >

Although interest in GIS has grown over the years, the number of GIS staff has not. The city has one full-time GIS employee who serves all city departments and one technician in the utilities department who counts GIS among his various duties.

The GIS supervisor is responsible for maintaining the entire GIS program, including editing and updating all the core datasets. With very limited staff time available for special projects, the city needed to find a way to make GIS more accessible to support departmental programs. It opted to enter into an Esri Enterprise License Agreement (ELA) for small governments. The agreement gives the City of Salina access to unlimited licenses for core Esri products, such as ArcGIS for Desktop, ArcGIS for Server, and ArcPad. Additionally, any employee using mapping applications can have the software installed on a work computer without needing an individual license.

As a result, every Salina Fire Department vehicle now has ArcPad with a self-contained, custom mobile program. The Fire Department in Salina has become the second-biggest user of GIS, just behind public works. The Fire Department spends vast amounts of time preplanning strategies to fight fires at certain locations; these locations are called target hazards because they present a specific, known hazard to public safety personnel. The preplanning involves both documentation and photography.

Figure 4.7 Every Salina Fire Department vehicle now has emergency information available digitally via ArcPad. Courtesy of City of Salina, Department of Public Works.

Prior to implementing the mobile program, this information was stored in books with page upon page of information that needed to be accessed during an emergency. This information is now available digitally in every Fire Department vehicle using a completely self-contained ArcPad-based mapping system. The target hazards are visible en route to a call and are displayed at the touch of a finger on the screen of the mobile computer. These computers also display information such as fire hydrants, aerial photography, and street addresses. All this information increases the situational awareness of the first responders in the few minutes it takes to reach the location of an emergency call.

Other top department users of GIS in Salina include planning and zoning for land-use issues, parks and recreation for bike and multiuse trails, public works for tracking traffic accidents, and utilities

CASE STUDY > > >

> ## "The Salina Department of Public Works has used GIS as an effective communications tool to illustrate and explain the status of our infrastructure and/or field situations to city staff, elected officials, and the public alike. Whatever the situation, we have found that GIS clarifies what we have, what we are doing, what could be done, and what we plan to do."
>
> Mike Fraser, Director, Department of Public Works, City of Salina, Kansas

for asset management and viewing "as-built" maps for construction and development projects. All departments consult with the GIS supervisor on an as-needed basis but essentially run their own GIS applications using data from the central GIS program. When training for employees is needed, the ELA with Esri enables the city to use the company's desktop training program.

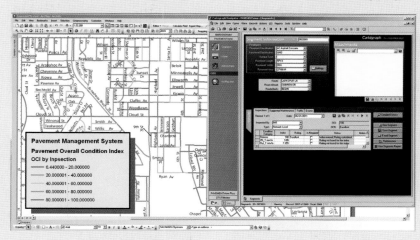

Figure 4.8 One of the many ways the city uses GIS maps is for pavement management. Courtesy of City of Salina, Department of Public Works.

Along the way, the GIS program has also grown to serve Salina citizens. In the beginning, any services provided to the public, such as street maps, were a by-product of the core mission to provide information to employees. Over time that practice has changed. As technology has evolved, it has become possible to deliver spatial information to the public simply and affordably. Delivering information to the public has become one of the core missions of the GIS program.

The city installed its first public mapping service in 2003. As budgets tightened and workloads increased, the program looked for new ways to respond to the demand for services and still stay within budget.

In 2011, the city underwent a significant update of its public property mapping website. A substantial investment of staff time and effort went into programming the website to enhance its capabilities,

CASE STUDY > >

Figure 4.9 Salina's public
web-mapping site has
extensive instructions
designed to allow users
with little to no GIS
experience to operate
the site. Courtesy of City
of Salina, Department of
Public Works.

which were based on requests from citizens over the years. The updated website allows citizens to do things such as save maps made online to PDF or JPEG files, export property information to text files or spreadsheet-compatible files, or search for street intersections. The website also has a much more robust help system, complete with video demonstrations, which can be accessed with a simple right-click of the mouse. Utilities information is also available to the public, including the location of water, wastewater, and fiber-optic lines. All of these things enable businesses and private citizens to access Salina data without a trip to city offices.

Although some printed maps are still available through the city, most are now provided via the public website. Among the most popular public uses of Salina's GIS program through the website are address locations and intersection mapping for the general citizenry, aerial photography for businesses and realtors, sewer line locations for plumbers and construction crews, and topology and geography for school students.

Beyond the website, the GIS program has produced other useful analyses for Salina citizens. When the local school district, Unified School District 305, had to adjust school boundaries, the city published this data, which allowed parents and potential home buyers to see which school(s) served a particular property. At the request of the city commission and local chamber of commerce, another project involved analyzing the north part of Salina to locate sites for a potential grocery store. The ArcGIS Spatial Analyst extension helped the city identify possible locations using downloaded census

CASE STUDY >

data, bus stop locations, and distances from major streets to then rank the vacant parcels. In the past, these types of analyses would normally be done by a consultant. The citizens may not hear about it, but the GIS program often works behind the scenes to help them out.

Salina has found that doing more with less, in this case less GIS personnel, can be done. To transition to a self-help GIS program, Salina team members offer the following tips:

- Remember that GIS is a customer service business. If you turn off customers, they will turn off your GIS.
- Treat all the users equally, from the smallest department to the largest.
- Reach out to all the departments. You can learn what they do, and they can learn how GIS can help them.
- If you don't have a GIS, don't be afraid to jump in. It can be as simple or complex as you want it to be, but it won't be anything until you start.
- Expand your GIS only to the limits of your ability to maintain it. This is why the self-service part of GIS is really helpful.
- Enlist the help of other departments. If a department wants to store data in your GIS, it should make a commitment to help maintain it.

CASE STUDY •

Using GIS to deploy smart meter technology in San Marcos, Texas

William Flynn, Public Services GIS/Technology Manager, City of San Marcos, Texas

Level of government: City
State/province: Texas
Country: USA
Population: 44,894

San Marcos, Texas, has made a practice of staying ahead of the curve when it comes to technology. In 2007, San Marcos leaders determined that the city needed to have a better understanding of the current state of its utilities infrastructure—for example, knowing where an electric outage had occurred or where a water leak might be located. The city's Public Services team members began researching smart meter technologies as a means of generating improved management information for customers and utilities.

San Marcos is unique in that the city owns and manages both the municipal water and electric utilities for the community. Having smart meter technology means better service for the citizens and businesses in San Marcos, but it also impacts the city's bottom line in terms of revenue generation. The city has about 30,000 meters, and it needed a system that worked with both utility types.

CASE STUDY > > > >

> ## Having smart meter technology means better service for the citizens and businesses in San Marcos, but it also impacts the city's bottom line in terms of revenue generation.

Staff research identified many benefits associated with implementing a smart grid system, including the opportunity for improved customer service and asset management. On the customer service front, the new system gives San Marcos access to more current information on use patterns among its customers, allowing them to adjust their use patterns during the same billing cycle if needed. For water service, the city can provide readings on the hour; for electric service, it can generate reports down to thirty-minute, or even fifteen-minute, intervals when needed.

Implementation of the new system started in the fall of 2008 with initial testing. Full deployment began in April 2009. GIS proved integral for planning the deployment of San Marcos's new grid technology in nearly all phases, including:

- Developing the deployment schedule
- Making the deployment and activation routes more efficient
- Mapping the line-of-sight analysis for the gateway and relay collectors, because the city sits at the beginning of the Texas Hill Country
- Producing maps for residents with the smart meter installation schedule
- Identifying network communication issues
- Visualizing assets
- Connecting with inventory
- Integrating with the utility billing system, work order/asset management system, automated outbound calling system, and smart meter data

One challenge the San Marcos team had to contend with was having different service boundaries for its electric utility than the city's political boundaries. The different boundaries necessitated that some San Marcos neighborhoods receive electric service from other providers. The negotiations with the neighboring electric utilities—the Pedernales (PEC) and Bluebonnet (BEC) Electric Cooperatives—allowed equipment to be installed in the affected neighborhoods that made it possible for the city's smart water meters to communicate with and report back to San Marcos's offices. GIS maps were used to identify locations for gateways and relays outside the electric utility's boundaries and helped determine how to establish communications in the mesh network in order to serve city residents who had smart water meters but not smart electric meters.

The electric utility hired a consultant to complete the smart electric meter deployment, which took about five and half months. Installation of meters on the water side was more challenging and took a much longer time to complete. The smart water meter deployment, which involved installing about 10,000 meters, was done by San Marcos water/wastewater crews over an eighteen-month period. Installations had to be coordinated and harmonized with the four billing cycles San Marcos had established for different areas of the city. Each address and its corresponding account number had to have electric and water meters read together, and multiple meter-reading routes had to be defined that fell within the billing cycles. San Marcos has about 121 routes spread across all the billing cycles.

CASE STUDY > > >

Figure 4.10 Workers installing the smart meters and the subsequent node activation phase. Courtesy of City of San Marcos, Texas.

In developing the deployment schedule for the water meters, a GIS analysis determined the number of water meter installs that needed to be made on each route. The water utility system had many more pieces of equipment involved and more special cases. The system uses nodes (wireless devices) to communicate with individual meter registers, and then transmits data to the central collector via a system of gateways and relays over the mesh network. Different sizes and types of meters had to be replaced as part of the deployment. Sometimes all the equipment needed to be replaced; sometimes the meter and register were compatible with the node; and sometimes the meter was fine, but the register was too old or wasn't compatible with the node. As a result, there were many different types of installation tasks that took different lengths of time to complete. At the same time, the city also had to consider its ten-year equipment replacement plan.

A number of other factors influenced the deployment schedule, such as the weather; the number of employees willing to work overtime on weekends; unforeseen distractions, such as water main breaks; and equipment shortages, including shortages of meters, registers, and nodes. Water meters that were due for reading could not be changed out, so there were numerous blackout dates. GIS analyses helped staff develop work plans for routing that accounted for all these variables and deployed the equipment as efficiently as possible.

Because the schedule for water meter installations was often difficult to predict due to these many challenges, the city also developed a communications plan that makes use of GIS. San Marcos created a "Smart Metering" section on the city's website that includes a map service updated every quarter to reflect revisions to the schedule. The online map service proved much more useful and costs less than sending print mailings with utility bills. Maps are also displayed in lobbies of city facilities. These tools enable customers to see deployment progress and better anticipate when they should receive their new equipment.

When the new meters were deployed, the city took the opportunity to record the GPS location of all the new meters, both water and electric. Although a street address can identify a site, field crews need to know the exact location of where to find a meter at, for example, an apartment complex or a golf course. In addition, even though the city has many employees with long service careers who know where the infrastructure is located, many of the newer employees do not have such a mental map. Recording the exact locations of as much of the infrastructure as possible into the city's GIS will make future management and maintenance work go more smoothly, saving staff time spent on the radio with dispatch or coming back to the office to consult with coworkers.

With the smart grid in place, the city began using GIS for asset management. City staff integrated the GIS with IBM Maximo, a work order and asset management system that allows the city to track the spatial locations of all maintenance work; find hot spots around town of certain types of activities and equipment failures; plan future target areas for infrastructure work, such as capital improvement plan (CIP) projects; and keep tabs on the flow of rotating equipment.

To collect all the infrastructure data, the Public Services Department purchased thirteen Trimble GPS units that were sent out with crews to identify the exact location of the city's meters on a property. The GPS units were purchased specifically for the use of capturing spatial data relating to meter locations, but the city has opted to also log additional needed data for all water/wastewater, electric, and storm water infrastructure, including the location of meters, service laterals, mains, manholes,

Figure 4.11 This ArcGIS dashboard has greatly assisted the City of San Marcos in monitoring the performance of the AMI (advanced metering infrastructure) network. With approximately 20,000 electric meters and 10,000 water meters in the field, office staff can get a spatial understanding of what areas of the network are not functioning properly. This graphic demonstrates how long it has been since each node has transmitted a meter reading over the network.

Courtesy of City of San Marcos, Texas.

fire hydrants, utility poles, transformers, junction boxes, and curb inlets, among other features. GIS is also deployed in the field using laptop computers, which gives field crews direct access to the system. In recent years, the city has moved almost completely away from the old hard-copy map books and atlases and instead looks at real-time data available through GIS.

The utilities use GIS for a number of other tasks as well, such as routing field crews, diagnostic work to determine what parts of town have had incidents reported, and analyzing consumption patterns to determine where any hot spots and cool spots may exist. The asset management and work order management systems also have been integrated so there is a continually updated record of what work has been completed at different sites by field crews. GIS is also linked to the utilities' outbound calling system, which allows messages to be sent out to residents, for example, if a storm comes through and the city needs to alert citizens when debris will be picked up.

The system has also been used to notify customers about planned electric outages and boil notices for water. "We used the billing system to get the contact information for the residents in particular neighborhoods, and will then send the message out in bulk. We're also in the process of collecting e-mail addresses, so that we have that medium as an option, too. We can circulate those messages out even more quickly than phone calls. Given our demographics in San Marcos, we've had to make our notifications bilingual, in both English and Spanish. We see a lot of potential uses in that, using GIS to pick the area for the analysis and then linking it to the customer database," notes William Flynn, Public Services GIS/Technology manager for the city.

CASE STUDY •